Terrorism and National Security Reform

Terrorism and National Security Reform demonstrates that blue-ribbon commissions can be powerful vehicles for policy change, overturning the conventional wisdom that views them only as devices for passing the buck. Jordan Tama explains how the unique political credibility of commissions can enable them to forge bipartisan consensus on tough policy challenges. He also shows that commissions are most valuable during a crisis, when policy makers face pressure to make changes but frequently cannot agree on what to do. Using an original database, case studies, and more than 200 interviews of policy makers and commission participants, Tama reveals how commissions have shaped Barack Obama's plan for ending the Iraq War, spurred the largest government and intelligence overhauls since 1947, and driven many other elements of U.S. counterterrorism policy. In an era of unrelenting partisanship and extreme polarization, this book shows that commissions are increasingly valuable policy-making tools.

Jordan Tama is Assistant Professor at American University's School of International Service and Research Fellow at AU's Center for Congressional and Presidential Studies. His scholarship and commentary have been published in *Presidential Studies Quarterly, Foreign Policy, TheAtlantic.com, The Hill, Asian Survey, International Affairs Review*, and other journals. He has served as a member of the Intelligence and Counterterrorism Expert Advisory Groups for Barack Obama's 2008 presidential campaign, as a speechwriter for former U.S. Representative Lee Hamilton, and as a contributor to the Princeton Project on National Security. He is a Fellow of the Truman National Security Project and holds a Ph.D. from Princeton University's Woodrow Wilson School of Public and International Affairs.

Terrorism and National Security Reform

How Commissions Can Drive Change During Crises

JORDAN TAMA
American University

CAMBRIDGE UNIVERSITY PRESS
Cambridge, New York, Melbourne, Madrid, Cape Town,
Singapore, São Paulo, Delhi, Tokyo, Mexico City

Cambridge University Press
32 Avenue of the Americas, New York, NY 10013-2473, USA

www.cambridge.org
Information on this title: www.cambridge.org/9780521173070

First published 2011

Printed in the United States of America

A catalog record for this publication is available from the British Library.

Library of Congress Cataloging in Publication data
Tama, Jordan, 1976–
    Terrorism and national security reform : how commissions can drive
change during crises / Jordan Tama.
        p.   cm.
    Includes bibliographical references and index.
    ISBN 978-1-107-00176-3 (hardback) – ISBN 978-0-521-17307-0 (pbk.)
    1. Executive advisory bodies – United States – Case studies.   2. Political planning –
    United States – Case studies.   3. National security – United States – Case studies.
    4. Terrorism – Government policy – United States – Case studies.   I. Title.
    JK468.C7T36   2011
    363.325′15610973–dc22   2010037102

ISBN 978-1-107-00176-3 Hardback
ISBN 978-0-521-17307-0 Paperback

To My Family

Contents

Figures and Tables

Acknowledgments

The inspiration for this book dates back to when I worked as a speechwriter for former U.S. Representative Lee Hamilton (D-IN), from 1999 to 2002. This was before the 9/11 Commission or Iraq Study Group had been created, but Lee served on several other panels then and was already establishing his reputation as a master of the commission form. Once at Princeton University's Woodrow Wilson School, where I pursued my Ph.D., my interest in commissions was further stoked by my involvement in the Princeton Project on National Security, a bipartisan study of national security strategy led by John Ikenberry and Anne-Marie Slaughter. I started to wonder: What impact do commissions generally have? I decided to write a dissertation that would attempt to answer this question, and thus this book was born.

In addition to providing this inspiration, Lee and Anne-Marie have been terrific mentors and have shaped my understanding of commissions through many conversations. I am also grateful to Anne-Marie for serving as one of my dissertation advisors and always making time to give me helpful feedback – even after starting a very demanding job as the State Department's Policy Planning Director.

It was my great fortune to have three other extremely dedicated advisors and mentors at Princeton. Bob Keohane, Christina Davis, and David Lewis each spent countless hours reading my work and discussing ways to improve it. Bob, who served as my dissertation committee chair, taught me how to conduct rigorous social science research. His frank and supportive advice was invaluable, especially as I navigated the most difficult part of the dissertation process: developing an argument and formulating a research design.

Christina taught my first international relations course at the Wilson School, and has been a wonderful mentor ever since. Her keen insights strengthened my work in many ways. Dave pressed me to consider tricky theoretical issues and wisely encouraged me to develop statistical tests of commission influence. I appreciate his kind willingness to continue advising me after moving from Princeton to Vanderbilt.

Several fellow Princeton doctoral students were very valuable sources of ideas and support. Jeff Colgan was like an extra advisor, commenting on drafts of all of my chapters and helping me work through tough methodological issues. Jessica Green and Mareike Kleine gave me much useful feedback on drafts as well. Other Princeton students and faculty members offered helpful comments on different iterations of my work at the international relations graduate research seminar.

Outside Princeton, I benefited from comments I received after presenting my findings at two meetings of the American Political Science Association and at my new home, American University, which has also provided a supportive and intellectually stimulating environment for completing revisions to the book. At AU, I am especially grateful to Gordon Adams, Boaz Atzili, David Bosco, Deborah Brautigam, Philip Brenner, Maria Green Cowles, Daniel Esser, Louis Goodman, Tamar Gutner, Dorle Hellmuth, Sikina Jinnah, Shoon Murray, Robert Pastor, Vidyamali Samarasinghe, Jim Thurber, Sharon Weiner, and Guy Ziv for their terrific guidance and warm friendship during my first year on the job.

I also thank several outstanding scholars who have blazed the trail of commission research and were helpful to me in various ways: Loch Johnson, who offered keen insights and discussed with me his experience on the Aspin-Brown Commission; Christopher Kirchhoff, with whom I had fruitful conversations about the impact of commissions over several dinners; Kenneth Kitts, who provided useful suggestions and sent me the dissertation on which his own book on commissions was based; and Amy Zegart, who gave me valuable feedback on an early version of this project and kindly shared with me her own commission data set.

In addition, I thank David Bosco, I. M. Destler, Ole Holsti, and the manuscript's anonymous reviewers for offering valuable comments and suggestions. Andrew Dallas and Kate Tennis provided excellent research assistance.

The heart of my research for this book consisted of more than 200 interviews of commission members, commission staff, and government officials. Their names are listed in Appendix C, except for those who requested anonymity. All of them were generous in taking the time to share their perspectives. The book would be much less informative without their many recollections and insights, and I am very grateful to all of them.

One person I interviewed merits special mention for going way above and beyond the call of duty. Jim Kurtz not only answered all of my questions about two commissions on which he worked, but also put me in touch with more than a dozen other people who were involved in various commissions.

I am grateful to the Woodrow Wilson School and the Lynde and Harry Bradley Foundation for their generous financial support of my research and writing. At Cambridge University Press, I thank Lew Bateman for his interest in my manuscript, and I thank Lew and Anne Lovering Rounds for their work shepherding it through the peer review and editorial processes. Rachel Nishan meticulously prepared the index.

I also thank Robert Hathaway and Robert Litwak for being excellent mentors over the years.

Special thanks go to my family – especially my parents Phil, Lanni, and Ellyn; my grandparents William, Elsa, and Joseph; my aunts Jillian, Rachel, and Julie; and my sister Gabriela – for their love and support, and for instilling in me a passion for learning, a good work ethic, and an interest in the world at large. I could never have written this book without all that they have taught me.

My wife Julia was tremendously helpful throughout this project as a thoughtful sounding board, a font of ideas, a superb editor, and my biggest cheerleader. She also made the four years I spent working on it a time of great joy. I am immensely thankful for her.

I

Commissioning Reform

On January 28, 2004, David Kay reported to Congress on his findings as head of the Iraq Survey Group, which President George W. Bush had formed to scour Iraq for weapons of mass destruction (WMD) after the 2003 U.S. invasion of that country. Kay testified that he had found no evidence of Iraqi WMD and that WMD stockpiles probably did not exist in Iraq at the time of the invasion.[1] His report was immediately seized on by prominent Democrats, who argued that it showed Bush took the country to war under false pretenses, and called for an independent investigation of the administration's use of intelligence (Schlesinger and Milligan 2004).

Within days of Kay's testimony, Bush created a presidential commission, chaired by former Senator Charles Robb (D-VA) and U.S. Court of Appeals Judge Laurence Silberman, to probe the intelligence community's capabilities and deficiencies related to foreign WMD programs.[2] Bush's action was principally motivated by a desire to defuse the political pressure generated by the failure to find WMD in Iraq. As the *Washington Post* reported, Bush sought "to get out in front of a potentially dangerous issue that threaten[ed] to cloud his reelection bid" (Milbank and Priest 2004). In response, Democratic leaders charged that the commission's mandate was inadequate because it did not cover how intelligence had been handled by the Bush White House (Allen 2004).

---

[1] Testimony by David Kay before the Senate Armed Services Committee, January 28, 2004.
[2] Executive Order 13328, issued February 6, 2004.

Given the Bush administration's deeply political motivation for establishing the Robb-Silberman Commission, expectations for its impact on intelligence policy were quite low. The commission's report, issued in March 2005, identified numerous intelligence shortcomings and offered seventy-four proposals for reform. But the reactions of many commentators remained focused on the limits to the commission's inquiry, implying that its only function was to deflect blame for the WMD fiasco away from the White House by making the intelligence community a scapegoat for it (Pincus and Baker 2005). A *New York Times* editorial asserted caustically that the commission "could have saved the country a lot of time, and considerable paper, by not publishing its report" (*New York Times* 2005).

However, the commission actually accomplished much more than taking the heat off the Bush administration: Its unanimous report sparked a variety of important reforms. After receiving the report, Bush ordered agency heads to inform White House Homeland Security Advisor Frances Fragos Townsend of their plans for implementing each commission proposal. During subsequent months, Townsend met frequently with those officials to press them to act on recommendations which they resisted (Bumiller 2005). This pressure from the White House led agencies to make major changes that they would not have otherwise made.

To take two examples, the commission proposed: (1) combining the intelligence, counterintelligence, and counterterrorism divisions of the Federal Bureau of Investigation (FBI) into a national security service subject to the budgetary authority of the director of national intelligence (DNI); and (2) placing several parts of the Justice Department under the authority of a new assistant attorney general for national security. The goal of these proposals was to integrate the FBI into the broader intelligence community and to break down bureaucratic walls between intelligence and law enforcement within the Justice Department (Commission on the Intelligence Capabilities of the United States regarding Weapons of Mass Destruction 2005, 29–32). Both recommendations were controversial within the administration because they threatened the turf of existing agencies and offices. FBI Director Robert Mueller opposed the national security service recommendation, and Justice Department officials were divided on the other proposal.[3] Yet the recommendations were endorsed

---

[3] Interview of FBI official, October 2007; interview of Justice Department official, November 2007; interview of senior Bush administration official, May 2009.

by Bush – leading within a year to the establishment of an FBI national security branch subject to the DNI's budgetary authority, and to the formation of a Justice Department national security division headed by a new assistant attorney general.[4]

Each of these reforms was triggered directly by the Robb-Silberman Commission. Before the commission reported, the White House had not considered such large-scale overhauls of the Justice Department and FBI.[5] Without the panel, the reorganization ideas would not have been placed on President Bush's radar screen, and Bush would not have acted to institute the changes over the objections of top agency officials. One Justice Department official said of the reforms, "They wouldn't have happened but for the commission."[6] Another administration counterterrorism official recalled, "There were lots of folks within the department and within the FBI who didn't want to make those changes, and they had to be overruled. It only happened because of the report."[7] A senior FBI official, acknowledging that the bureau opposed reorganization, agreed that it occurred because the commission prompted Bush to press for implementation of its proposals.[8]

The commission also influenced many other reforms, including the formulation of new standards for conducting intelligence analysis and the establishment of "mission managers" under the DNI to oversee all intelligence efforts on priority subjects, such as North Korea and Iran.[9] Some of these changes were facilitated by the contemporaneous establishment of the DNI post. One intelligence official commented, "[DNI] John Negroponte's entire strategic plan for transforming the IC [intelligence community] was modeled on [the commission's] report."[10]

More broadly, the commission's substantial impact was made possible by the Iraq WMD scandal that prompted the panel's formation in the first place and placed pressure on the Bush administration to reform intelligence. Commission member William Studeman noted, "Our recommendations came at a time when the IC needed to get some focus for

---

[4] "Bush Administration Actions to Implement WMD Commission Recommendations," White House memorandum, June 29, 2005; Public Law 109–177, enacted on March 9, 2006.
[5] Interview of senior Bush administration official, May 2009.
[6] Interview of Justice Department official, November 2007.
[7] Interview of Bush administration official, February 2008.
[8] Interview of FBI official, October 2007.
[9] "Office of DNI Progress Report – WMD Recommendations," Office of the DNI, July 27, 2006.
[10] Interview of intelligence official, May 2008.

reform and transformation, and when serious round turns needed to be taken."[11]

In short, the scandal created a window of opportunity for reform, which the Robb-Silberman Commission seized. The WMD fiasco placed pressure on administration officials to improve intelligence, but the commission's report was necessary to catalyze important policy and organizational changes.

The Conventional Wisdom about Commissions

The story of the Robb-Silberman Commission illustrates how a commission established to quiet a furor can also drive major reforms. Yet the conventional wisdom about commissions is that their reports do little more than gather dust on bookshelves. Commentators typically see the appointment of a commission during a crisis as a symbolic action that relieves policy makers of political pressure but does not lead to policy change. One *Washington Post* reporter quipped, "There are two ways to bury something in Washington: 1) Dig a hole in the ground, insert something and cover it. 2) Appoint an advisory commission to report on whatchamaycallit" (Causey 1987). In a similar vein, a *New York Times* headline declared, "Commissions Are Fine, But Rarely What Changes the Light Bulb" (Rosenbaum 2005).

The statements of many policy makers are not any more charitable. When John McCain proposed forming a commission to study the U.S. financial crisis during the 2008 presidential campaign, Barack Obama mocked the idea as "the oldest Washington stunt in the book," implying that a commission would not help solve the problem (Shear 2008). In a different context, former Defense Department official James Bodner observed, "Most commissions are created for reasons other than producing results. And most commissions don't produce results."[12]

The conventional view of commissions is captured well by a joke Lloyd Cutler, White House Counsel to Presidents Jimmy Carter and Bill Clinton, used to tell: "A retiring president leaves his successor three envelopes to be opened, in sequence, to learn what to do each time he faces a serious crisis. The first envelope says 'Blame your predecessor.' The second says 'Appoint a commission.' The third says 'Prepare three envelopes.'"[13]

---

[11] Interview of William Studeman, October 30, 2007.
[12] Interview of James Bodner, April 23, 2008.
[13] I am grateful to I. M. Destler for relaying this joke.

Some scholars share the view that commissions rarely spur policy change. Mark Fenster claims that the influence of commissions "seems to fall within a narrow range – from marginal to nil – and rare is the commission whose proposals are actually adopted into law or regulatory rule" (Fenster 2008, 1242). Daniel Byman asserts that commissions "are like bees: They sting once and then die" (Byman 2006). Kenneth Kitts, author of the only book other than this one on national security commissions, describes them as damage control devices rather than as institutions that contribute to reform (Kitts 2006). Even some commission members have a dim view of the influence of advisory panels. Sidney Drell, who has served on many panels, commented, "Commissions don't have batting averages that are as good as those of good baseball hitters."[14]

In spite of this conventional wisdom, an occasional commission garners widespread praise for triggering major reform. To cite two examples, many observers have credited the 9/11 Commission with inducing enactment of the 2004 law that created the DNI and lauded a panel chaired by Alan Greenspan in 1983 for breaking a deadlock on Social Security reform (Kaplan and Whitelaw 2004; Tolchin 1983). More generally, some scholars assert that commissions often play important roles in spurring organizational change or fostering consensus on controversial measures (Campbell 2002; Pfiffner 2009b; Wolanin 1975).

Research Questions and Existing Knowledge

These contrasting opinions frame the questions that motivate this book: Are the 9/11 and Greenspan Commissions anomalies, as the conventional wisdom would suggest, or do many commissions prompt significant reforms? How can a commission spark reform that would not happen without it? Why are some commissions influential whereas others are not?

Before proceeding, a word about the kind of commissions I am discussing. For the purposes of this book, I define a commission as a temporary panel of two or more people – including at least one private citizen – created by an act of Congress or executive branch directive. The body also must only possess informal advisory power and must be mandated to produce a final report within four years.[15]

---

[14] Interview of Sidney Drell, January 25, 2008.
[15] A standard definition of a commission does not exist. Mine draws heavily on definitions by the 1972 Federal Advisory Committee Act and by other scholars (Tutchings

Such commissions are a staple of American politics. In national security policy alone, the executive branch and Congress form new panels nearly every year. (I use the terms "commission" and "panel" interchangeably.) Moreover, some panels, such as the 9/11 Commission and the 2006 Iraq Study Group (or Baker-Hamilton Commission), attract great public interest.

Yet relatively few scholars have examined the impact of commissions. In the first systematic study of the issue, Thomas Wolanin traced the government's response to ninety-nine commissions and found that roughly half of them had an important recommendation acted on by the executive branch or Congress (Wolanin 1975, 131–139). A decade later, David Filtner argued, based on case studies of eight commissions addressing social policy, that panels can educate the public and legitimize new ideas (Filtner 1986, 151–180). More recently, James Pfiffner concluded, in a survey of twenty-three panels, that some of the past century's most important changes in government organization resulted from the work of commissions (Pfiffner 2009b).

In addition, several excellent studies have focused on national security commissions. Kenneth Kitts found, in a study of five such panels, that commissions can help the president deflect criticism and remain in control of policy making (Kitts 2006, 174). Christopher Kirchhoff concluded, based on an examination of three disaster investigations, that commissions have a special capacity to identify deficiencies in government institutions (Kirchhoff 2009). In the intelligence arena, Michael Warner and Kenneth McDonald determined that four intelligence reviews led to important reforms, whereas Amy Zegart found that the vast majority of intelligence commission proposals were not implemented during the decade before September 11, 2001 (Warner and McDonald 2005; Zegart 2006; Zegart 2007). In a case study, Loch Johnson concluded that the 1996 Aspin-Brown Commission bolstered the intelligence community's public reputation (Johnson 2004).

Taken together, these rich studies have generated many valuable insights about commissions. But they have left some large gaps. Most importantly, scholars have not fully explained how and when commissions can induce

1979, 11–12; Wolanin 1975, 7; Zegart 2004, 369). My definition excludes ad hoc panels formed by standing bodies such as the Defense Science Board and the National Research Council. It also excludes the Base Realignment and Closure (BRAC) commissions, whose recommendations on base closings must be accepted or rejected by the president and Congress without revision. This formal proposal power gives BRAC commissions a different source of influence than commissions that only possess informal advisory power.

government reforms, or tested hypotheses about the impact of commissions while controlling for relevant variables. These gaps leave us without a clear understanding of why some commissions are more influential than others. In addition, with the exception of a study by Colton Campbell, scholars have tended to focus on panels created by the president, thereby neglecting the role of congressional commissions (Campbell 2002).

Overview of the Argument

In this book, I attempt to fill these gaps by formulating and testing a theory of commission influence while revealing the broader importance of commissions for policy making. I demonstrate that far from just being ways to pass the buck or avoid blame, commissions can be valuable tools for driving reform on important issues.

Simply put, Congress and the president often need help making policy. Excessive partisanship, fierce turf battles, and supermajoritarian requirements for the passage of legislation (e.g., the sixty votes needed to end a Senate filibuster) frequently prevent the president and Congress from adopting badly needed reforms. Although many commissions are created for reasons other than changing policy, they are often powerful vehicles for overcoming these obstacles to reform by forging bipartisan consensus. Their value is only increasing as the American political system becomes more polarized, making it all the more difficult for elected officials to forge consensus themselves. Commissions are one of the best antidotes to polarization.

The power of commissions lies in their unique form of political credibility. This credibility stems from their independence, stature, and bipartisanship – a special combination of characteristics that distinguishes commissions from both the executive branch and Congress. Commissions can have tremendous impact because a unanimous report by a politically diverse, prestigious, and independent panel sends a powerful signal to policy makers and the public that its proposals are both sound and politically palatable. These commission proposals can thereby become the focal point of a reform debate, prompting elected officials to adopt them. By contrast, technical expertise is not usually the source of a commission's appeal. The impact of most commissions is driven more by their political credibility than by their specialized knowledge.

Yet the possession of political credibility is not sufficient for a commission to spur change. After all, many commissions possess credibility but fail to have a major impact. The most important condition that enables a commission to turn its credibility into influence is the existence of a crisis on the issue addressed by the panel.

In the political world, a crisis is a moment of heightened political pressure stemming from an unexpected event. Since political pressure is hard to measure, in this book I define a crisis more simply as a situation marked by a disaster or government scandal (the two kinds of events that can suddenly generate intense pressure on policy makers). Using this definition, I classify commissions into two types: 1) crisis commissions, which are established by the executive branch or Congress in response to a disaster or scandal; and 2) agenda commissions, which are created by Congress or the executive in the absence of a crisis to advance a policy goal.

Challenging the conventional wisdom, I argue that crisis commissions often do trigger policy change – even if they are formed primarily to defuse political pressure. They have this effect by taking advantage of windows of opportunity for reform opened by disasters or scandals. Since crises make the status quo unpopular, they create demand for proposals that can serve as focal points for reform efforts. Crisis commissions often generate such proposals, thereby boosting the prospects for reform and, if reform does occur, shaping exactly how policy changes. On the other hand, agenda commissions usually do not prompt change because it is very difficult to overturn the status quo without the impetus provided by a crisis. My argument therefore contains a certain irony: Commissions formed to deflect pressure tend to trigger more reform than commissions established to influence policy.

Two other factors also greatly influence the likelihood of a commission sparking policy or organizational change: whether a commission is formed by the executive branch or by Congress, and whether its mandate is narrow or broad. Executive branch commissions have greater impact than congressional commissions because they can be appointed more quickly and tend to be less politically polarized, enabling them to reach consensus and to complete their work while a window of opportunity for reform remains open. At the same time, commissions with relatively narrow mandates spur more reform than panels of broader scope because a narrow charge makes it easier for a commission to achieve unanimity and to advocate effectively for the adoption of its recommendations.

Testing the Argument

Although my argument, spelled out in greater detail in Chapter 2, applies to commissions that operate in any policy area, I test it on commissions that examined national security issues. Chapter 3 analyzes an original data set of all fifty-one national security commissions that reported between the beginning of the Reagan administration and the end of 2006.[16] This data set includes information on numerous variables that might contribute to commission outcomes, as well as two original measures of commission impact. The analysis represents the first effort to use statistical tests that control for relevant variables to probe the factors that shape commission influence. A battery of tests determines that the evidence matches my theory's expectations.

I supplement this statistical analysis with case studies, which span Chapters 4–6. In these case studies, I investigate the impact of eight commissions that investigated terrorist threats or attacks. The case studies demonstrate that commissions have played a central role in the U.S. response to terrorism during the past three decades, shaping many major national security decisions. In each case, I assess whether the commission was directly responsible for important policy changes, and I evaluate whether my theory explains the outcome.

The first of these case study chapters discusses three terrorism commissions that were created by the executive branch during the 1980s, in response to bombings by Hezbollah and Libya that killed hundreds of Americans at U.S. facilities in the Middle East and aboard a transatlantic civilian flight.[17] My analysis shows that these crisis commissions had powerful effects, influencing the 1984 U.S. withdrawal from Lebanon and triggering reorganizations of the State Department and Federal Aviation Administration. In each instance, the commission's political credibility enabled it to establish a reform focal point at a time when policy makers faced pressure to make changes but could not otherwise agree on reforms.

Chapter 5 picks up the story of terrorism commissions in the late 1990s, when Al Qaeda replaced Hezbollah, Libya, and Iran as the greatest terrorist threat to the United States. The chapter compares two commissions that were created after Al Qaeda's bombing of U.S. embassies in Africa in August 1998: an executive branch commission that catalyzed important upgrades to embassy security, and a congressional commission

---

[16] I am grateful to Amy Zegart for sharing with me her commission data set, which provided some of the foundation for mine.

[17] The panels are the Commission on Beirut International Airport Terrorist Act of 23 October, 1983 (the Long Commission), the Secretary of State's Advisory Panel on Overseas Security (the Inman Panel), and the President's Commission on Aviation Security and Terrorism (the Lockerbie Commission).

on terrorism that did not spur reform.[18] I also explain how the *USS Cole* Commission, formed after Al Qaeda's bombing of a Navy destroyer in October 2000, sparked important changes in military force protection policies.

Chapter 6 focuses on Al Qaeda's September 11, 2001 attack and two related panels: the Hart-Rudman Commission and the 9/11 Commission.[19] The Hart-Rudman Commission's story unfolds in two parts. Its scant impact before 9/11 illustrates how difficult it is for agenda commissions to spark change, whereas its ability to shape the establishment of the Department of Homeland Security after 9/11 shows how a panel can spur reorganization in the wake of a crisis. The 9/11 Commission's impact was even greater: It induced the creation of the DNI post and a host of other counterterrorism reforms. The commission's catalytic effect was driven by the magnitude of the 9/11 attack, the panel's remarkable bipartisan cohesion, and the commission's persistent advocacy on behalf of its proposals.

The final chapter evaluates the influence of the Iraq Study Group, which received a cool reception from President Bush and congressional leaders but ultimately had a substantial impact by shaping the Iraq platform of then-Senator Barack Obama as he launched his presidential bid. The concluding chapter also explains why my argument should apply to commissions on issues other than national security, considers whether commissions generally give good advice, and offers tips for policy makers interested in forming a commission or advancing reform.

[18] The panels are the Accountability Review Boards on the Embassy Bombings in Nairobi and Dar Es Salaam on August 7, 1998 (the Crowe Panel) and the National Commission on Terrorism (the Bremer Commission).

[19] Formally, these panels are the United States Commission on National Security/21st Century and the National Commission on Terrorist Attacks upon the United States.

PART ONE

PATTERNS OF COMMISSION INFLUENCE

2

A Theory of Commission Influence

This chapter sets the framework for the book's empirical analysis by formulating a theory of commission influence. The theory is grounded in the notions that a special impetus is often needed to induce Congress and the president to adopt reforms, and that commissions are uniquely capable of providing this impetus. I explain why obstacles to reform often exist and how the distinct political credibility of commissions enables panels to overcome them. I also outline the circumstances in which commissions are likely to be able to turn their credibility into impact.

The Drivers of Commission Impact

Any theory of commission influence must begin with an understanding of why policy makers form panels in the first place. Prominent political science theories argue that policy makers often delegate authority to institutions in order to obtain expertise or facilitate the reaching of agreement (Epstein and O'Halloran 1999; Hawkins et al. 2006b). Scholars have developed and tested these and other theories by examining delegation to congressional committees, government agencies, regulatory bodies, permanent advisory panels, and international institutions (Balla and Wright 2001; Hawkins et al. 2006a; Kiewiet and McCubbins 1991; Lewis 2003).[1]

---

[1] Although some definitions of delegation are restricted to grants of authority to actors with formal power, other definitions encompass grants of authority to provide advice (Bradley and Kelley 2008, 3). Delegation to commissions would fall within such broader definitions of delegation.

Scholars of ad hoc commissions, for their part, have identified many reasons why policy makers form commissions, including to obtain ideas, build consensus, generate political cover, defuse public pressure, preempt an unwanted initiative, overcome congressional gridlock, or circumvent bureaucratic obstructionism (Campbell 2002; Dean 1969; Filtner 1986; Halperin 1961; Kitts 2006; Marcy 1945; Popper 1970; Tutchings 1979; Wolanin 1975; Zegart 2004). Yet scholars differ in the emphasis they put on these various motivations. In the area of national security, Amy Zegart argues that most commissions are established to provide information, whereas Kenneth Kitts contends that they are typically formed to deflect criticism and conduct damage control (Kitts 2006; Zegart 2004).

Of course, the creation of any commission does not necessarily have a single overriding motivation. To the contrary, nearly every commission has multiple purposes (Wolanin 1975, 26). I recognize there are many specific reasons Congress and the president form commissions, from avoiding blame to seeking consensus.

But my theory goes beyond existing scholarship by generating hypotheses of commission influence based on the political context surrounding the establishment of panels. Commissions are often formed as part of a policy struggle between Congress and the president in which one or both branches of government seeks to move policy closer to its preferences. In the following pages, I explain why commissions are only likely to influence this policy struggle when there exists a crisis that makes the status quo unpopular.

Agenda and Crisis Commissions

Policy makers frequently establish commissions in situations of disagreement about how to proceed on a given issue. This disagreement could be between the president and Congress, within Congress, or within the executive branch. When the president and Congress are at odds, one of the branches might form a commission as part of its effort to pressure the other branch to agree to a policy change that it favors – based on the expectation that the commission will make recommendations that are relatively close to its own preference. When the dispute lies within Congress, legislators seeking a change in existing policy might try to establish a commission in the hope that it will help build broader support for that reform. And when executive agencies cannot agree, the president might establish a commission in order to force a resolution of the issue. I label all of these commissions created under conditions of disagreement (and in the absence of a crisis) "agenda commissions," because they represent

FIGURE 2.1. Context of agenda commission.

attempts to advance an agenda that faces opposition. My theory focuses on the situation of disagreement between the president and Congress, which is the most common and significant, but it applies to the other types of disputes also.

A simple model helps to illustrate my argument. To see the context of "agenda commissions," consider a one-dimensional policy space in which P represents the president's preference in a given policy area, C represents Congress's preference, and Q represents the status quo. (I treat Congress and the president as unitary actors in this section to simplify matters.) As Figure 2.1 illustrates, Q would usually lie someplace in between P and C. Given this baseline situation, the president would typically form a commission when seeking to move policy closer to P, whereas Congress would normally establish a panel when it wants to shift policy toward C.

Agenda commissions are unlikely to spark policy change, however, because it tends to be very difficult to change the status quo in the absence of a crisis. In general, politics is marked by a strong bias in favor of maintaining the status quo (Baumgartner and Jones 1993, 47–54; Halperin and Clapp 2006, 99; Zegart 2007, 57–59). This bias is bolstered in American politics by the need for new legislation to be approved by the president and two houses of Congress, and by the Senate's supermajoritarian requirement of sixty votes to cut off a filibuster (Tsebelis 1995, 307–310). Keith Krehbiel's "pivotal politics" model and the "revolving gridlock" model of David Brady and Craig Volden assert that these features of the U.S. political system prevent policy changes from happening whenever the status quo is "moderate" – that is, in between the preferences of the president and pivotal legislators, such as the sixtieth senator needed to break a filibuster (Brady and Volden 1998; Krehbiel 1998). Figure 2.1 depicts this situation.

The same logic suggests that the recommendations of agenda commissions generally will not be supported by both the president and Congress. Congress and the president are only likely to support proposals that lie closer to their preferences than the status quo, and it is not possible for a commission to make such proposals when the status quo already lies between their preferences. In the context of Figure 2.1, if a commission's proposals lie between P and Q, the president will back them, but

Congress will not. If they lie between C and Q, they will be supported
by Congress, but not by the president. The upshot is that agenda commissions are unlikely to lead to policy change.[2] A Clinton administration
White House official put this more bluntly: "Commissions created by one
party to foist a policy preference on another party are usually a recipe for
spinning wheels, wasting time, and deadlock."[3]

By contrast, policy change is much more likely to happen in the wake
of a crisis. Numerous scholars have noted that crises create windows of
opportunity for policy change (Birkland 2006; Checkel 1997; Goldstein
1989; Haas 1992; Hall 1989; Ikenberry 1993; Keeler 1993; Kingdon
1995; Legro 2005). These windows open because crises discredit existing
policies and institutions and generate public pressure on elected officials
to make significant reforms. Increased public attention during crises can
also help overcome the resistance of interest groups or bureaucrats to
reforms by giving policy makers a new set of public rewards for action
to counterbalance that resistance (Cohen, Cuellar, and Weingast 2006,
708). Harold Gehman, the chairman of two commissions formed after
disasters, quipped, "A crisis is a wonderful catalyst for Washington to
act."[4] Obama White House Chief of Staff Rahm Emanuel made much the
same point during the 2008 presidential transition when he commented
about the financial crisis: "You never want a serious crisis to go to waste"
(Seib 2008).

Policy makers often form commissions during a crisis to defuse public
pressure, deflect attention, or delay action. Indeed, the establishment of
crisis commissions is often criticized by pundits because of these common
motivations. But crisis commissions are also typically established in the
context of policy disagreement between the branches, just like agenda
commissions. The crucial difference in terms of their potential to influence reform is that crisis commissions are often set up at a time when

---

[2] The infrequency with which agenda commissions influence policy raises an important
question: Why do policy makers form agenda commissions if those panels are unlikely
to spark reform? There are four reasons: (1) Occasionally, an agenda commission does
influence policy, as explained later in this chapter. Because the creation of a commission
tends to be relatively inexpensive for policy makers, forming a panel can be worth the cost
even if the odds of success are relatively low. (2) A congressional agenda commission is
sometimes formed as a concession to members of Congress who cannot obtain the votes
necessary to pass a substantive measure. (3) An agenda commission sometimes shapes
public debate even when it does not spark policy change. (4) An agenda commission has
the potential to be influential at a later date if a crisis occurs after it reports.

[3] Interview of Clinton administration official, January 2008.

[4] Interview of Harold Gehman, January 17, 2008.

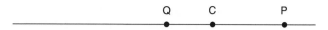

FIGURE 2.2. Context of crisis commission.

the status quo is unpopular, making it "extreme" relative to the preferences of both Congress and the president. This situation – post-crisis, but before policy reform – is depicted in Figure 2.2, where Q lies to the left of both P and C. The status quo is now extreme because the crisis has generated public pressure that shifts the preferences of the president and Congress in the same direction, whereas the status quo remains unchanged.[5] These preference changes make the political environment ripe for reform, regardless of the main motivation of the president or Congress in forming a commission.

To use an example, consider preferences for aviation security policies. Before a crisis, the president might favor stricter regulations than the status quo, and Congress might favor looser ones. However, after a terrorist attack on one or more airplanes, both Congress and the president are likely to back tighter regulations, though they will probably still disagree about what those policies should entail and how strict they should be. Until the policies are changed, the status quo will be extreme relative to the preferences of both branches. Figure 2.2 describes this situation, which is ripe for a change to someplace between the new preferences of the president and Congress.

Yet reform does not happen easily or automatically after a crisis, because entrenched bureaucratic interests often put up powerful resistance to reform, and bargaining obstacles can prevent policy makers from reaching mutually beneficial agreements. For instance, policy makers often have limited information about the preferences and negotiating strategies of other legislators. These shortcomings can prevent policy makers from identifying areas of agreement, thereby blocking the adoption of new policies (Tallberg 2006b, 24–27).

---

[5] The difference between agenda and crisis commissions, as depicted in Figures 2.1 and 2.2, is probabilistic, not absolute. The status quo is not necessarily moderate during the operation of all agenda commissions or extreme during the work of all crisis commissions. For instance, in some cases a crisis can lead to a further polarization of congressional and presidential positions. However, the tendency of presidential and congressional preferences to shift in the same direction during a crisis implies that agenda commissions are more likely than crisis commissions to coexist with moderate status quos, whereas crisis commissions are more likely to operate when the status quo is extreme.

In addition, the policy-making process is typically characterized by the existence of multiple equilibria (Garrett and Weingast 1993, 179). In this situation, political bargaining does not have a unique and predictable outcome; instead, there are multiple policy options that could obtain the support of a majority (Riker 1986, 146). When multiple equilibria exist, policy makers frequently fail to reach any agreement, because there is no obvious way for them to choose one of the possible outcomes (Garrett and Weingast 1993, 175–176).

The Importance of Focal Points

Negotiation problems and multiple equilibria give commissions an opportunity to influence policy because they generate demand for a focal point. I define a focal point as a proposal or idea around which political debate revolves in a given policy area.[6] Nearly fifty years ago, Thomas Schelling noted the value of focal points as a means of solving coordination problems, citing the example of proposals by investigative bodies: "Fact-finding reports...tend to draw expectations to a focus, by providing a suggestion to fill the vacuum of indeterminacy that otherwise exists: it is not the facts themselves, but the creation of a specific suggestion that seems to exercise influence" (Schelling 1960, 68). Although Schelling did not say what kind of fact-finding reports he had in mind, his claim applies perfectly to commissions. Yet no other commission scholar has elaborated on his assertion.

Since Schelling offered this insight, analysts of other types of political institutions have emphasized that focal points do not always emerge in situations of multiple equilibria without the active intervention of an institution, political leader, or policy entrepreneur. In European politics, Geoffrey Garrett and Barry Weingast contend that a 1979 European Court of Justice ruling provided a necessary focal point for negotiations over how to organize the European market, and Jonas Tallberg and Derek Beach claim that the European Union presidency and secretariat shape outcomes by making proposals that provide focal points for further bargaining among governments (Beach 2004, 423; Garrett and Weingast 1993; Tallberg 2006a). In American politics, Roderick Kiewiet and Matthew McCubbins argue that congressional party leaders play a comparable role, exploiting "the sheer prominence of their position to stake out a highly visible focal point on key issues, thus encouraging support to

---

[6] A standard definition of a focal point does not exist in political science. My definition captures the essence of most uses of the term by other scholars.

coalesce around one of possibly many acceptable alternatives" (Kiewiet and McCubbins 1991, 44–45). All of this scholarship underscores that a political actor can spark policy change when there is not a single equilibrium outcome by publicizing a particular option that becomes viewed as the default choice or basis for negotiation.

A focal point influences policy in part by helping to overcome the political system's status quo bias. This bias is especially strong when there exist multiple prominent alternatives to the status quo, rather than a single alternative (Kahneman, Knetsch, and Thaler 2000). Thus, even when existing policy is discredited in the wake of a crisis, it is often necessary for consensus to develop around a single alternative before change occurs (Birkland 2006, 20; Kingdon 1995, 178–179; Weaver 2000, 35). As Jeffrey Legro writes, "In cases where a single alternative idea exists, a more natural focal point of opposition is available and it is easier for those disenchanted with the old ideas to coordinate and effect change" (Legro 2005, 35).

A commission's recommendations can provide this focal point. The proposals do not need to be original to serve this purpose; indeed, frequently commissions make recommendations that have been discussed or proposed previously by other people. But a commission can add substance and heft to preexisting policy ideas and, by advocating them, make them more widely known and accepted than competing proposals. In this way, its recommendations can become the most salient and attractive option to policy makers.

A commission's ability to establish a focal point in the situation of multiple equilibria is enhanced by the prevalence of bounded rationality and the frequency with which policy makers satisfice. Bounded rationality refers to the general inability of decision makers to canvass all alternatives systematically, whereas satisficing describes people's common practice of making choices by selecting the first available option that meets their goals (Simon 1955; Simon 1982). These tendencies suggest that a commission's proposal does not have to be the best possible option in order to become a focal point. It only has to be minimally acceptable to policy makers.

Moreover, policy makers often have only vague preferences regarding specific policy choices. Generally they have clear policy goals, such as combating terrorism or reducing poverty, but lack specific preferences on the best means to achieve those goals. The vagueness of these preferences gives a commission added opportunity to shape policy makers' positions and influence policy outcomes. This opportunity is likely to be greatest

FIGURE 2.3. Opening for crisis commission.

in the wake of a crisis, because a crisis tends to generate new uncertainty about future developments and about which policies are likely to achieve policy makers' objectives.[7]

Figure 2.3 depicts the opportunity presented to a commission in a situation of multiple equilibria following a crisis. In this situation, the president and Congress agree on the direction in which policy should be changed, but disagree on the amount of that change. (The president favors greater change than Congress in the diagram, but the model would also apply if Congress supports more change than the president.) In principle, policy could move to any place between the status quo (Q) and A – the point that is as far from Congress's preference (C) as is Q. Within this range, any policy is preferable to the status quo for both the president and Congress, and thus any option could win their support. Yet negotiating problems, including the lack of an obvious way of settling on a specific option, can prevent Congress and the president from reaching agreement on their own. In other words, demand exists for a focal point. A commission can step into this leadership void by issuing a recommendation that lies somewhere between Q and A – that is, a proposal that both branches prefer to Q. This recommendation within the zone of possible agreement can provide the single prominent alternative to the status quo that is needed to prod Congress and the president to agree on policy change.[8]

Picking up the aviation security scenario, a commission formed after a terrorist attack on one or more airplanes has the potential to trigger changes to aviation security policy by providing a focal point at a time when multiple equilibrium outcomes exist. This opportunity was presented

[7] Bounded rationality, satisficing, and the vagueness of policy preferences are not necessary conditions for the operation of my focal point argument, but they represent additional reasons why a focal point can have a powerful effect.

[8] Not all places between Q and A are equally likely to become a focal point. If a commission recommends a policy that is only slightly to the right of Q, it will not be very attractive to Congress or the president because it represents only a small change from the status quo. By the same token, if the panel's proposal is just a little to the left of A, it will be relatively unappealing to Congress because it is nearly as far from Congress's preference as is the status quo. In either case, the recommendation is unlikely to gain broad enough political support to become a focal point. A proposal that represents a marked improvement over the status quo from the perspective of both political branches is more likely to do so.

to the President's Commission on Aviation Security and Terrorism (the Lockerbie Commission), which was established by George H. W. Bush in response to the bombing of Pan Am Flight 103 over Lockerbie, Scotland by Libyan agents in December 1988. The bombing killed 270 people, placing political pressure on Congress and the president to bolster security policies. But policy makers did not reach agreement on significant reforms during the next year and a half.

When the Lockerbie Commission reported in May 1990, its recommendations quickly became the focal point for the debate over legislative fixes. Members of Congress introduced legislation to adopt the commission's proposals just six weeks after the panel reported, leading to enactment of a major law, the Aviation Security Act, in November 1990.[9] That act adopted most of the commission's recommendations, including creating a new system of federal security managers at domestic airports, mandating tighter controls over checked baggage and airport personnel, and requiring that the government notify the public of threats to aviation under certain circumstances. In Chapter 4, I show that this legislation would probably not have been enacted without the impetus provided by the commission.

To use another example, the 9/11 Commission was also established in response to an attack on aviation, but Congress and the president had already made major changes in aviation security policy, such as the federalization of baggage screeners, by the time the commission reported in July 2004. As a result, the commission's impact occurred in other policy areas, where demand for a focal point still existed. Most notably, prior to the release of the commission's report, there was no momentum on Capitol Hill for broad reform of the intelligence community. Even those policy makers interested in intelligence reform lacked consensus on which changes should be adopted.

The commission's proposal to establish a director of national intelligence generated momentum for reform and provided a focal point that dominated political debate in subsequent months. The Bush administration and powerful legislators opposed creating a DNI before the commission reported, but the idea gained such strong public support due to the panel that it was enacted into law – along with numerous other commission proposals – by the Intelligence Reform Act of December 2004.[10] In Chapter 6, I explain how the commission drove the DNI's

[9] This act is Public Law 101–604.
[10] This act is Public Law 108–458.

establishment, which represented the most significant reorganization of the intelligence community in nearly sixty years.

This discussion of crisis and agenda commissions generates my first hypothesis: *Commissions established after a crisis are likely to have a greater impact on policy than commissions formed in the absence of a crisis.*

This hypothesis challenges the conventional wisdom that crisis commissions only serve as damage-control devices that rarely lead to policy change. It also counters a claim by historian Hugh Davis Graham that commissions formed during crises have less influence than panels created in other circumstances (Graham 1985, 9–10).

Executive and Congressional Commissions

Although demand for a focal point tends to be greatest following a crisis, the existence of a crisis does not guarantee that a commission will spark reform. Other variables, including the source of a commission's authority and the scope of its mandate, shape the likelihood that a commission will construct a focal point.

Commissions can be established in three ways: by statute, presidential order, or agency directive. I label commissions established by statute "congressional commissions" and call panels formed by the president or an agency "executive commissions." My theory implies that executive commissions should influence policy more often than congressional commissions, for three reasons.

First, an executive commission is more likely than a congressional commission to issue recommendations while demand for a focal point still exists. Understanding why this is the case requires relaxing the unitary-actor assumption that I adopted previously to describe the president and Congress. In reality, the president is a much more unified actor than Congress. Although executive-branch agencies often disagree with each other, the president directs action for the executive as a whole, enabling it to make decisions relatively quickly. By contrast, congressional decision making is highly fragmented – spread across two houses and numerous committees, and complicated by divisions between political parties (Moe and Wilson 1994). This fragmentation makes it relatively hard for Congress to act with alacrity.

The different speeds of action of Congress and the executive shape the relative ability of congressional and executive commissions to construct a focal point. The president or an agency head can form a commission and appoint its members quite quickly – often within weeks. But when members of Congress seek to establish a commission, the slow pace of the legislative process frequently allows the passage of many months, or even years, before its authorizing statute is enacted, and additional months typically go by before its members are appointed.

The latter delay results from the sharing of appointment power among multiple policy makers. Whereas the members of executive commissions are typically appointed by a single official, for congressional commissions appointment power is often divided among four or more members of Congress, such as the Republican and Democratic leaders of the House and Senate as well as the president. If some or all of these policy makers oppose the commission's existence or do not consider it to be a priority, which is frequently the case, they are likely to drag their feet in naming their appointments. The extent of these delays is evident in my data set of all fifty-one national security commissions that reported between 1981 and 2006. (The data set is described in more detail in Chapter 3.) An average of twenty-two months transpired between the authorization of congressional commissions and the completion of their work, whereas the average duration of executive commissions was just nine months.

This difference implies that it is relatively difficult for a congressional commission to influence policy, even in the wake of a crisis, because a window of opportunity for reform may close by the time the panel issues recommendations. This window could close because the president and Congress agree on policy change before the commission reports. For instance, in terms of Figure 2.3, policy could move from Q to someplace between C and A while the panel is operating, making additional reform unlikely. Alternatively, a congressional commission's delays can enable the window of opportunity to close because they allow political pressure for reform to dissipate. In other words, the preferences of the president and Congress revert to their precrisis preferences, making the status quo moderate again, as in Figure 2.1, and eliminating demand for a focal point.

Second, executive commissions are more likely than congressional commissions to be designed in a way that facilitates the issuance of unanimous recommendations. As explained in more detail later in this chapter, unanimity is critical to the construction of a focal point, because it sends a powerful signal to policy makers about the political acceptability of a commission's recommendations. When the president or an agency head appoints a commission, that official can structure the panel so that unanimity is likely – for instance, by keeping the number of commissioners relatively low and appointing a group that is not extremely diverse ideologically.

By contrast, the design of congressional commissions tends to be more haphazard because it is shaped by the messy legislative process and multiple principals. For instance, whereas a senator's initial proposal for a commission might call for a panel of eight members, the president and other members of Congress might press for a larger commission so that their own allies or supporters will be appointed to it. The compromises necessary to authorize the commission could result in a panel of twelve people – rather than eight – complicating the achievement of unanimity. In this way, the influence of legislative compromises on the structure of commissions is similar to their role in the establishment of new agencies, leading to panels that, like agencies, are not necessarily designed to be effective (Moe 1989).

The sharing of appointment power for congressional commissions among Republicans and Democrats also tends to generate panels that are more divided along partisan or ideological lines than executive commissions. Party leaders have an incentive to appoint partisans or ideologues to congressional commissions in order to ensure that they are not imbalanced in favor of loyalists of the opposing party. Because partisans and ideologues tend to be less open to changing their viewpoint or compromising, their presence on a commission makes it more difficult for the panel to reach consensus, and thereby makes the construction of a focal point less likely.

Third, executive commissions have the potential to spark reform even in the absence of a crisis because of Congress's relative disunity. As I argued earlier, a commission is generally unlikely to induce policy change when the status quo lies between the preferences of Congress and the president. But reform in the direction favored by the president can sometimes occur in this situation nevertheless. Consider Figure 2.4, in which R represents the recommendation of an executive agenda commission. (R is to the right of Q because executive commissions tend to recommend policies that the president prefers to the status quo.) Whereas the president favors moving policy to R, Congress does not. However, if Congress is closely divided on the issue, the president might only need to sway a few legislators in order to induce Congress to support a change to R. The commission's advocacy of its recommendation, combined with the many levers of influence available to the president, can sometimes lead these key legislators to change their

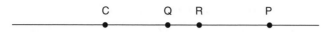

FIGURE 2.4. Executive commission recommendation.

FIGURE 2.5. Congressional commission recommendation.

stance in accord with the commission's proposal.[11] In other words, the fragmentation of Congress can allow the president, with the assistance of the commission, to peel off enough members of Congress to shift C to a point where it is closer to R than to Q, allowing the adoption of R.

On the other hand, the more unitary character of the executive makes it very difficult for a congressional commission to induce a substantial shift in P. In the context of a moderate status quo, a congressional agenda commission is likely to propose a policy between Q and C, as in Figure 2.5, where R represents the recommendation. (Congressional commissions are apt to propose policies that Congress prefers to the status quo because most, if not all, of their members are usually appointed by congressional leaders.) In this situation, the president's preference is highly unlikely to shift to the left of Q absent heavy public and congressional pressure, which few panels can generate.

In addition to these generic differences between executive and congressional commissions, executive commissions enjoy a particular advantage in national security affairs. It is well-established that the president exerts greater influence than Congress over foreign and defense policy (Bartels 1996, 17; Hilsman 1993, 311; Howell and Pevehouse 2007, 9; Wildavsky 1966). The president's dominance of national security affairs suggests that policy is usually more likely to move in the direction favored by the president than toward the preference of Congress. Because the proposals of executive commissions tend to be more attractive to the president than the recommendations of congressional commissions, they are more likely to be adopted.

---

[11] The presidential levers of influence can include offering members of Congress concessions on other issues that are important to them, making the issue space, in effect, multidimensional.

This discussion of executive and congressional panels generates my second hypothesis: *Executive commissions are likely to have a greater impact on policy than congressional commissions.*

This hypothesis has not previously been tested by any scholars. Most commission scholarship has focused on presidential panels, neglecting the proliferation of congressional commissions since the 1970s.

The Scope of Commission Mandates

A commission's ability to establish a focal point is also affected by the scope of its mandate. Some panels are given broad mandates to investigate wide swaths of policy, such as national security strategy or the functions of the intelligence community. Other commissions are asked to examine more specific issues, such as the threat of terrorism or the role of women in the armed forces. Still other panels are formed to study issues as narrow as a specific weapons system.[12]

One might expect commissions with broad mandates to have greater impact because they should generate wider interest among policy makers and the public. After all, more people are interested in America's national security strategy than in whether to procure a single weapons system. Moreover, the proposals of commissions of broad scope should tend to be more important than those of panels with more restricted mandates. But commissions of broad scope face a countervailing challenge that tends to limit their influence sharply: Their mandate to examine a wide range of problems and agencies makes it difficult for them to shape policy on any single issue.

Recall that a focal point is a proposal or idea around which political debate revolves in a given policy area. Even if a crisis creates demand for a focal point, a commission's recommendations are unlikely to become that focal point without advocacy by the panel's numbers to call attention to the proposals and gain backing for them from key policy makers. A narrow mandate is more conducive to a successful advocacy effort, because it allows the commission to target its promotion efforts on the relatively small number of agencies or congressional committees that have jurisdiction over the issue addressed by the panel. By contrast, successful advocacy is harder for a commission of broad scope, because the greater number of issues or agencies it examines brings an increase in the

---

[12] Typically, commissions formed by executive-branch agencies investigate more specific issues than do presidential or congressional panels, but some agency panels have very broad mandates and some congressional and presidential commissions have quite narrow ones.

number of involved policy makers. Put another way, a commission can lobby one or two agencies or committees much more readily than it can lobby a broad cross-section of the government.

Moreover, a commission with a broad mandate is less likely to have an effective champion in Congress or the executive. When a panel's scope is limited, a single member of Congress or an executive-branch official with a keen interest in the issue can sometimes drive adoption of the commission's recommendations through one piece of legislation or directive. However, the proposals of a commission of broad scope can rarely be adopted through a single measure, and responsibility for adopting them tends to be diffused throughout government. This diffusion of responsibility diminishes any individual policy maker's incentive or capacity to pursue the adoption of those recommendations.

Relatedly, a narrow mandate simplifies a commission's task of reaching consensus on specific proposals. A commission of broad scope may be unable to achieve such consensus because it cannot deliberate intensively on all of the issues it must cover. This disadvantage can diminish a commission's impact in one of two ways: (1) If the commission's recommendations are not unanimous, they are unlikely to become a focal point. (2) If the proposals are unanimous but vague, they will not be easily transferable into legislation or regulations. Representative Mac Thornberry (R-TX) explained, "A lot of commissions will say, 'The government needs to work together better,' or 'We need Middle East peace to stop terrorism.' But that's not particularly helpful when you go to a legislative counsel and need to put something down in black and white in a bill. When a recommendation is more specific, you can introduce it."[13]

This discussion of commission mandates generates my third hypothesis: *Commissions with narrow mandates are likely to have a greater impact on policy than panels with broader mandates.*

This hypothesis conforms with assertions by other scholars that commissions with limited mandates are more influential (Drew 1968, 47; Popper 1970, 44). But my argument offers the fullest explanation of why this is the case, and the empirical analysis in subsequent chapters represents the first effort to test this hypothesis rigorously.

Moreover, the hypothesis is worth investigating because it challenges other political science theories. In their work on international institutions, Barbara Koremenos, Charles Lipson, and Duncan Snidal argue that it is beneficial for an institution to have a broad mandate, because

---

[13] Interview of Mac Thornberry, April 3, 2009.

that breadth creates room for issue linkage and trade-offs, which facilitate the reaching of agreements (Koremenos, Lipson, and Snidal 2001, 786). Their argument suggests that commissions of broad scope should be more likely to resolve deadlocks between Congress and the president. However, my expectation is that commissions with narrow mandates should prompt political bargains more often, because they can more easily reach consensus on specific proposals and advocate effectively on behalf of those recommendations.

Still, this hypothesis must be accompanied by a caveat: If a commission of broad scope does succeed in forging political agreement, its impact will tend to surpass that of a commission with a narrow mandate that triggers change. For instance, a commission that catalyzes an overhaul of the process for funding all national security agencies should be considered more influential than a panel that sparks reform of one division within a single agency. My argument is simply that commissions with broad mandates succeed so rarely that they are less influential on average than panels with more circumscribed charges.

An Illustrative Comparison: The Scowcroft and Webster Commissions

A brief comparison of two commissions illustrates the benefits associated with executive-branch authorization and a narrow mandate. On January 3, 1983, Ronald Reagan established the President's Commission on Strategic Forces (the Scowcroft Commission).[14] Reagan's purpose in forming this agenda commission was to increase congressional support for funding production and deployment of the MX intercontinental ballistic missile (ICBM), which the Democratic-controlled House of Representatives had rejected in December 1982.[15] (The Republican-led Senate backed funding the MX.) Reagan gave the panel, which was chaired by Brent Scowcroft and included prominent Republicans and Democrats, a narrow mandate: to review America's modernization program for strategic arms, particularly the ICBM.

The commission's unanimous report, issued on April 11, 1983, recommended a congressional-executive bargain: deploying the MX promptly, as the administration wanted, and developing a smaller ICBM known as the Midgetman, which was favored by many Democrats but opposed

[14] Executive Order 12400.
[15] Interview of Robert McFarlane, May 21, 2008; interview of Thomas Reed, November 15, 2007.

by the Pentagon (President's Commission on Strategic Forces 1983). The commission promoted its compromise aggressively to both Congress and the administration, persuading the White House to endorse development of the Midgetman and gaining the backing of House Democrats with great influence on defense issues, such as Les Aspin (D-WI) and Al Gore (D-TN), for its MX proposal.[16] This advocacy effort succeeded in catalyzing the House to approve funding for the MX on May 25, 1983 (Kitts 2006, 90–93; Wrenn 1984, 11–12).[17]

In interviews, numerous Reagan administration and congressional officials involved in the MX debate credited the commission with turning the tide in favor of the missile.[18] Then–Deputy National Security Advisor Robert McFarlane observed, "Funding wouldn't have been provided without the commission."[19] The commission also triggered the appropriation of funds in 1983 for developing the Midgetman as part of the panel's bipartisan compromise.[20] Scowcroft described the bargain: "People who liked the MX swallowed the Midgetman, and people who liked the Midgetman swallowed the MX."[21]

The commission's large impact was facilitated by its executive-branch authorization and narrow scope. The executive-branch authorization enabled the panel to be appointed very quickly, which allowed it to report within just three months – before the House was due to vote again on the MX. Its executive origin also helped by producing a commission with moderate, but not great, ideological diversity: All of the panel's members supported a strong national defense, though they joined the panel with varied views on the MX and other strategic arms.[22] This limited diversity eased the commission's effort to reach consensus.

---

[16] Interview of John Deutch, December 5, 2007; interview of Thomas Reed, November 15, 2007; interview of Brent Scowcroft, July 10, 2007; interview of James Woolsey, November 8, 2007.

[17] The House bill was H.R. 113. The bill was later folded into the 1983 Department of Defense Appropriations Act, Public Law 98–112.

[18] Interview of James McCarthy, October 31, 2007; interview of Robert McFarlane, May 12, 2008; interview of Thomas Reed, November 15, 2007; interview of John Vessey, July 18, 2007; interview of Reagan administration official, May 2008; interview of congressional aide, April 2008.

[19] Interview of Robert McFarlane, May 12, 2008.

[20] Interview of James McCarthy, October 31, 2007; interview of Thomas Reed, November 15, 2007. The funds were provided by the 1983 Department of Defense Appropriations Act, Public Law 98–112.

[21] Interview of Brent Scowcroft, July 10, 2007.

[22] Interview of Brent Scowcroft, July 10, 2007; interview of James Woolsey, November 8, 2007.

The commission's narrow scope further simplified the panel's task of formulating unanimous and specific recommendations, and it permitted the commission to focus its advocacy on a limited number of key policy makers – namely, senior White House officials and a few House Democrats with great influence on defense issues. The panel's ability to sway Aspin, Gore, and other Democrats who previously opposed funding the MX illustrates how an agenda commission can help an administration peel off key legislators, even in the absence of a crisis.

By contrast, the history of the Commission on the Advancement of Federal Law Enforcement (the Webster Commission) reveals some of the disadvantages associated with congressional authorization and a broad mandate. This crisis commission, chaired by former Director of Central Intelligence and FBI Director William Webster, was created after a series of disasters that called into question the quality and purpose of federal law enforcement agencies: the 1992 shooting of several civilians by U.S. Marshals and FBI agents in Ruby Ridge, Idaho; the 1993 siege of a Branch Davidian compound in Waco, Texas by FBI and Bureau of Alcohol, Tobacco, and Firearms (ATF) agents, which ended in a fire that killed eighty-six people; and the 1995 Oklahoma City bombing.[23] The commission's authorizing statute, enacted in April 1996, instructed the panel to review federal law enforcement operations and priorities for the 21st century, including the capability to investigate and deter terrorism.[24]

Even before the commission began operating, congressional disagreement about its mission hampered its work. Some members of Congress wanted the panel to highlight abuses by the FBI, others wanted it to focus on strengthening the government's ability to prevent terrorist acts, and still others wanted it to offer proposals for consolidating law enforcement agencies.[25] The commission's report explains that these different conceptions made setting up the panel contentious, causing lengthy delays: "Months passed before an appropriation for the Commission's work was enacted and almost 2 years went by before the full, five-member complement of Commissioners was appointed" (Commission on the Advancement of Federal Law Enforcement 2000, 23).

The panel's unanimous 185-page report, issued in January 2000, covered the management of law enforcement agencies, terrorism, international

---

[23] The legislation was the Antiterrorism and Effective Death Penalty Act of 1996, Public Law 104–132.

[24] I classify the panel as a national security commission because its mandate covered the issue of terrorism.

[25] Interview of Lee Colwell, December 7, 2007; William Webster, December 4, 2007.

crime, and cyber crime. It lacked a central theme, though, beyond the commonplace conclusion that America should "move now on an urgent basis to prepare to detect these criminal activities at the source, counter them in all appropriate ways, and protect Americans to every extent possible" (Commission on the Advancement of Federal Law Enforcement 2000, 15). The commission's proposals included folding the Drug Enforcement Agency (DEA) into the FBI, transferring part of the ATF to the FBI, bolstering the attorney general's law enforcement authorities, and restricting the federalization of crimes that can be dealt with at the state level.

The report had no discernible impact: None of its principal recommendations was adopted at the time. In the Clinton administration's only public comments on it, Treasury Secretary Lawrence Summers and Attorney General Janet Reno noted that the administration had already considered and rejected the idea of merging the ATF and DEA into the FBI.[26] Just three senators attended the sole congressional hearing on the report.[27]

The commission's lack of influence was due to two main factors. Most important, the federal law enforcement crisis of the early to mid-1990s had become a distant memory to the public and most policy makers by the time the commission reported in 2000 – a major downside of the long delays that attended the panel's establishment. A window of opportunity for policy change existed during the Clinton administration's first term, when it considered reorganizing law enforcement agencies, but that window closed several years before the commission reported.

Second, the commission's broad scope complicated its task of generating public interest in its proposals. Webster explained: "This was a broad study on a whole range of federal law enforcement issues, covering a lot of agencies.... We didn't say the system is broken. We didn't have one big recommendation to get people's attention."[28]

The Political Credibility of Commissions

Thus far, I have argued that commissions can catalyze policy change by creating reform focal points, and that they are more likely to do so if they

---

[26] Statement of Treasury Secretary Lawrence H. Summers and Attorney General Janet Reno, February 1, 2000.
[27] Hearing of the Senate Judiciary Subcommittee on Criminal Justice Oversight, February 3, 2000.
[28] Interview of William Webster, December 4, 2007.

are formed in the wake of a crisis, established by the executive, and given a narrow mandate. All of this leaves unanswered an important question: Why do Congress and the president need commissions to generate focal points? In this section, I explain how the unique political credibility of commissions distinguishes them from other political actors and institutions, enabling them to create focal points when others cannot do so.

Presidents, party leaders, and congressional committee chairs have significant agenda-setting power, but these policy makers frequently lack strong political credibility, because other actors consider them to be biased or motivated by partisan, electoral, or ideological concerns. Moreover, their proposals often lie to one side of the political spectrum, offering little appeal to those on the other side. By contrast, commissions have less inherent agenda-setting power – indeed, they lack any formal proposal power – but tend to have far greater political credibility. This credibility, deriving from the political diversity, independence, and stature of commissions, enables them to generate focal points.

The importance of political credibility as the key source of commission influence is illuminated by considering the choice to establish a commission in the context of other policy-making options. When executive-branch officials or members of Congress are interested in taking action in a given policy area, they have the following choices: They can propose or adopt new measures themselves, delegate to the bureaucracy or to a standing advisory body, or form a commission.

There are two principal reasons why policy makers might not act on their own: (1) they might not have enough information to decide on a policy option, or (2) they might be unable to win sufficient backing from other policy makers for their preferred choice. If insufficient information is the reason, they can usually call on existing agencies for advice because agencies possess or have access to all manner of expertise. Yet sometimes policy makers mistrust the information provided by agencies, suspecting that it is biased (Beckman 1981, 228; Bimber 1996, 37–41; Halperin and Clapp 2006, 176–177; Newmann 2003, 75). In these instances, they can turn to standing advisory bodies, such as the Government Accountability Office, National Academy of Sciences, and Defense Science Board, or to federally funded research and development centers (FFRDCs), such as RAND and the Institute for Defense Analyses. These bodies, which conduct dozens of government-sponsored national security studies every year, specialize in providing expert, impartial advice on technical policy issues. Given these existing options for expert advice, policy makers should not generally need to form commissions in search of technical information. As Larry Halloran, the former staff director of a House government reform subcommittee, commented about Congress, "We can get expertise whenever we want it."[29]

Instead, policy makers are likely to establish commissions when they seek political advantage – that is, when they lack sufficient backing for their agenda and are seeking to bolster that support. In these cases, expert information is likely to be less important than political credibility. James Lindsay writes, "Expertise matters most on scientific and technical issues, but these are the issues least likely to be at the core of the debate between the two ends of Pennsylvania Avenue. Congress and the president struggle far more often over what are essentially *political* judgments" (Lindsay 1994, 181). When making these political judgments on policy issues, elected officials are more likely to be swayed by a bipartisan commission comprised of people whom they know and respect than by an agency that lacks independence or impartiality, or by an expert panel that lacks stature in Washington.

Unanimity Out of Diversity
Scholarship on congressional committees sheds light on how the bipartisanship and ideological diversity of commissions contribute to their political credibility. Thomas Gilligan and Keith Krehbiel argue that congressional committees shape policy making by providing the rest of Congress with signals about the political feasibility of policy options (Gilligan and Krehbiel 1990; Krehbiel 1991). Committees are most informative, Gilligan and Krehbiel assert, if they are political microcosms of their parent chamber, with an ideologically diverse membership whose median preference matches that of the chamber. When such committees approve bills, those bills tend to receive majority backing on the floor, because legislators take cues from committee members who share their philosophical bent, and legislators can assume that they would not be able to achieve an outcome more to their liking on the floor than their like-minded colleagues were able to achieve within the committee.

Commissions can provide a powerful signal of the political acceptability of their proposals in much the same way. Other things being equal, this signal is strongest when a commission is bipartisan and an ideological microcosm of the broader policy-making community. (In practice, nearly all commissions are bipartisan, but their ideological diversity varies.) If a commission consisting of liberal Democrats, centrists, and conservative

[29] Interview of Larry Halloran, March 24, 2009.

Republicans issues a unanimous report, policy makers and interested citizens of all affinities will tend to conclude that the commission's proposals accord with their own preferences because at least one panel member is ideologically similar to them. This expectation conforms to the results of studies that have found that people defer to the judgment of others who are believed to be like themselves (Cialdini 2001, 120).

Political diversity only bolsters a commission's impact, however, if the commission is able to reach consensus. John Zaller argues that when an ideologically diverse group of political figures agrees on a policy issue, the attentive public tends to support the group's prescription, but when such a group divides, the public tends to become polarized too (Zaller 1992, 8–11). The same logic applies to the recommendations of commissions. Whereas a unanimous commission report signals clearly to policy makers and the public that its proposals are politically palatable, a divided report muddies the signal, preventing a commission from generating a focal point. Given the lower likelihood that a very diverse commission will achieve unanimity, the relationship between diversity and impact cuts two ways. A commission must be fairly diverse in order to release a meaningful political signal, but too much diversity can make a commission less likely to be influential.

In fact, most commissions do reach consensus. (Thirty-five of the fifty-one commissions in my data set of national security commissions produced unanimous reports.) This tendency contrasts sharply with the practice of congressional committees, which rarely agree unanimously on legislation. Commissions possess a special ability to reach consensus even when they are relatively diverse, because of their small size and the privacy and relative depoliticization of their deliberative environment.

Small group size has several beneficial effects: It enables extensive face-to-face interaction among members, gives each member a greater stake in the group's work, encourages a sense of common purpose, and makes it easier for members to reconcile their differences (Olson 1965; Verba 1961). As one senior staff member of a commission observed, "The bigger a commission is, the more likely it is to get gridlocked and the more frustrated the members become that they don't have enough of a slice of what the commission is doing."[30] In addition, small groups tend to exercise greater influence on the beliefs of their members than do larger ones, making it more likely that individuals will change their opinions in the direction of the majority view. Sidney Verba contends that most

---

[30] Interview of Michael Bayer, November 20, 2007.

groups retaining these characteristics consist of considerably fewer than twenty people (Verba 1961, 12). The median number of members of the commissions in my data set is ten, suggesting that most commissions have these attributes.[31]

The unusual deliberative environment of commissions is as important as their size in facilitating consensus. Commissions are one of the only institutions where prominent political figures of different parties and perspectives deliberate intensively in a private setting that is relatively insulated from political pressures. This is important because privacy and depoliticization are necessary conditions for deliberation in which people consider seriously alternative views (Checkel 1997; Checkel 2001, 562–563). Whereas congressional committee hearings have neither of these characteristics, commission deliberations are generally private, and they are somewhat depoliticized because panel members do not typically hold public office during the time of their commission service. Their detachment from the permanent institutions of government can soften partisan instincts, thereby facilitating compromise (Wolanin 1975, 32–33). Former Secretary of State James Baker, who has served on many panels, quipped, "It helps to have 'has-beens' on commissions because they have no political ax to grind."[32]

Commission members are also typically freed from the constraint of having to satisfy the parochial concerns of constituents and interest groups, which often limits the ability of members of Congress to reach agreement. Brian Jenkins, an advisor to several national security panels, noted, "Commission discussions aren't taking place in public, so there's no point in posturing."[33] Self-interest further contributes to the tendency to seek consensus on commissions. Commissioners know that if they do not achieve unanimity, their report is unlikely to have much impact.

There is much anecdotal evidence that these special attributes of commissions – small size, privacy, and depoliticization – spark changes of opinion and facilitate the reaching of consensus (Filtner 1986, 81; Halperin 1961, 381; Larsen 1975, 24–25; Short 1975, 85–88; Templeton 2005, 168–203; Wolanin 1975, 152). David Filtner has written, "The transforming aspect of the commission experience is such that, on the

---

[31] Some scholars have asserted that small commissions are more influential than large ones, but have not explained why this is the case or rigorously tested the proposition (Popper 1970, 17; Tutchings 1979, 33).

[32] Interview of James Baker, June 2, 2007.

[33] Interview of Brian Jenkins, December 18, 2007.

best commissions, members go in thinking they know the tune and come out singing a new song" (Filtner 2004).

The national security commissions that are the subject of this book include many examples of such changes of opinion. For instance, on the 2006 Iraq Study Group (ISG), James Baker, Lawrence Eagleburger, and Charles Robb were persuaded to support the withdrawal of most U.S. troops from Iraq and a change in the remaining troops' mission to training Iraqi forces and conducting counterterrorism operations.[34] Former Secretary of State Eagleburger recalled, "From the beginning of the war, I had felt that we need to stay in Iraq until we accomplish our goals. I opposed withdrawal. But when I came on board the ISG and read the background papers, I was horrified by the descriptions of conditions on the ground and the condition of our military. Reluctantly, I adjusted my view."[35]

Independence and Stature

The relative frequency of opinion changes within commissions reflects the large amount of independence possessed by panels – another attribute that contributes to their credibility. This independence is grounded in the autonomy of commissions, which makes them somewhat unpredictable.

Commissions, like other institutions, pursue their own interests subject only to the constraints imposed upon them by their relationship with their sponsors (Kiewiet and McCubbins 1991, 5). As commissions conduct their work, these constraints can be significant because panels must rely on the executive branch and/or Congress for funding, logistical support, and access to information (Fenster 2008, 1258). By the time commissions write their reports, these sources of dependency are reduced or even eliminated, but another constraint remains: Commissions generally want policy makers to adopt their recommendations. This desire suggests that their proposals should not stray too far from what key policy makers support.

Nevertheless, many commissions issue findings and recommendations that diverge significantly from their sponsors' preferences. Rhett Dawson, staff director of two national security commissions, colorfully described this phenomenon: "Once you create a commission, it's like watching a hog learning to ice skate. That hog is going to go wherever it

---

[34] Interview of Lawrence Eagleburger, January 24, 2008; interview of Charles Robb, July 23, 2007.
[35] Interview of Lawrence Eagleburger, January 24, 2008.

wants to go."[36] Perhaps the most remarkable instance of such skating is the Commission on Marijuana and Drug Abuse, established by Richard Nixon, which recommended to Nixon that marijuana should be decriminalized – a proposal that could not have been further from Nixon's own position (DeParle 1983).

Two of the commissions in my data set provide more recent examples. The 1997 Federal Advisory Committee on Gender-Integrated Training and Related Issues, appointed by Clinton administration Defense Secretary William Cohen, recommended instituting gender-segregated basic training in all branches of the armed services, even though Cohen and the leadership of the Army, Navy, and Air Force favored maintaining gender-integrated basic training (Federal Advisory Committee on Gender-Integrated Training and Related Issues 1997). Contemporaneous newspaper coverage indicates that the recommendation greatly surprised Pentagon officials (Priest 1997).

A decade earlier, a majority on the 1987 Secretary of State's Advisory Committee on South Africa, appointed by Reagan administration Secretary of State George Shultz, reported that the administration's strategy of constructive engagement toward South Africa had "failed," and called for the establishment of multilateral sanctions on South Africa (Secretary of State's Advisory Committee on South Africa 1987). The report was so sharply at odds with the administration's policy that the State Department tried to prevent reporters from obtaining a copy of it.[37] Shultz noted, "When you appoint a high-powered commission, you're rolling the dice a bit. You don't know whether they'll agree with your policies."[38]

Indeed, the independence of commissions underscores that a policy maker's decision to appoint a panel is a risky strategic choice. For instance, in forming a crisis commission, a president is gambling that the panel is more likely to defuse political pressure facing the White House than to increase such pressure through a report that criticizes the administration. This gamble may pay off most of the time, but sometimes it does not. Still, the intensity of political pressure during a crisis often leads the president to make this risky choice.

This unpredictability of commissions derives in part from the stature and reputations of the commissioners themselves. Commissioners are often people of significant standing, such as former members of

---

[36] Interview of Rhett Dawson, June 25, 2007.
[37] Interview of Michael Clough, November 14, 2007.
[38] Interview of George Shultz, February 22, 2008.

Congress or cabinet officials. Such individuals might be somewhat loyal to a given president or to other policy makers, but they also know that their own reputations are at stake when their commission issues its report. If the report is viewed as a whitewash, their reputations may suffer. This concern was probably one reason why James Baker endorsed the Iraq Study Group's highly critical assessment of conditions in Iraq in late 2006, despite his close ties to George W. Bush. One person involved in the study group noted that Baker cares greatly about his reputation and how he will be viewed by history.[39] He therefore had an incentive to support findings that would be well-received by the broader policy-making community – even if they were unfavorable to the Bush administration.

Combined with the diversity and stature of commissions, their independence enhances their impact by generating a perception that they are relatively unbiased and trustworthy. Studies have shown that people are more persuaded by information when it is provided by a person or institution that is perceived to have these characteristics (Chaiken 1980; Druckman 2001a; Wu and Shaffer 1987). Relatedly, psychologists have found that people decide what to think of a message based on cues about its source. For instance, experiments by James Druckman show that people are far more likely to support a policy proposal if it is made by a political party with which they identify (Druckman 2001b). In the same way, I expect that in many cases policy makers and interested citizens support a commission's recommendations without carefully evaluating them because they respect the panel's members. Former Representative Mickey Edwards (R-OK) notes, "Often it's not what was said that makes the difference; it's who said it."[40]

Research by Andrew Rich further underscores the importance of stature, diversity, and independence: He argues that think tanks are more credible when they are well-known and are perceived to be nonideological and independent of narrow groups of supporters (Rich 2004, 12, 84–86). Similarly, these attributes serve as the principal sources of the credibility of commissions, enabling them to construct focal points and generate support for their proposals.

Returning to the example of the Scowcroft Commission, its bipartisanship, independence, and stature enabled it to persuade Congress to approve funding for the MX when the Reagan administration could not

---

[39] Interview, April 2007.
[40] Interview of Mickey Edwards, May 23, 2007.

do so on its own. The White House needed to form a commission to win congressional approval of the MX because Democrats distrusted the administration's chief defense spokesperson: Defense Secretary Caspar Weinberger (McFarlane 1994, 223–224). The membership on the commission of highly regarded Democrats, such as Carter administration officials John Deutch and William Perry, gave the panel's unanimous report much broader political appeal than any statements of the Reagan administration. Commission member James Woolsey recalled, "We were successful because we could go up to the Congress with a group that spanned the parties and was very prestigious and sounded like members of Congress."[41]

Advocacy

Still, highly credible commissions that issue unanimous reports can fail to establish a focal point if they do not promote their recommendations intensively. Successful commissions do more than just carry out their mandate to investigate and report; they also act as policy entrepreneurs, using all of their persuasive power to press policy makers to adopt their proposals (Kingdon 1995, 179–183).

Andrew Rich has found that the influence of think tanks is correlated with the amount of resources they invest in marketing (Rich 2004, 155). The same principle applies to commissions. Indeed, many commission members identify advocacy or lack of it as a key factor explaining their panel's success or failure. Harold Brown, chairman of the 1996 Commission on the Roles and Capabilities of the United States Intelligence Community (the Aspin-Brown Commission), cited inadequate promotion as a reason for that panel's modest impact: "To get anything through Congress, you need a full-court press with lots of media exposure. I didn't do it. We didn't make a big push."[42]

The Aspin-Brown Commission was not atypical in this respect. Most panels stop operating shortly after releasing their final report, and their members return to focusing on their regular professional work. But the experience of some panels, such as the 9/11 Commission, which promoted its recommendations persistently, suggests that extra advocacy can play a critical role in helping to focus the attention of policy makers on commission proposals.

---

[41] Interview of James Woolsey, November 8, 2007.
[42] Interview of Harold Brown, June 5, 2007.

This discussion of the credibility of commissions generates the expectation that panels are likely to be most influential if they: (1) are bipartisan and moderately diverse ideologically; (2) have relatively few members; (3) are composed of people of great stature; (4) issue unanimous reports; and (5) promote their recommendations intensively.

The empirical analysis of subsequent chapters investigates whether my sample of national security commissions confirms these expectations, providing valuable additional tests of my theory of commission influence.

The Path from Commission Creation to Policy Change

Figure 2.6 diagrams my argument's causal chain. The diagram depicts the stages of a commission's lifespan and variables that contribute to a panel's impact. No single variable is necessary or sufficient for a commission to exert influence, but each variable can make influence more or less likely.

The causal chain begins with the key conditions related to a commission's formation that are the subject of my three hypotheses: the existence or absence of a crisis, a panel's source of authority, and the scope of its mandate.[43] These initial conditions are followed by important aspects of a commission's composition and output, most of which are elements of its political credibility: the diversity, size, and stature of its membership; the unanimity of its report; and its advocacy efforts. Each of these variables makes a distinct contribution to a commission's impact.

The arrows in the diagram represent directions of influence and show that many of the variables are shaped by others that precede them in the causal chain. In the wake of a crisis, a commission is more likely to be established by the executive than by Congress because the executive can act more quickly – so an arrow connects those two variables. In addition, commissions formed by the president should attract members of greater stature than panels established by Congress or by an agency, and congressional commissions should be more ideologically diverse than executive panels. Moving to the bottom of the diagram, panels with broad mandates are likely to be large to enable the representation of more perspectives and constituencies; large and very diverse commissions are less likely to issue unanimous reports; and commissions that reach consensus

---

[43] I consider source of authority and scope to be initial conditions because they are set before a commission is appointed, but they are not exogenous because they are determined by the policy makers that form a panel.

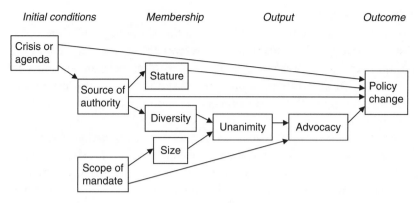

FIGURE 2.6. Causal chain of commission influence.
Note: Arrows represent directions of influence

are more likely to promote their recommendations intensively. An arrow also connects "scope of mandate" to "advocacy," because commissions of broad scope must lobby more policy makers to trigger reform.

My theory treats the variables representing initial conditions as the principal explanatory variables because they come earliest in the causal chain. But I expect these initial conditions only to explain partially the impact of commissions. In other words, if two commissions are established in the same context and manner but vary in their political credibility, their impact should differ. For instance, if one of the commissions includes members of great stature and issues a unanimous report, and the other panel is composed of people of lesser standing and fails to reach consensus, the former commission will be more likely to catalyze policy change.[44]

Alternative Hypotheses

My argument, of course, is not the only plausible explanation of commission influence. There are at least two other plausible hypotheses concerning the impact of commissions.

[44] This discussion raises an important question: Why would commissions with the same initial conditions vary in their composition? Even holding constant the existence or absence of a crisis, a panel's source of authority, and its scope, the membership's stature can vary because policy makers with the power to name commissioners sometimes do not consider a commission to be a priority and therefore appoint people of low stature. Similarly, the membership's diversity can vary, because in some cases the policy makers appointing commissioners may themselves span a broader ideological spectrum than in other instances.

Expertise Hypothesis

Commissions might be more likely to influence policy when they possess greater expertise. This notion represents the prominent view in the political science literature that policy makers often delegate authority to institutions in an effort to obtain specialized information (Epstein and O'Halloran 1999, 54–55; Hawkins et al. 2006b, 13–14). The argument highlights the complex and technical character of many public policy issues, asserting that policy makers often turn to commissions for advice because they lack sufficient knowledge to make policy decisions.

Many commission scholars identify expertise as a key characteristic of panels. Amy Zegart contends that most foreign policy and national security commissions are formed to generate new information or ideas, an argument that implies that panels possessing greater expertise should be more influential (Zegart 2004, 388–389). Similarly, Christopher Kirchhoff argues that a commission's expertise is its most important political resource, and Terrence Tutchings claims that commissions have greater impact when they possess large staffs and conduct extensive research (Kirchhoff 2009, 175; Tutchings 1979, 83–89).

Their argument generates the first alternative hypothesis: *Commissions possessing more expertise are likely to have a greater impact on policy than commissions with less expertise.*

Illusory Impact Hypothesis

A second alternative hypothesis rejects altogether the idea that commissions influence policy. This hypothesis represents the conventional wisdom – described in Chapter 1 – that commissions typically only serve symbolic purposes, such as deflecting political pressure or avoiding blame. In this view, commissions do not spur reform, or, in more nuanced terms, do so only rarely.

This perspective argues that the apparent impact of many commissions is illusory. When policy makers adopt a commission's proposals, they are doing so not because they were influenced by the commission, but because they wanted to make those policy changes anyway. Typically, according to this argument, the same conditions that cause policy makers to create commissions also lead those policy makers to make reforms that commissions propose. For instance, the adoption of the recommendations of a crisis commission results from the pressure generated by the crisis itself, not from the commission, and the apparent impact of executive commissions only reflects the president's preexisting interest in changing policy. In other words, the reforms that follow the reports of crisis or executive commissions would be made even if the panels had not existed.

This view is expressed in the second alternative hypothesis: *Commissions rarely cause policy change to occur.*

I test the expertise and illusory impact hypotheses, along with my own hypotheses, in Chapters 3–6.

Conclusion

The theory developed in this chapter contends that the independence, stature, and bipartisanship of commissions give them a special capacity to trigger policy or organizational change. Yet commissions are only likely to drive reform in certain circumstances. The most important of these circumstances is the existence of a crisis, which creates a window of opportunity for a panel to spur change by making the status quo unpopular, and by generating demand for proposals that can command broad political support. Commissions are also more likely to trigger reform if they are established by the executive branch and given a narrow mandate, because those characteristics make it easier for panels to reach consensus, report quickly, and promote their proposals effectively.

The remaining chapters of this book test the validity of my argument and of the alternative hypotheses that commissions rarely influence policy or that they do so by providing specialized expertise. Chapter 3 uses statistical tools to determine whether my hypotheses and the expertise hypothesis are supported by a data set of fifty-one national security commissions. The case studies in Chapters 4–6 investigate the impact of eight commissions that probed terrorist threats or attacks, evaluating whether the commissions catalyzed important reforms that would not have otherwise occurred, and whether my theory explains the outcomes.

3

The Impact of National Security Commissions

In Chapter 2, I explained how a commission's distinct political credibility can enable it to catalyze reform. My argument generated three hypotheses about the conditions in which panels are most likely to spur change: Commissions have greater impact on policy if they are (1) formed in response to a crisis, (2) established by the executive branch, or (3) given a narrow mandate. I also formulated two alternative hypotheses that represent other plausible views of commission influence: (1) Panels have more impact on policy if they possess greater expertise, and (2) commissions rarely cause policy change to occur.

In this chapter, I test my hypotheses and the first alternative hypothesis through statistical analysis of an original data set of all fifty-one commissions that reported on national security issues between 1981 and 2006.[1] (The second alternative hypothesis is tested in Chapters 4–6.) The analysis features two original measures of commission impact and, to my knowledge, represents the first effort to investigate the sources of a commission's ability to shape policy through rigorous statistical testing. Although limiting the analysis to national security commissions might reduce my ability to draw general conclusions about all commissions, this restriction enables me to evaluate in some depth the impact of every commission over a twenty-six-year period. Chapter 7 considers whether commissions addressing issues other than national security might have different patterns of influence.

---

[1] I am grateful to Amy Zegart for sharing with me her commission data set, which provided some of the foundation for mine.

I tried to minimize the use of statistical jargon in this chapter, but readers without any background in statistics may wish to skip to Chapter 4.

The Data

To test the hypotheses, I created a data set of all commissions that reported on national security issues from the beginning of the Reagan administration in 1981 to the end of 2006. (Appendix A describes how I constructed the data set.) I chose to go back in time no further than the Reagan administration, because my assessment of the impact of commissions relies in part on interviews, and many of the people involved in earlier panels are now deceased or not available to be interviewed.

I determined whether to classify a panel as a national security commission by examining its official mandate. I included in the data set any commission whose mandate explicitly concerned U.S. policies, programs, or strategies to prevent or respond to threats to U.S. security, or to promote peace or security overseas.[2] This approach generated a data set comprising fifty-one commissions that examined various defense, intelligence, homeland security, and foreign policy issues.[3] (Appendix B lists all fifty-one commissions.)

Impact Measures: The Dependent Variables
In order to obtain assessments of commission influence that can be compared across panels, I measured the impact of these fifty-one commissions on government policy in two ways: first, by asking over 200 commissioners, panel staff, and government officials to rate their impact; and second, by determining whether their principal recommendations were fully or partially adopted by the government within two years. Although neither of these measures is a perfect indicator of a commission's influence – such an indicator does not exist – each measure generates reliable and valid information about a panel's overall impact. Moreover, employing two measures of impact enables me to probe their validity

---

[2] This definition excludes strictly historical inquiries and commissions whose mandates only concern administrative issues. I also excluded from the data set panels that only issued classified reports.

[3] Based on my definition, a few commissions are included in the data set even though they might not seem to concern national security based on their title. For instance, the 1987 Secretary of State's Advisory Committee on South Africa is included because its charter instructed it to recommend measures to promote peaceful change in South Africa, which fits my definition of promoting international peace or security.

by determining their correlation. If they are highly correlated, that gives me added confidence that each of them represents a relatively accurate measure of commission influence.

INTERVIEWEE EVALUATIONS. I assembled the first measure by surveying the people who know more about this topic than anyone else: commissioners and panel staff, as well as government officials who had direct responsibility for issues addressed by panels. This time-intensive approach has not been employed by other scholars. Yet it generates data that are highly informative about commission influence and facilitate statistical analysis.

I requested interviews with the chair(s) and staff director of each of the fifty-one commissions. For many panels, I also sought interviews with other commissioners and senior staff and with executive-branch and congressional officials who covered the commission's issue area. Roughly 80 percent of the people I contacted agreed to be interviewed. In all, I conducted 209 interviews in person, over the phone, or via e-mail between May 2007 and April 2009. The interviewees included eleven current or former members of Congress, seventeen former cabinet-level officials, and the chair(s), vice chair, and/or staff director of forty-seven of the fifty-one commissions. Thirty-seven percent of the interviewees served on more than one commission or had responsibility for issues addressed by multiple panels. In such cases, the interviews covered each of those commissions. Some of the interviews were conducted off the record to enable interviewees to speak more freely.

Among other questions, I asked each person the following: "How would you rate the commission's impact on policy on a scale of one to five, with one representing no impact and five representing very large impact?" Altogether, the interviews generated 341 responses to this question. (There were more responses than interviews because many interviewees rated multiple commissions). The number of responses per commission ranged from two to twenty, with a median of six. For each panel, I calculated the mean rating based on these responses. The mean scores, which I label *policy impact*, vary widely across commissions and are normally distributed. For all fifty-one commissions, the average *policy impact* score is 2.95, the standard deviation is .86, the minimum is 1.33, and the maximum is 4.61.

These data have an obvious potential reliability problem: Interviewee evaluations are subjective and can reflect a respondent's biases. But this danger does not undermine the data's utility, because there is no reason to expect that interviewee biases are correlated with any of my explanatory variables. The most significant systematic bias I expect is that commission members and staff are likely to provide higher impact ratings than are government officials because people who serve on a commission have a vested interest in its success. In addition, commission chairs and staff directors might tend to offer more favorable assessments than other members and staff because chairs and staff directors have the greatest personal stake in panels. On the other hand, interviewees who dissented from a panel report might tend to provide lower ratings than other respondents.

To account for these possible biases, I control for whether an interviewee was a commissioner or staff person, served as the chair or staff director, or dissented from the report in some of the regressions whose results are presented later in this chapter. I also investigated the possibility that the assessments of interviewees who rated multiple panels differed systematically from those of respondents who rated only one panel, but I did not find any evidence of a significant difference between these classes of responses.

Any other biases among interviewees should be random, reflecting idiosyncratic personal characteristics, such as their level of frankness or the size of their egos. Such random biases can make it more difficult to find a statistically significant relationship between explanatory and dependent variables, but they do not undermine the reliability of regression results (Lewis 2007, 1077).

THE ADOPTION OF KEY RECOMMENDATIONS. As a second measure of impact, I investigated whether the principal recommendations of commissions were fully or partially adopted by the government within two years of the panel's report. I chose the time frame of two years, because that should be long enough for many proposals to work their way through the legislative or regulatory process and, if a recommendation is adopted more than two years after a commission reports, the connection between the commission and that policy change is likely to be tenuous.

To identify principal recommendations, I first determined whether the commission report prioritized six or fewer proposals.[4] If it did, I classified

---

[4] I decided to investigate the adoption of no more than six recommendations per commission because of the large amount of time required to determine whether some proposals were adopted. Because many commissions issue dozens of recommendations, it was not feasible for me to determine whether all of the proposals of fifty-one panels were adopted.

them as the principal recommendations. (I excluded vague proposals whose adoption cannot be determined objectively, such as recommendations for the president to exert leadership or for the government to improve the coordination of policy on a certain issue. I also excluded recommendations that did not require any policy change.)

If the commission report did not prioritize six or fewer recommendations, I identified key proposals by (1) asking commission chairs and staff directors what they considered to be the principal recommendations, and (2) noting which proposals were given the most attention in coverage of the commission's report on the day after its release in a sample of four prominent and ideologically diverse newspapers: the *Chicago Tribune*, *New York Times*, *Wall Street Journal*, and *Washington Post*. If more than six recommendations were mentioned in these newspapers, I selected the proposals mentioned closest to the beginning of the articles as the principal ones. Altogether, this method generated 196 principal recommendations for forty-nine commissions. The average number of key proposals per commission is four, with a minimum of one and a maximum of six. For two of the fifty-one commissions in my data set, I could not identify any principal recommendations according to the method described in this paragraph.[5] Those two commissions are therefore excluded from the analysis that uses this dependent variable.

Taking this set of 196 principal recommendations, I then used publicly available sources – including government reports, legislation, transcripts of congressional hearings, statements by policy makers, and published articles – to try to determine whether each recommendation was fully adopted, partially adopted, or not adopted within two years. In instances where I could not determine with certainty from these sources whether a proposal was fully or partially adopted, I asked interviewees and other government officials with expertise on the issue whether it was fully or partially adopted. Ultimately, I was able to determine with confidence whether 192 of the 196 proposals were fully or partially adopted within two years. I dropped the remaining four proposals from the statistical analysis. In all, 44 percent of the 192 recommendations were fully adopted, 17 percent were partially adopted, and 39 percent were not

---

[5] In one of these cases – the 1999 Congressional Commission on Military Training and Gender-Related Issues – the only recommendation highlighted by my sources was for a continuation of existing policy. In the other case – the 1998 Commission to Assess the Ballistic Missile Threat to the United States – the only unclassified proposal was too vague for me to determine whether it was adopted.

adopted.[6] I label this three-category dependent variable *adoption* (0 = not adopted, 1 = partially adopted, 2 = fully adopted).

The fact that nearly half of key commission proposals were fully adopted provides suggestive evidence that at least some commissions do influence policy. But these data do not indicate whether policy changes would have occurred without a commission's work. The case studies in subsequent chapters address this issue more directly by investigating whether commissions were directly responsible for important reforms.

Clearly, it should be easier for the government to adopt some recommendations than others. In particular, recommendations that are highly specific and require enactment of a statute (rather than just executive-branch action) should be the least likely to be fully adopted. To account for this variation in the difficulty of adopting proposals, I determined whether each proposal required congressional action and formulated a metric for the specificity of recommendations. This metric defines highly specific recommendations as ones calling for a concrete and precisely described action. For instance, proposals to create an agency to do x or to increase spending on y by $z are highly specific, whereas a recommendation to boost spending on y by an unspecified amount is not highly specific. All of the regression results discussed later in this paper that treat *adoption* as the dependent variable control for whether each proposal is highly specific or requires congressional action to be adopted.

Explanatory and Control Variables

I also measured sets of explanatory and control variables. The three explanatory variables – *crisis*, *executive*, and *scope* – represent the conditions that my theory highlights as the key drivers of commission influence. The control variables represent other panel characteristics that might affect commission outcomes.

---

[6] I classify a proposal as adopted when it is enacted into law or becomes official executive-branch policy. This classification does not consider whether a recommendation is fully implemented. Because many policies are adopted without being fully implemented, a standard of implementation would generate lower scores on this variable. In a study of twelve governmental and nongovernmental commissions that made recommendations on intelligence reform from 1991 to 2001, Amy Zegart finds that only about 10 percent of their proposals were fully implemented (Zegart 2005; Zegart 2006; Zegart 2007). I consider the standard of adoption to be a reasonable measure of commission impact because the implementation of a reform after it has been adopted usually depends on factors beyond a commission's influence.

EXPLANATORY VARIABLES. *Crisis*: I use this binary variable to test my hypothesis that commissions are more influential if they are established in response to a crisis. In Chapter 2, I described two kinds of commissions: crisis commissions, which are established in response to a disaster or scandal; and agenda commissions, which are formed in the absence of a crisis to advance a policy goal. I classified each of the fifty-one commissions in the data set as a crisis or agenda commission by determining from contemporaneous newspaper coverage, interviews, and other sources whether a disaster or scandal on the issue addressed by the commission preceded its formation. If a panel's establishment was preceded by a disaster or scandal, I labeled it a crisis commission; if not, I labeled it an agenda commission. In making these classifications, I defined a disaster as a terrorist attack or other event involving the loss of American lives, and I defined a scandal as an incident or accusation of government wrongdoing or fraud. This method identified twenty-four crisis commissions and twenty-seven agenda commissions. *Crisis* takes a value of one for crisis commissions and zero for agenda commissions in my statistical models.

Executive: I employ this dichotomous variable to test my hypothesis that executive-branch commissions have greater impact than congressional commissions. The data set includes twenty-six executive commissions and twenty-five congressional commissions. *Executive* takes a value of one for commissions that were authorized by the executive branch unilaterally and a value of zero for commissions authorized by statute.

Scope: This binary variable enables me to test my hypothesis that a narrow mandate facilitates commission impact. I define a commission of narrow scope as one whose mandate concerns a single issue, challenge, or event, *and* is focused on a single agency, program, or policy.[7] I classify all other commissions as panels of broad scope. For instance, the 1984–1985 Chemical Warfare Review Commission is classified as possessing narrow scope, because its mandate to review the adequacy of America's chemical weapons posture concerned a single issue managed by a single agency (the Army). On the other hand, the 1995–1996 President's Advisory Board on Arms Proliferation Policy is categorized as having broad scope, because its mandate to identify policy options to inhibit the

---

[7] I treat the departments of the Army, Navy, and Air Force as separate agencies, but as a robustness check I employ an alternative definition treating the Defense Department as a whole as a single agency.

proliferation of conventional weapons and related equipment and technologies spanned multiple agencies, programs, and policies. Using this method, I identified seventeen commissions with narrow mandates and thirty-four panels of broad scope. *Scope* takes a value of one for commissions with narrow mandates.

CONTROL VARIABLES. *Stature*: I use this continuous variable as a control based on my expectation that the stature of commission members contributes to a panel's influence. The measure is based on the prominence of the most senior positions held by commissioners at any point in their careers, rated on a scale of zero to five. For instance, five refers to a president; four refers to a vice president or leader of the House or Senate; three refers to a member of Congress, cabinet secretary, or Supreme Court justice; two refers to an agency head or the secretary or chief of staff of one of the armed services; one refers to a Senate-confirmed official, general, admiral, or federal judge; and zero refers to none of these. I also assign values on this scale to prominent positions outside the federal government. For example, governors receive a rating of three, CEOs of Fortune 500 companies are scored as two, and heads of academic institutions or think tanks are labeled as one.[8] The overall measure of a commission's stature represents the average value assigned to that panel's commissioners.

Large: I employ *large* as a control because I expect that large commissions have less impact, in part because they are less likely to reach consensus. This binary variable indicates whether the number of commissioners on a panel is at least one standard deviation greater than the average size of a commission. Because the mean commission size is 10.7 members and the standard deviation is 5.0, all commissions composed of 16 or more members are classified as large commissions. Eight of the fifty-one commissions fit this definition.[9]

Unanimous: This dichotomous variable indicates whether a commission's final report was unanimous. I classify any report containing a dissenting opinion, additional view, or footnote by one or more

---

[8] Other people would surely assign values on this scale somewhat differently, but for the purpose of my empirical analysis the most important aspect of this metric is that I created it before I measured the stature of individual commissions. This means that the scale was not biased by my own knowledge of the data.

[9] I expect *large* to be more informative than a continuous variable measuring the number of commissioners on a panel, which I label *size*, because I expect the relationship between membership size and impact to be nonlinear. However, I employ *size* and *size squared* as robustness checks.

members as nonunanimous.[10] This approach identified thirty-five unanimous commission reports and sixteen nonunanimous ones. I use *unanimous* as a control because I expect that unanimous reports are more influential.

Advocacy: This variable allows me to test my expectation that intensive advocacy by commissions on behalf of their recommendations boosts the impact of panels. The continuous measure is based on my interviews of commission members and staff, in which I asked them: "How would you rate the commission's effort to promote its recommendations after the report was issued on a scale of one to five, with one representing no promotion and five representing very extensive promotion?" (I did not ask government officials who did not serve on a commission to make this assessment because I expect them to be less knowledgeable about this variable.) For each commission, I generated a mean *advocacy* score by averaging these ratings.

Agency: This dichotomous variable measures whether a panel was established by an executive-branch agency official, rather than directly by the president or by Congress. It takes a value of one for agency commissions and zero for panels authorized by statute or by presidential directive. I include *agency* as a control because I expect that, within the category of executive commissions, panels formed directly by the president have greater impact than panels established by agency officials.

Salience: This variable measures the salience of the issue addressed by each commission, with salience defined as the amount of public attention given to an issue. I include it as a control because commissions might be more likely to influence policy when they address issues that are in the national spotlight. I measure the variable by counting the number of front-page articles in the *New York Times* and *Washington Post* on the issue examined by a panel during the ninety days prior to the commission's official authorization. (I use the natural log of *salience* in the regressions.) Because crises often generate heavy media coverage, *crisis* and *salience* are correlated (correlation coefficient = .30), but this correlation is modest because some scandals and disasters attract relatively little public attention, and some issues, such as the missions of the armed forces, are highly salient in the absence of a crisis.

---

[10] As a robustness check, I only classify a report as nonunanimous if it contains a dissenting opinion or additional view in the body of the report text.

Staff: This continuous variable measures the size of a commission's staff. (I use the natural log of *staff* in the regressions.) I include it to test the alternative hypothesis that commissions with more expertise have greater impact. In general, a larger staff should imply more expertise because many staff members are experts on the commission's topic. However, since *staff* is not a perfect measure of expertise, I employ two other proxies for expertise as robustness checks in the statistical analysis: (1) *budget*, which measures the total expenses of a commission; and (2) *experience*, which measures the proportion of a commission's members that previously worked directly on the issue addressed by the panel.[11] Like *staff*, each of these variables measures expertise imperfectly, but they provide additional tests of the expertise-based alternative hypothesis.

One variable that is not included as a control also merits mention. A panel's political diversity is an important part of my theory of commission influence, because such diversity shapes a panel's political credibility and its ability to reach consensus. However, I do not include a control for political diversity in my primary regression models, because the data set does not include any commissions with at least one member of one political party and no members from the other party – meaning there is not variation in whether the panels are bipartisan – and other measures of diversity are highly imperfect. Still, I employ two such measures as robustness checks: whether a panel has an even number of Republicans and Democrats (*evenly bipartisan*), and how commissioners and staff rate a panel's ideological diversity on a scale of one to five (*diversity*).[12]

A First Look

As a first look at the relationships among the principal variables of interest, Table 3.1 presents cross-tabulations of the explanatory and

---

[11] In some cases, *budget* might provide a better estimate of expertise than *staff*, because a panel can use funding to pay consultants who are not full-time staff members. However, I was only able to obtain precise budget figures for thirty-six of the fifty-one commissions. For the remaining fifteen commissions, I estimated the total budget based on partial budget data, the size of the staff, and the number of months the commission operated.

[12] The latter measure is highly imperfect because the retrospective ratings are likely to be heavily influenced by whether a commission achieved unanimity. Still, it is a reasonable supplement to the more objective, but less fine-grained, *evenly bipartisan* measure.

TABLE 3.1. *Policy impact scores and proposal adoption rates for commissions with different characteristics*

Variable	Number of commissions	Mean policy impact rating	Number of proposals	Fully adopted proposals
Context				
Crisis	24	3.43	102	57 (56%)
Agenda	27	2.52	90	28 (31%)
Authority source				
Executive	26	3.35	104	60 (58%)
Congress	25	2.54	88	25 (28%)
Scope				
Narrow	17	3.35	50	34 (68%)
Broad	34	2.75	142	51 (36%)
Commission size				
Small	8	3.17	28	16 (57%)
Medium	35	2.95	131	57 (44%)
Large	8	2.74	33	12 (36%)
Report				
Unanimous	35	3.20	132	65 (49%)
Nonunanimous	16	2.40	60	20 (33%)
TOTAL	51	2.95	192	85 (44%)

dependent variables. The figures show large differences in both measures of commission influence – *policy impact* and *adoption* – for each of the explanatory variables (*crisis, executive,* and *scope*), conforming to my predictions. All of these differences are statistically significant ($p < .01$ or $p < .05$, two-tailed), meaning it is highly unlikely that they are coincidental. Although the cross-tabulations do not provide definitive support for my hypotheses because they do not control for other relevant variables, they provide suggestive evidence that the existence of a crisis, executive-branch authorization, and narrow scope facilitate commission impact.

The first rows in the table show that crisis commissions outperformed agenda commissions by large margins on both impact measures. Crisis commissions received mean ratings on *policy impact* that are .89 higher than the ratings of agenda commissions – a big gap for a one-to-five scale in which the standard deviation for the mean ratings is .86. The difference between crisis and agenda panels on *adoption* is also substantial: 56 percent of the principal recommendations of crisis commissions were fully adopted within two years, whereas that rate was only 31 percent for agenda commissions.

The differences in *policy impact* and *adoption* between executive and congressional commissions are similarly large. Whereas executive commissions received average impact ratings of 3.35 and saw 58 percent of their principal recommendations get fully adopted, the comparable scores for statutory panels are 2.54 and 28 percent. (As expected, among executive commissions there is also a significant difference between presidential and agency panels, though these data are not presented in Table 3.1: Presidential commissions score higher than agency panels on both dependent variables.)

My third principal explanatory variable – *scope* – reveals slightly less variation on *policy impact*, with commissions of narrow scope receiving ratings that are .60 higher than panels of broad scope. However, there is great variation between commissions of broad and narrow scope on *adoption*, as the recommendations of panels with narrow mandates were fully adopted nearly twice as often as those of commissions with broad mandates.

Table 3.1 also includes cross-tabulations for two control variables: *large* and *unanimous*. Panels with sixteen or more commissioners score lower on *policy impact* and *adoption* than smaller commissions, as I expected, but the differences between large panels and small or medium-sized ones are not statistically significant.[13] On the other hand, there are statistically and substantively significant differences between unanimous and nonunanimous panels on both dependent variables, in the direction that I expect. Unanimity corresponds to jumps of .80 on *policy impact* and 16 percent in the proportion of proposals that are fully adopted – gaps that are both statistically significant ($p < .01$).

High-Impact and Low-Impact Commissions

A closer examination of commissions that score particularly high or low on the impact measures provides additional insight into the importance of a crisis, executive-branch authorization, and a narrow mandate. I

---

[13] Small panels are those with five or fewer commissioners (i.e. at least one standard deviation smaller than the mean panel size). Medium-sized commissions have between six and fifteen members.

classified all commissions as high-impact, medium-impact, or low-impact panels based on their *policy impact* ratings. Commissions that received scores greater than one standard deviation above the mean are high-impact panels, whereas those with scores at least one standard deviation below the mean are low-impact commissions. This categorization creates groups of ten high-impact commissions and ten low-impact panels, presented in Tables 3.2 and 3.3.

The groupings suggest that the three explanatory variables account for a great deal of a commission's impact. Of the ten high-impact commissions, eight have at least two of the following three characteristics: establishment after a crisis, authorization by the executive branch, and narrow scope. By contrast, only two of the ten low-impact commissions possess at least two of those characteristics. This difference between the high-impact and low-impact commissions suggests that the variables are particularly influential when they are present or absent in combination.

Tables 3.2 and 3.3 also suggest that the two dependent variables are very strongly correlated. I created a mean adoption score for each commission, which represents the average value on *adoption* for all of a panel's principal proposals. Because *adoption* is a three-category ordinal variable, the mean adoption scores can vary from zero to two, with zero assigned to commissions that did not see any of their key proposals get fully or partially adopted, and two assigned to panels that had all of their principal recommendations get fully adopted. The tables show that those panels receiving very high-impact ratings from interviewees also tended to have most of their proposals adopted, whereas those commissions receiving very low interviewee ratings tended to perform far worse in terms of proposal adoption. Only two of the ten low-impact commissions have a mean adoption score of one or higher. By contrast, all ten high-impact panels achieved that adoption rate.

In fact, the two dependent variables are highly correlated for the full data set. Across all of the commissions, the correlation coefficient between interviewee impact ratings and the mean adoption score per commission is .69. This very strong correlation between *policy impact* and *adoption* gives me added confidence that each of them is a valid and relatively accurate measure of a commission's influence.

The importance of the explanatory variables is also revealed by a comparison of two other sets of commissions: (1) crisis commissions formed by the executive branch with a narrow mandate, which should be the most likely of all panels to have a substantial impact; and

TABLE 3.2. *High-impact commissions*

Commission	Context	Authority source	Scope	Policy impact rating	Mean adoption score
9/11 Commission	Crisis	Congress	Broad	4.61	1.00
USS *Cole* Commission	Crisis	Executive	Broad	4.33	1.80
President's Commission on Strategic Forces	Agenda	Executive	Narrow	4.30	1.33
Secretary of State's Advisory Panel on Overseas Security	Crisis	Executive	Narrow	4.29	1.40
President's Blue Ribbon Commission on Defense Management	Crisis	Executive	Broad	4.25	1.60
Accountability Review Boards on the Embassy Bombings in Nairobi and Dar es Salaam	Crisis	Executive	Narrow	4.13	2.00
President's Commission on Aviation Security and Terrorism	Crisis	Executive	Broad	4.03	1.80
Long-Range Air Power Review Panel	Agenda	Congress	Narrow	4.00	2.00
Panel to Review the V-22 Program	Crisis	Executive	Narrow	3.92	2.00
Commission on the Intelligence Capabilities of the United States regarding WMD	Crisis	Executive	Broad	3.90	1.67

TABLE 3.3. *Low-impact commissions*

Commission	Context	Authority source	Scope	Policy impact rating	Mean adoption score
Joint Security Commission 2	Agenda	Executive	Broad	2.00	0.00
Secretary of State's Advisory Committee on South Africa	Agenda	Executive	Narrow	2.00	1.00
U.S. Commission on Improving the Effectiveness of the UN	Agenda	Congress	Narrow	2.00	0.00
National Advisory Committee on Children and Terrorism	Crisis	Congress	Narrow	1.97	0.75
Commission on the Advancement of Federal Law Enforcement	Crisis	Congress	Broad	1.75	0.00
Commission on Security and Economic Assistance	Agenda	Executive	Broad	1.71	1.00
Commission on Merchant Marine and Defense	Agenda	Congress	Broad	1.50	0.00
President's Advisory Board on Arms Proliferation Policy	Agenda	Congress	Broad	1.50	0.00
Commission to Assess the Organization of the Federal Government to Combat the Proliferation of WMD	Agenda	Congress	Broad	1.39	0.00
Commission on the Assignment of Women in the Armed Forces	Agenda	Congress	Broad	1.33	0.00

(2) agenda commissions authorized by statute with a broad mandate, which should be the least likely to exert influence. Nine commissions fall into the first category, and all of them have ratings on *policy impact* that are greater than the mean for all commissions. By contrast, thirteen fit into the second category, and all but one of them scores below average on *policy impact*. Notably, the panel that rates surprisingly high – the 2001 Commission to Assess United States National Security Space Management and Organization – possesses a distinct characteristic that accounts for its impact: It was chaired by Donald Rumsfeld at the end of the Clinton administration. In interviews, commission members and government officials agreed that Rumsfeld's appointment as secretary of defense after the election of George W. Bush enabled the commission to influence policy more than it otherwise would have, because Rumsfeld was able to use his position in the Defense Department to adopt some of the commission's proposals.[14]

These groups of commissions also offer suggestive evidence of the importance of a commission's makeup and ability to reach consensus, holding constant a panel's initial conditions. Among the thirteen congressional agenda commissions possessing broad mandates, seven issued unanimous reports and six did not. Those that achieved unanimity have mean ratings on *policy impact* of 2.43, whereas those that failed to reach consensus have average scores of only 1.86, a substantively large and statistically significant difference. Panel size seems to contribute to the ability to reach consensus within this group. The seven unanimous commissions comprised an average of nine commissioners, whereas the six nonunanimous panels had an average of twelve members.

Data for the full set of fifty-one commissions provide more preliminary evidence of the importance of a panel's size, which is in turn shaped by its scope. My theory contends that a narrow mandate is beneficial in part because of the following causal chain: Commissions of narrow scope tend to require fewer members, smaller panels are more likely to reach consensus, and commissions issuing unanimous reports are more likely to promote their recommendations aggressively. The data support each of these claims. Commissions of broad scope have an average of twelve members, whereas panels with narrow mandates have an average of just eight commissioners. In addition, *size* (representing the number of

---

[14] Interview of Pete Aldridge, January 26, 2008; interview of Duane Andrews, January 11, 2008; interview of Stephen Cambone, February 6, 2008; interview of Charles Horner, January 28, 2008; interview of Douglas Necessary, December 4, 2007.

commissioners on a panel) has a strong negative correlation with *unanimous* (correlation coefficient = −.49), indicating that smaller panels are far more likely than larger ones to achieve consensus.[15] *Unanimous* is also moderately correlated with *advocacy* (correlation coefficient = .20), suggesting that panels engage in more advocacy if they reach consensus.

Other data further illustrate the importance of commission size. In my interviews, I asked panel members and staff to rate the average level of commitment of the commissioners to their panel's work on a scale of one to five, with one representing very low commitment and five representing very high commitment. Based on these responses, I generated an average *commitment* score for each commission. This variable has a strong negative correlation with the size of a panel's membership (coefficient correlation = −.40), implying that commissioners develop a significantly greater stake in a panel's work if its membership is relatively small. This greater sense of commitment is probably one reason why smaller panels achieve consensus more often.

Additional statistics offer evidence in support of my argument about the advantages possessed by executive commissions. In Chapter 2, I assert that executive commissions are more influential than congressional commissions in the wake of a crisis, in part because they are more likely to issue recommendations while a window of opportunity for reform still exists. Among the twenty-four crisis commissions in my data set, those established by the executive produced their final report in an average of seven months, whereas those authorized by Congress did so in an average of twenty-one months.[16] This huge discrepancy supports my theory's contention that congressional commissions take much longer to get set up because their members are typically appointed by several different policy makers, some of whom may drag their feet in naming commissioners if they do not consider the panel to be a priority. I suspect that the big difference in the duration of executive and congressional panels accounts for a significant portion of the gap in their impact.

By contrast, the data set provides weaker support for my argument that executive-branch panels are more likely than congressional commissions

---

[15] *Unanimous* and *large* are also correlated, but not quite as strongly. Their bivariate correlation coefficient is −.29.

[16] These lengths of time are measured from the date of the commission's official charter or authorizing legislation to the date of its final report. Taking into account the additional delays that often accompany efforts to enact authorizing legislation for congressional commissions would make the gap between the duration of executive and congressional panels even greater.

to achieve unanimity. Of the executive commissions, 73 percent issued unanimous reports, whereas 64 percent of the congressional panels did so. Although the greater rate of unanimity for executive commissions conforms to my expectation, the difference is not statistically significant.

An Illustrative Comparison: The Packard and Deutch-Specter Commissions

A brief comparison of a pair of commissions further illustrates how the existence or absence of a crisis and a panel's source of authority can heavily shape a commission's prospects for driving reform. The President's Blue Ribbon Commission on Defense Management (known as the Packard Commission after its chair, David Packard) was established by Ronald Reagan in July 1985 in response to a major procurement scandal involving the Defense Department. For months, Congress and the media had been chastising the Pentagon for purchasing items ranging from ashtrays to toilet seat covers at wildly exorbitant prices. National Security Advisor Robert McFarlane encouraged Reagan to form the commission in an effort to restore confidence in the Defense Department and rebuild support for the administration's defense agenda.[17]

The Packard Commission conducted its work while the congressional armed services committees were debating proposed legislation on military reorganization, which became enacted as the landmark Goldwater-Nichols Act in September 1986. By issuing a unanimous interim report in February 1986 – just seven months after Reagan established the panel – the Packard Commission shaped the Goldwater-Nichols Act in two important ways (President's Blue Ribbon Commission on Defense Management 1986a).[18] First, its recommendation to establish a vice chairman of the Joint Chiefs of Staff influenced Congress's decision to do so through the legislation. Arnold Punaro, who served at the time as minority staff director of the Senate Armed Services Committee, observed that the commission's proposal was one of the key reasons the committee included the vice chairman provision in the act: "Without the commission's clout, it's anybody's guess whether we could have gotten the votes for that [provision]."[19]

---

[17] Interview of Mike Donley, October 29, 2007; interview of John Douglass, September 26, 2007; interview of Robert McFarlane, May 12, 2008; interview of Paul Stevens, April 25, 2008.

[18] The commission's final report was issued in June 1986 (President's Blue Ribbon Commission on Defense Management 1986b). Most of its recommendations were the same as those in the interim report.

[19] Interview of Arnold Punaro, December 19, 2007.

Second, the commission's proposal to create an under secretary for acquisition to overhaul procurement policy induced Congress to establish that position as part of the Goldwater-Nichols Act. This reform was not being considered in Congress before the commission proposed it, and it would not have been adopted absent the panel's recommendation, according to several congressional and administration officials who worked on the issue at the time.[20]

The Packard Commission would have been unable to shape the Goldwater-Nichols Act in these ways if it took much longer to be appointed and issue its report. Its authorization by the president was therefore critical to its impact, as was the pressure for reform generated by the procurement scandal. Other commission recommendations, including a proposal for a new NSC planning process for the formulation of defense budgets, were adopted separately by President Reagan in a national security decision directive issued in April 1986.[21] In my data set, the Packard Commission scores very high on both dependent variables: Four out of five principal recommendations were fully adopted, and a total of ten interviewees gave it an average rating on *policy impact* of 4.25.

The Packard Commission's influence contrasts sharply with that of one of the congressional agenda commissions in my data set: the Commission to Assess the Organization of the Federal Government to Combat the Proliferation of Weapons of Mass Destruction (the Deutch-Specter Commission, after its chair and vice chair, John Deutch and Arlen Specter). Senator Specter (R-PA) introduced legislation to establish the commission in 1996 in an effort to build political support for reforms that he favored: instituting new export restrictions designed to prevent proliferation and establishing a White House position to coordinate the government's antiproliferation policies. Specter had been unable to achieve passage of legislation adopting such reforms, because the Clinton administration sought to preserve policy flexibility with respect to arms exports and opposed the idea of establishing a proliferation czar.[22]

Once the commission was authorized, its low priority in the White House and partisan squabbling in Congress created substantial delays

[20] Interview of Mike Donley, October 29, 2007; interview of John Douglass, September 26, 2007; interview of Ken Krieg, November 12, 2007; interview of Arnold Punaro, December 19, 2007.
[21] National Security Decision Directive 219, issued on April 2, 1986.
[22] Interview of Suzanne Spaulding, June 26, 2007; interview of Clinton administration official, January 2008.

in the appointment of commissioners. (Appointment power was divided between congressional leaders and the president). Although the panel's authorizing legislation was enacted in October 1996, it did not report until July 1999. The commission's principal recommendations were to establish an interagency council for combating proliferation led by a new national director for combating proliferation, and to create a government-wide budget category for proliferation-related programs (Commission to Assess the Organization of the Federal Government to Combat the Proliferation of Weapons of Mass Destruction 1999).

These proposals were not adopted, and the commission's impact was very small, for three primary reasons: (1) Several Republican commissioners dissented from the panel's report, undermining its bipartisan credibility. (2) The Clinton administration was not seeking to change its overall approach to proliferation policy. (3) A crisis did not exist to generate pressure for reform. As Gary Samore, who served then as NSC Senior Director for Nonproliferation and Export Controls, commented, "We didn't ask for this commission.... Nobody had any appetite for organizational changes. Reorganization doesn't make sense unless there's a pressing need to do it."[23] None of the commission's three principal recommendations was fully or partially adopted, and the commission scores second-lowest among all of the panels in my data set on *policy impact*, with an average rating by seven interviewees of 1.39.

Results of Statistical Tests

The cross-tabulations, descriptive statistics, and illustrative examples discussed so far provide some preliminary evidence in support of my hypotheses, but controlled statistical tests are necessary to test other plausible explanations of the correlations between the explanatory and dependent variables. In the absence of tests that control for variables that could affect commission outcomes, I cannot exclude the possibility that the correlations presented earlier are due to factors other than those highlighted by my theory. For instance, crisis commissions might score higher than agenda commissions on the dependent variables because they address issues that are more salient. Regressions enable me to investigate such possibilities.

I conducted regressions for various models, controlling for other variables that might be relevant. In one set of regressions, I used interviewee

---

[23] Interview of Gary Samore, April 21, 2008.

impact ratings as the dependent variable; in another, I used *adoption*. Overall, the results strongly support each of my hypotheses and offer little support for the expertise alternative hypothesis.

Interviewee Ratings as the Dependent Variable
Because *policy impact* is continuous and normally distributed, I estimated a series of regressions with this dependent variable using ordinary least squares.[24] Table 3.4 presents the results for six models.

The unit of observation varies among these models because two modeling approaches are sensible. In the first three models, the unit of observation is a commission, and the dependent variable represents the average impact rating for each panel. In the fourth, fifth, and sixth models, the unit of observation is a single interviewee response, and the dependent variable represents individual respondent ratings. The first modeling approach, using a commission as the unit of observation, is more intuitively appealing because it assigns a single impact score to each panel. But the second modeling approach has two advantages: (1) It accounts for variation in the number of respondents per commission. (2) It enables me to control for interviewee characteristics that might be correlated with impact ratings. The results using the two approaches are broadly similar.

Models 1 and 4 represent the base model, featuring the explanatory variables (*crisis, executive,* and *scope*) and variables representing the expertise hypothesis (*staff*) and controls (*agency* and *salience*). Models 2 and 5 add two control variables representing key attributes of a commission's membership: *stature* and *large*. Finally, Models 3 and 6 add *unanimous* and *advocacy* – important elements of a commission's output.[25] I do not include *stature, large, unanimous,* or *advocacy* in the base model, because I expect them to be endogenous to one or more of the explanatory variables, but I include them in these other models because I expect them to exert independent influence on the dependent variable

---

[24] Although my interview question asks respondents to rate the policy impact of commissions on a scale of one to five, implying a discrete variable, many interviewees gave responses consisting of fractions (e.g. 3.5), and the mean rating on *policy impact* for each commission represents an average of multiple scores. In practice, therefore, the variable is continuous for both modeling approaches described in this section.

[25] Because many interviewees did not rate the extent to which a commission promoted its report, Model 6 uses average ratings on *advocacy* for each commission, rather than individual interviewee scores for this variable. As a robustness check, I ran the same regression using individual ratings of *advocacy*. The results of that regression were broadly similar to those presented in Model 6, except that *executive* lost its statistical significance, probably because the number of observations dropped from 317 to 167.

TABLE 3.4. *Contributors to the impact of commissions on policy*

Variable	Model 1	Model 2	Model 3	Model 4	Model 5	Model 6
Crisis	.63***	.63***	.57***	.62***	.60***	.61***
	(.21)	(.21)	(.17)	(.22)	(.21)	(.13)
Executive	.71**	.82**	.69***	.48	.59*	.57***
	(.30)	(.32)	(.26)	(.34)	(.31)	(.20)
Scope	.58**	.41	.48**	.66***	.51*	.46**
	(.24)	(.25)	(.21)	(.25)	(.26)	(.19)
Stature		.18	.01		.19	−.02
		(.16)	(.13)		(.14)	(.10)
Large		−.33	−.10		−.33	−.15
		(.29)	(.24)		(.22)	(.20)
Unanimous			.34*			.43**
			(.18)			(.17)
Advocacy			.39***			.43***
			(.09)			(.07)
Staff	.11	.07	.02	.18	.14	.06
	(.12)	(.12)	(.09)	(.14)	(.13)	(.07)
Agency	−.44	−.45	−.39	−.38	−.39	−.40**
	(.30)	(.30)	(.24)	(.29)	(.28)	(.19)
Salience	.04	.02	.04	.10	.07	.05
	(.06)	(.06)	(.05)	(.06)	(.05)	(.03)
Interviewee was member or staff				.02	.04	.12
				(.17)	(.16)	(.17)
Interviewee was chair or director				.20	.21	.21
				(.14)	(.14)	(.14)
Interviewee dissented from report						-.23
						(.30)
Number of commissions	51	51	51	51	51	51
Number of interviewee responses				341	341	341

Note: The dependent variable is a continuous variable measuring the policy impact of a commission on a scale of one to five, with one representing no impact and five representing very large impact. In Models 1, 2, 3, the unit of observation is a commission. In Models 4, 5, 6, the unit of observation is a single interviewee response, and observations are clustered by commission because they are not independent. Table entries are coefficients of an ordinary least squares regression, with standard errors in parentheses.
*** $p < .01$, ** $p < .05$, * $p < .1$ for two-tailed tests.

too. Models 4, 5, and 6 also control for respondent characteristics that I expect to be correlated with interviewee ratings of impact: whether the interviewee was a commissioner or staff person, served as the commission chair or staff director, or dissented from the panel report.[26]

Crisis, the first explanatory variable, is highly significant both statistically and substantively in the hypothesized direction in all six models. Its coefficient ranges from .57 to .63, meaning that, holding other variables constant, a commission's impact on policy is estimated to increase by about .6 on a one-to-five scale if it is established in response to a crisis – a large amount considering that the standard deviation of *policy impact* is .86. The results strongly support my hypothesis that crisis commissions are more influential than agenda commissions.

The results for *executive* are similar in degree. Executive commissions outperform congressional commissions by a margin of .48 to .82 across the six models, implying that a panel's impact rating increases by at least half a point on the one-to-five scale if it is authorized by the executive rather than by statute. These results are statistically significant in five of the six models, representing rather strong evidence for my hypothesis that executive-branch authorization bolsters a commission's influence.

The third explanatory variable, *scope*, generates results that provide solid support for my hypothesis that commissions have greater impact if they are given a narrow mandate. The results across the six models indicate that a commission's impact on policy jumps by roughly .5 or .6 if its scope is narrow. These results, like those for *executive*, are statistically significant in all but one model.

Whereas the results in Table 3.4 provide solid backing for each of my three hypotheses, they do not support the expertise hypothesis. *Staff* (measuring the size of a commission's staff) does not obtain statistical significance in any of the models, though its coefficient is positive, as the hypothesis would expect. This result suggests that expertise is not an important source of commission impact. Because *staff* is an imperfect measure of expertise, I also tested the same models with two other proxies for expertise: *budget* (measuring the total expenses of a commission) and *experience* (measuring the proportion of commissioners with previous

---

[26] I only include the control for whether an interviewee dissented from the report in Model 6 because Models 4 and 5 do not control for unanimity. Absent the control for unanimity, a control for whether an interviewee dissented would serve, in effect, as a proxy for nonunanimity because dissent only exists in cases where unanimity is not achieved. The results of Models 4 and 5 would therefore be misleading if the control for dissent was included in those models.

experience working on the issue dealt with by a panel). The results when using *budget* or *experience* are not presented in Table 3.4, but neither of these proxies neared statistical significance in any model.

Table 3.4 includes mixed results concerning the importance of control variables that represent elements of a commission's makeup and output. *Stature* and *large* are not statistically significant in any model, suggesting that the prominence and size of a commission's membership might not shape a panel's impact independently. However, the results in Models 3 and 6 imply that a commission's ability to reach consensus and its conduct of advocacy shape its impact to a large extent. In both models, a commission's impact rating rises by about .4 if its report is unanimous or if its advocacy efforts increase by one standard deviation. (Recall that *advocacy* represents interviewee assessments of the extent to which a commission promoted its recommendations). These results are statistically significant, representing striking evidence that a commission's impact is not entirely predictable based on its context and initial conditions. In particular, they suggest that panels are substantially more influential when they promote a unanimous report intensively.

Proposal Adoption as the Dependent Variable

As additional tests of my hypotheses, I investigated which variables contribute to the adoption of key recommendations by estimating ordered logit regressions in which the dependent variable is *adoption*. The results are presented in Table 3.5.

The variables employed in the three models in Table 3.5 correspond to the variables used in the two groups of three models in Table 3.4. Model 1 represents the base model, Model 2 adds variables representing commission membership, and Model 3 adds variables representing panel output. The only difference between these models and those in Table 3.4 is that these models include two indicator variables to control for whether a recommendation is highly specific or requires congressional action because those characteristics should shape the difficulty of adopting a proposal. Because the substantive significance of the results in Table 3.5 is not easy to interpret, Table 3.6 shows the substantive significance of key variables of interest for Model 3.

In all three models, *crisis*, *executive*, and *scope* are statistically and substantively significant in the expected directions, providing more strong evidence in support of my hypotheses. The existence of a crisis increases the odds of a recommendation being fully adopted by 16 percent in every model. The importance of *executive* and *scope* is even greater: The odds

TABLE 3.5. *Contributors to the adoption of commission recommendations*

Variable	Model 1	Model 2	Model 3
Crisis	.65*	.66*	.65*
	(.35)	(.36)	(.37)
Executive	1.59***	1.77***	1.71***
	(.40)	(.40)	(.44)
Scope	1.56***	1.39***	1.33**
	(.49)	(.54)	(.55)
Stature		.20	.19
		(.29)	(.32)
Large		−.39	−.25
		(.41)	(.47)
Unanimous			.31
			(.40)
Advocacy			.04
			(.17)
Staff	.38*	.35	.32
	(.22)	(.22)	(.22)
Agency	−1.21***	−1.30***	−1.26***
	(.44)	(.42)	(.45)
Salience	−.03	−.05	−.06
	(.09)	(.09)	(.09)
Specificity of recommendation	−1.07***	−1.06***	−1.05***
	(.33)	(.33)	(.32)
Recommendation requires congressional action	−.59*	−.59*	−.60*
	(.33)	(.34)	(.35)
Cutpoint 1	−2.58	−2.46	−2.13
	(.76)	(.83)	(.93)
Cutpoint 2	−1.66	−1.54	−1.21
	(.73)	(.82)	(.91)
Number of commissions	49	49	49
Number of recommendations	192	192	192

Note: The dependent variable is a three-category ordinal variable expressing the extent to which a recommendation is adopted (0 = not adopted, 1 = partially adopted, 2 = fully adopted). Observations are clustered by commission because they are not independent. Table entries are coefficients of an ordered logistic regression, with standard errors in parentheses.

*** $p < .01$, ** $p < .05$, * $p < .1$ for two-tailed tests.

TABLE 3.6. *Effects of key variables on the adoption of recommendations*

Variable	Change in Probability of Full Adoption
Crisis	.16 (−.01, .33)
Executive	.39 (.22, .57)
Scope	.32 (.08, .56)
Salience	−.03 (−.10, .05)
Staff	.08 (−.03, .18)

Note: For indicator variables (*crisis, executive*, and *scope*), the coefficients represent the change in the probability of a recommendation being fully adopted if the variable changes from zero to one. For continuous variables (*salience* and *staff*), the coefficients represent the change in the probability of a recommendation being fully adopted if the variable increases by one standard deviation. For all variables, 95 percent confidence intervals are in parentheses. The results are calculated using the estimates from Model 3 in Table 3.5.

of a proposal being fully adopted jump by roughly 40 percent if a commission is established by the executive rather than Congress, and increase by about a third if a panel's mandate is narrow instead of broad.

Considered in conjunction with the results of the regressions employing interviewee impact ratings as the dependent variable, these results powerfully confirm my hypotheses that commissions are more influential if they are established in the wake of a crisis, formed by the executive, and given a narrow mandate.

Tables 3.5 and 3.6 also provide further information on the validity of the expertise hypothesis. *Staff* is statistically significant in Model 1 ($p < .1$), and the results for all three models imply that if the size of a commission's staff increases by one standard deviation, the odds of a proposal being fully adopted increase by 8 or 9 percent. But *staff* does not obtain statistical significance in Models 2 and 3, calling into question the variable's importance. Furthermore, neither of the two other measures of expertise – *budget* and *experience* – nears statistical significance in any of the models when it replaces *staff* as a proxy for expertise. (These alternative specifications are not presented in Table 3.5). Therefore, there exists, at most, quite limited evidence that a commission's expertise contributes to the adoption of its recommendations. Because none of the expertise measures is statistically significant in the regressions treating impact ratings as the dependent variable, expertise seems, according to the totality of the results, to have little importance as a source of commission influence.

As in Table 3.4, the control variables representing features of a commission's membership – *stature* and *size* – are not statistically significant in Table 3.5, though the signs on their coefficients conform to the expectations of my theory. The biggest difference between Table 3.4 and Table 3.5 concerns the variables representing a commission's output: *unanimous* and *advocacy*. Whereas these variables are highly significant in Table 3.4, they do not approach statistical significance in Table 3.5. In addition, combinations of the four membership and output variables are not statistically significant in joint significance tests when the adoption of key recommendations is the dependent variable. These results challenge my expectation that a commission's makeup, ability to reach consensus, and advocacy contribute independently to its impact. Given the discrepancy between Tables 3.4 and 3.5 in the results for *unanimous* and *advocacy*, I cannot reach a definitive conclusion from the regressions about their independent importance. It is possible, however, that their significance is masked in Table 3.5 by the multicollinearity described earlier among several of the explanatory and control variables, including *scope*, *large*, *unanimous*, and *advocacy*.

Checking the Results

To further probe the accuracy of my regression models, I compared the models' predictions to the actual outcomes for each of the two dependent variables. These comparisons revealed strong correlations between the predicted and observed outcomes, providing more evidence that the models capture most of the key drivers of commission influence.[27]

I also investigated the robustness of the regression results by including other variables in the models and measuring some variables differently. I examined whether the nature of a crisis affects the impact of commissions by distinguishing between panels formed after disasters and those created after scandals; I found that both types of crisis boost a commission's impact. By adding an interaction term for *crisis* and *executive*, I further determined that a crisis bolsters commission influence regardless of whether a panel is formed by the executive or Congress, and that executive-branch authorization facilitates the impact of both crisis and agenda commissions. In addition, I found that the use of different measures of commission scope, size, and unanimity, and the inclusion of two

---

[27] Correlation coefficients for the predicted and actual values range from .46 to .84 across all of the models presented in Tables 3.4 and 3.5. The correlations are strongest (between .69 and .84) when using mean impact ratings as the dependent variable, because the average rating of all interviewees for a given commission is more predictable than the impact rating of an individual interviewee or the adoption of an individual commission recommendation.

measures of the political diversity of commissions, did not significantly change the results for *crisis, executive*, or *scope*.[28]

I also probed whether variables related to the political context of commissions contribute to their impact. I expected commissions might have less impact under divided government, when the president is unpopular, or at the end of a president's term, because the enactment of legislation is complicated by divided government, and a weak or outgoing president tends to have less capacity or incentive to make major policy changes. However, I found no support for these expectations.[29] I also found no evidence that patterns of commission influence differ depending on the identity of the president at the time a panel reports. In all of these cases, moreover, the principal results were unchanged by the inclusion of the additional variables.

Conclusion

This chapter's statistical analysis indicates that national security commissions are much more likely to influence policy when they are formed in response to a crisis, established by the executive branch, or given a narrow mandate. These findings represent strong evidence in support of the theory that I developed in Chapter 2, and they call into question the conventional wisdom that crisis commissions rarely lead to policy change. On the other hand, the statistical tests generate mixed results on whether the achievement of unanimity and intensive advocacy by a panel shape commission influence independently of the three explanatory variables. At the same time, the results offer little support for the alternative hypothesis that specialized expertise drives a commission's appeal.

Of course, these findings leave unanswered the critical question of whether policy changes made in accord with commission recommendations would have been made even if the panels never existed. That

---

[28] The alternative measure of *scope* treats the entire Defense Department as a single agency, rather than treating the departments of the Army, Navy, and Air Force as single agencies. For panel size, I replaced *large* with continuous variables representing the number of commissioners on a panel (*size*) and the square of that number (*size squared*). The diversity measures are whether a commission had an even number of Republicans and Democrats, and how a commission's members and staff rated its ideological diversity on a scale of one to five in interviews.

[29] I coded presidential approval for each commission based on the most recent Gallup poll prior to its report. I obtained the Gallup data at www.presidency.ucsb.edu/data/popularity. php. For timing in the election cycle, I included variables measuring whether a report was issued in the first or last year of a presidential term.

question is investigated in Chapters 4–6 by probing how eight commissions contributed to counterterrorism policy making. My analysis of those commissions shows that some panels do in fact spark major reforms that would not occur without them. The case studies also provide rich support for my argument, which is not directly tested in this chapter, that commissions are able to have a powerful influence on politics because they possess a unique form of political credibility.

PART TWO

COMMISSIONS AND COUNTERTERRORISM POLICY

4

Responding to the First Wave of Anti-American Terrorism

At 6:21 A.M. on October 23, 1983, a Hezbollah operative drove a large Mercedes-Benz truck toward a compound at Beirut's international airport that housed U.S. Marines deployed as part of a peacekeeping force in Lebanon. After crashing through a concertina-wire barrier and an open gate in a fence, the driver rammed the yellow truck over a wall of sandbags into the lobby of the four-story cement building where the Marines were sleeping. Before guards could respond, the suicide bomber detonated the huge mass of explosives in the truck – the equivalent of six tons of TNT – producing the largest nonnuclear explosion on earth in four decades (Wright 2001, 70). The ferocious blast instantly turned the building into rubble, crushing most of its occupants. The death toll was 241 U.S. servicemen, nearly all of them Marines. It remains the largest loss of American military life in a single incident since the Battle of Iwo Jima in World War II (Wright 2008).

Today, when Americans think of terrorism targeted at the United States, they think of Al Qaeda and 9/11. But anti-American terrorism first became a major threat during the 1980s, when it was perpetrated primarily by Hezbollah – with support from Iran – and Libya. The bombing of the Marine barracks, which led to the withdrawal of U.S. troops from Lebanon, was the most politically momentous attack of that era, but several other attacks claimed many American lives. Suicide bombers belonging to Hezbollah targeted the U.S. Embassy in Beirut with truck bombs in April 1983 and September 1984, killing a total of nineteen Americans and more than sixty Lebanese. In December 1985 and April 1986, Libyan operatives exploded bombs at two European airports and a disco in Berlin, killing twenty-two people, including six Americans. And on December 21, 1988, a bomb placed by a Libyan agent destroyed Pan Am Flight 103 over Lockerbie, Scotland, killing 180 Americans and 90 people of other nationalities.

During this first era of large-scale anti-American terrorism, the U.S. government established three commissions that examined terrorism. These three panels – each of which spurred policy change – are the subject of this chapter. The first commission, chaired by Robert Long, was formed by Secretary of Defense Caspar Weinberger in the immediate wake of the Marine barracks bombing. Its scathing critique of the U.S. intervention in Lebanon increased pressure on President Ronald Reagan to withdraw the Marines, and contributed significantly to Reagan's decision to pull them out quickly. The second, chaired by Bobby Inman, was created by Secretary of State George Shultz in 1984 in response to the successive bombings of U.S. embassies. Its report triggered the creation of a corps of professional diplomatic security officers and the adoption of new embassy security standards that remain in existence today. The third commission, led by Ann McLaughlin (now Korologos), was established by President George H. W. Bush in 1989 to examine the Lockerbie bombing. Like the Inman Panel, it sparked major changes in how the government protects against terrorism, but in the area of aviation, rather than diplomatic, security. All three commissions remain among the more influential national security panels of recent decades.

This is the first of three chapters presenting case studies of commissions that dealt with terrorism. Whereas this chapter covers the terrorism commissions of the 1980s, Chapters 5 and 6 discuss panels that operated during the next wave of anti-American terrorism, which was spearheaded by Al Qaeda starting in the 1990s. I focus on terrorism in these chapters to give them a thematic coherence and to take advantage of the fact that the commissions in my data set that examined terrorism varied in their context and characteristics, offering a rich sample of cases for in-depth study. Although the three commissions analyzed in this chapter were all formed by the executive branch in response to a crisis, the panels discussed in Chapters 5 and 6 include congressional and agenda commissions.

Analytically, I have two principal goals in Chapters 4–6. First, I seek to determine whether commissions catalyzed important reforms. My approach is to consider how events would have unfolded if a commission had not existed. If I find that a reform would not have occurred without a panel's work, I can conclude that the commission was directly responsible for the policy change. This type of analysis enables me to test the validity of the conventional wisdom about commissions, encapsulated in the alternative hypothesis that commissions rarely trigger reform.

Second, I aim to further test my theory of commission influence by probing whether it explains the impact of individual panels. The statistical tests I conducted in Chapter 3 strongly supported my hypotheses that commissions are more influential when they are (1) formed in response to a crisis, (2) established by the executive branch, or (3) given a narrow mandate. However, case studies are better suited than statistical tests to probe whether my theory accurately captures the process through which commissions contribute to reform. For instance, case studies can determine whether I am correct in arguing that commissions have a special ability to engage in genuine deliberation and to achieve consensus, and in claiming that political credibility – grounded in independence, stature, and ideological diversity – is the primary source of their ability to drive policy or organizational change. In Chapters 4–6, I test this argument by investigating whether the cases support the following implications of the argument:

- It should be common for commission members to change their stance on an issue during the panel's work.
- It should be common for commissions to issue findings and recommendations that their sponsors do not support.
- Influential commissions should possess a combination of independence, stature, and ideological diversity that other political institutions lack.
- Policy makers should praise the independence, stature, and bipartisanship of commissions when endorsing for panel proposals.
- The recommendations of commissions that issue unanimous reports should be supported by Democrats and Republicans.

By the same token, these chapters provide additional tests of the alternate hypothesis that expertise, rather than political credibility, is the key source of a commission's appeal. This alternative view generates its own implications:

- Influential panels should possess specialized knowledge that other political institutions lack.
- Policy makers should laud the expertise of commissions when describing their support for panel proposals.

I draw conclusions about the respective merits of the political credibility argument and the expertise hypothesis by determining whether the cases provide more support for one or the other of these sets of implications.

The Long Commission and Intervention in Lebanon

In 1982, Lebanon was the scene of fierce fighting involving Israel, Syria, the Palestine Liberation Organization (PLO), and Lebanese militias. Lebanon's government was unable to control the chaotic conflict, and it requested the intervention of international peacekeepers. In August, President Reagan deployed 800 Marines as part of a multinational force with the limited mission of facilitating the evacuation of the PLO from Beirut. This mission was completed on September 10, creating temporary calm in the capital. But four days later, Lebanese President-elect Bashir Gamayel was assassinated, triggering a new spasm of violence, including the massacre of hundreds of Palestinians by Christian Phalangists at the Sabra and Shatila refugee camps. In response, Reagan inserted a larger contingent of 1,400 Marines into Beirut as part of a new multinational force composed of U.S., French, Italian, and British troops. The goal of the second deployment was to assist the Lebanese army in gaining control over the Beirut area, and to establish an environment that would facilitate the withdrawal of Israeli and Syrian forces from Lebanon.[1]

The second deployment got bogged down, however, as the warring parties proved unable in subsequent months to uphold cease-fire and withdrawal agreements. At the same time, a new militia, trained by Iran's Revolutionary Guards, emerged with the goal of expelling Israel's army and the Western peacekeepers from Lebanon. This group, which only later became widely known as Hezbollah, or "Party of God," quickly learned to employ suicide attacks very effectively. Its first major strike was the April 1983 bombing of the U.S. Embassy in Beirut, which killed seventeen Americans. The bombing of the Marine barracks followed in October.[2] That attack was synchronized with the explosion just twenty seconds later of a truck bomb elsewhere in Lebanon that killed fifty-eight

---

[1] My account of the Lebanese conflict and the U.S. intervention in Lebanon draws on Robin Wright's scholarship and the reports of the Long Commission and the House Armed Services Investigations Subcommittee that investigated the Marine barracks bombing (Commission on Beirut International Airport Terrorist Act 1983; Investigations Subcommittee of the House Committee on Armed Services 1983; Wright 2001).

[2] A group called Islamic Jihad took responsibility for the bombings, but experts believe that Islamic Jihad was a *nom de guerre* of Hezbollah, which only declared its identity publicly in 1985 (Associated Press 2003; Goldberg 2002).

French paratroopers, producing a combined death toll of 299 U.S. and French troops in one of the first instances of coordinated suicide bombings (Goldberg 2002).

The huge loss of American life in the Marine barracks bombing sparked intense criticism of the deployment by members of Congress, even though Congress had authorized the deployment for eighteen months just a few weeks before the disaster. Democrats and Republicans now called on the administration to clarify the role of the U.S. troops in Lebanon, arguing that the existing mission was unclear and left the troops vulnerable to attack. Senator Sam Nunn (D-GA), the ranking minority member on the Senate Armed Services Committee, expressed the prevailing frustration: "Our forces in Lebanon now are not a deterrent; they're hostages" (Roberts 1983). But in the immediate aftermath of the attack, only a minority of Democrats and hardly any Republicans advocated the rapid withdrawal of the Marines.

Two weeks after the bombing, Secretary of Defense Caspar Weinberger established the Commission on Beirut International Airport Terrorist Act of October 23, 1983 (the Long Commission) with a rather narrow mandate: to examine the rules of engagement and security measures in place before and after the attack. Weinberger named five people to the commission: retired Navy Admiral Robert Long, who served as the chairman; Carter administration Under Secretary of the Navy Robert Murray; Army General Joseph Palastra; retired Marine Corps General Lawrence Snowden; and retired Air Force General Eugene Tighe.

Weinberger had multiple reasons for creating the commission. First, he needed to respond to public and congressional criticism that followed the bombing. Because the military chain of command was directly involved in events related to the attack, only an independent commission consisting primarily of retired officers could have the perception of impartiality required to conduct a credible investigation.[3] Second, Weinberger most likely wanted there to be an alternative to a probe already begun by the Investigations Subcommittee of the House Armed Services Committee, which could be expected to criticize harshly the Defense Department – and perhaps Weinberger himself – given the Democrats' majority control of that committee.

Third, and most important in terms of the commission's potential to influence policy, Weinberger hoped the commission would increase

---

[3] Interview of Richard Grunawalt, February 14, 2008; interview of Joseph Palastra, April 9, 2008.

pressure on the Reagan administration to end the Lebanon deployment. Weinberger and the Joint Chiefs of Staff had opposed the U.S. intervention in Lebanon from the outset, because they did not think the mission was clearly defined or necessary to protect national security (Lehman 1988, 309; Shapiro and Hiatt 1983; Weinberger 1990, 144). In authorizing the deployment, Reagan had overruled their objections and sided with Secretary of State Shultz and National Security Advisor Robert McFarlane, who favored intervening as a means of maintaining stability in the region.[4]

Weinberger saw the Marine barracks bombing as an opportunity to raise new questions about the merits of the intervention, and he surely realized that a critical commission report could bolster his case for withdrawal. Then–Secretary of the Navy John Lehman pointedly recalled, "Cap [Weinberger] established the commission to isolate what went wrong, and everyone knew that clarifying that would show what an ill-advised mission it had been from the beginning."[5] Weinberger asked the commission to report quickly – an indication both of the urgency of the issue and of Weinberger's hope that the report would weaken support for the deployment.

The Commission's Indictment

The commission's unanimous report, issued on December 20, 1983 – just six weeks after the panel's establishment – offered a searing indictment of many aspects of the design and execution of the Lebanon mission (Commission on Beirut International Airport Terrorist Act 1983). The commission blamed the entire chain of command for failing to ensure the security of the Marines in Lebanon, stating that the Marines were not trained or organized to deal with terrorist threats effectively, were not provided with timely intelligence on threats, and were not given a consistent set of rules of engagement. In addition, the panel argued that the Marines were left in a vulnerable position because the United States increasingly sided with the Christian-dominated Lebanese government in the multisided conflict without giving the Marines sufficient authority to protect themselves against antigovernment forces such as Hezbollah.

More broadly, the commission contended that America had placed too much emphasis on military involvement in Lebanon, at the expense of diplomacy. In its most politically charged recommendation, it proposed

---

[4] Interview of Robert McFarlane, May 21, 2008.
[5] Interview of John Lehman, February 27, 2008.

that the National Security Council "undertake a re-examination of alternative means of achieving U.S. objectives in Lebanon," including "a more vigorous and demanding approach to pursuing diplomatic alternatives" (Commission on Beirut International Airport Terrorist Act 1983, 8). Although the commission did not call explicitly for a withdrawal, this recommendation was widely interpreted in the administration, Congress, and the media as an endorsement of the withdrawal option.

Recognizing how much the report could undermine the administration's Lebanon policy, the White House directed the Pentagon not to conduct a briefing on its contents and declined to make the report available to reporters. One administration official said that "the less said about the Long report the better," because he feared it would become a rallying point for opponents of the deployment (Cannon 1983). The military service chiefs were also unhappy with the commission report because it blamed the entire chain of command for failures in Lebanon and argued that security measures put in place after the bombing remained inadequate.[6] But Weinberger wanted the report to be declassified so that its criticisms of the deployment would be heavily publicized. As he notes in his memoirs, "The Commission's findings placed before the public many of the arguments I had been making privately for well over a year" (Weinberger 1990, 163). Weinberger released the report to the public on December 28, five days after its findings were disclosed.

Congressional Opinion Changes

The report received extensive media coverage – it was the lead story in the *New York Times* and *Washington Post* on the day it was released – and its impact on the debate over Lebanon policy was felt immediately. When the commission reported, most leading Democratic and Republican political figures had not yet called for a withdrawal, despite any misgivings they may have had about the intervention. With two months having already passed since the Marine barracks bombing, congressional support for the deployment remained strong enough to enable it to continue. However, the commission's powerful criticism of the mission influenced the positions of key leaders on both sides of the political aisle, placing new pressure on the administration to change its policy.

In the days after the report was issued, Speaker of the House Tip O'Neill (D-MA), House Minority Leader Robert Michel (R-IL), and leading Democratic presidential candidate Walter Mondale reassessed or

---

[6] Interview of Joseph Palastra, April 9, 2008.

reversed their backing of the deployment. On December 27, Michel suggested that the administration should consider moving the Marines to ships off the coast of Lebanon – a remarkable change of position for a leader of the president's own party. The next day, a senior aide to O'Neill told a journalist that the speaker was reconsidering his stance on the intervention after reading the commission report (Taubman 1983a). And on December 31, Mondale called for an immediate withdrawal of the Marines for the first time (Peterson and Schram 1984).

For some of these political figures, the commission may have triggered the change in their position by giving them political cover to support a U.S. pullout. They may have felt less vulnerable to political charges of being weak on security or undermining the troops once they could point to a unanimous report by a commission of distinguished military officials in making the case for withdrawal.

At the same time, public support for the Lebanon deployment deteriorated. A mid-January poll by the *New York Times* and *CBS News* found that 49 percent of Americans favored withdrawing the Marines, whereas 38 percent supported continuing the deployment. These figures represented a dramatic change from late October, shortly after the Marine barracks bombing, when only 35 percent of respondents supported withdrawal – despite the very high death toll from the attack (Weisman 1984).[7] Nearly universal praise of the commission's report in the media surely contributed to this change in public opinion. Out of seventeen editorials and op-eds that discussed the report in the three months after its release in the *Chicago Tribune*, *New York Times*, *Wall Street Journal*, and *Washington Post* – a sample of prominent and ideologically diverse newspapers – all but one of the columns endorsed the commission's findings.

The commission's report was not the only document that influenced the raging debate over Lebanon policy. The Investigations Subcommittee of the House Armed Services Committee had released its own study of the Marine barracks bombing just four days before the commission reported.[8] Like the commission, the subcommittee was highly critical of the conduct of the U.S. military operation, and it urged the Reagan administration to review whether the continued deployment of U.S.

---

[7] I could not find any polling data on this issue between late October 1983 and January 1984.

[8] This subcommittee report was not approved by the full armed services committee until six weeks later, on January 31, 1984.

troops was justified. However, three Republicans on the subcommittee wrote a dissenting opinion, arguing that it was unfair to criticize the mission with "20-20 hindsight" (Investigations Subcommittee of the House Committee on Armed Services 1983, 76–78).

Given the issuance of this congressional report just a few days before the commission reported, it is difficult to separate the impact of one from that of the other. Indeed, the similarities between the two reports allowed each of them to amplify the message of the other. Mondale pointed to both reports when announcing his decision to call for a withdrawal: "I have just completed reviewing the Long Commission and House Armed Services Committee reports. I am now convinced that U.S. Marines must be withdrawn from Lebanon" (*New York Times* 1984a).

But several factors strongly suggest that the commission was more influential than the congressional subcommittee. First, the commission report received much more attention than did the subcommittee report. During the ninety days after each report was issued, the subcommittee report was mentioned by 43 articles in the *Chicago Tribune*, *New York Times*, *Wall Street Journal*, and *Washington Post*, whereas 118 articles referred to the commission report – nearly three times as many.[9] Second, leading politicians only changed their position on the deployment after the commission reported. Third, key members of Congress indicated that the commission exerted particularly large influence on their views. A senior aide to Speaker O'Neill commented that O'Neill attached special significance to the commission report because of his high regard for Long, who was widely viewed as a person of great independence and integrity (Rogers and Greenberger 1983). Similarly, House Foreign Affairs Committee Chairman Dante Fascell (D-FL) noted that a unanimous report by a military commission criticizing a deployment was especially powerful (Taubman 1983a). By contrast, the bipartisan credibility of the congressional subcommittee report was diminished by the fact that three of the five Republicans on the subcommittee dissented from it.

Journalists covering the debate over Lebanon policy also concluded that the Long Commission report was the key tipping point in the debate. An editorial in the *Wall Street Journal* stated, "Washington observers are saying that the rapid erosion of congressional support results not from the October 23 truck bombing, but from the highly critical report of

---

[9] I conducted these searches in LexisNexis using a wide array of search terms, including "committee," "subcommittee," "panel," and "commission," in order to identify any article that might refer to either report.

Admiral Robert Long's investigating commission" (*Wall Street Journal* 1984). That claim may have overstated the case, because the bombing was the impetus for the commission and a necessary condition for its impact, but the statement reflected the prevailing view of the commission's singular importance.

Reagan Withdraws the Troops

By further eroding public and congressional support for the Lebanon mission, the commission strengthened the hand of those administration officials, like Weinberger, who favored a withdrawal. Weinberger used the commission report to reopen discussions in the administration about the wisdom of remaining in Lebanon, and he cited the report in late December when recommending to Reagan that the United States shift its focus in Lebanon to diplomacy (Taubman 1983b; Weinberger 1990, 168–169). Secretary of State Shultz and National Security Advisor McFarlane continued to advocate continuing the mission, however, and Reagan maintained the existing policy through January.

With the administration stalemated, members of Congress began to push for withdrawal more aggressively. On February 1, the caucus of House Democrats approved a draft resolution calling for the withdrawal of the Marines. The resolution explicitly cited the Long Commission's recommendation of "a reassessment of alternative means to achieve United States objectives in Lebanon" in making its case for withdrawal (*New York Times* 1984b). The next day, a group of leading Democrats in foreign policy, including House Foreign Affairs Committee Chairman Fascell, House Armed Services Committee Chairman Les Aspin (D-WI), Representative Lee Hamilton (D-IN), and Senators Joe Biden (D-DE), Gary Hart (D-CO), and Claiborne Pell (D-RI), introduced companion measures in the House and Senate calling for the "prompt and orderly withdrawal" of the U.S. troops in Lebanon.[10] Many of these members of Congress, including Fascell, Aspin, and Hamilton, had supported the deployment until the Long Commission reported.

In the face of this growing congressional and public opposition, Reagan finally sided with Weinberger over Shultz and McFarlane, and on February 5 he ordered the Marines to begin a withdrawal from Lebanon. Administration officials told journalists off the record that Reagan's decision was motivated in part by the growing congressional opposition to the deployment and by concern that the Lebanon mission could hurt

[10] These measures were H.CON.RES. 248 and S.CON.RES. 92.

Reagan's reelection prospects (Cannon and Hoffman 1984). The pullout occurred quickly: By February 26, all of the U.S. troops had left Lebanon for ships offshore. The rest of the multinational force departed by April, ending the Western intervention without the achievement of peace or stability. The Lebanese war continued until 1990.

Assessing the Commission's Impact

Of course, the Long Commission was not primarily responsible for the U.S. withdrawal. The most important catalyst of the pullout was the massive loss of American life from the truck bombing. The killing of 241 Marines in a single day heightened public and congressional discontent with the Lebanon mission, creating a window of opportunity for policy change. But the bombing alone did not prompt Congress or the administration to support a rapid withdrawal. Until the Long Commission reported, Congress was unable to articulate a coherent and credible alternative to existing policy, because Democrats were divided on the deployment and most congressional Republicans remained loyal to the Reagan administration. At the same time, Weinberger was constrained from criticizing the mission publicly because he served the president.

As described in the previous section, leading political figures, including O'Neill, Michel, and Mondale, only called for a pullout after the commission's strong criticism of the U.S. intervention established a focal point for the Lebanon debate and gave Republicans and Democrats cover to call for withdrawal. By that time, two months had already passed since the bombing, implying that those same political figures might not have endorsed a pullout absent the commission's work. Furthermore, the pressure generated after the commission reported by the growing public and congressional opposition to the deployment contributed to Reagan's decision to withdraw the Marines.

In interviews, the three surviving members of the Long Commission agreed that their report helped to stimulate the withdrawal.[11] Key Reagan administration officials with responsibility for Lebanon policy at the time also said the report had a powerful impact. McFarlane commented that the commission increased pressure on the administration because it "lent standing to congressional concerns," adding that "withdrawal was due in part to the Long Commission."[12] In his memoirs, Navy Secretary

[11] Interview of Robert Murray, July 20, 2007; interview of Joseph Palastra, April 9, 2008; interview of Lawrence Snowden, January 28, 2008.
[12] Interview of Robert McFarlane, May 12, 2008.

John Lehman stated unequivocally that "the public impact of the report demolished support for the mission" (Lehman 1988, 318). Chairman of the Joint Chiefs John Vessey had a somewhat different view, asserting that Reagan would have ultimately decided to withdraw the Marines regardless of the commission, but he agreed that the commission shaped the public debate over the deployment.[13]

The Long Commission also influenced policy through a set of recommendations it made concerning counterterrorism policies. The commission proposed that the government establish an all-source intelligence fusion center to provide tailored intelligence to U.S. military commanders in areas of high threat or conflict. Such a center was created by the Central Intelligence Agency in January 1984 (Ignatius 1984). More generally, the commission argued that the military should develop doctrine, plans, and training regimens to defend against and combat terrorism. Weinberger ordered the implementation of this recommendation, and several former officials and experts said that it sparked the development of important new counterterrorism doctrine and training by the military services.[14]

What factors, then, account for the Long Commission's significant influence? Although the crisis generated by the Marine barracks bombing was the essential background condition enabling the commission's impact, the panel's indictment of the Lebanon intervention was particularly powerful because the commission represented the military establishment. Its stature, mostly nonpartisan makeup, and unanimity gave it tremendous political credibility and meant that its report, unlike that of the House armed services subcommittee, could not be dismissed as a partisan document. The commission's military credentials and unanimity also gave elected officials political cover to endorse withdrawal – cover that a split congressional subcommittee could not provide them.

The commission's authorization by Weinberger and its narrow mandate also facilitated its impact. Most important, its creation by Weinberger reflected his hope of using the report to persuade Reagan to end the deployment. This preexisting interest meant that the commission was likely to have a powerful advocate within the administration to promote the report if it criticized the intervention. However, authorization by the executive branch, rather than by Congress, was also essential to the panel's

---

[13] Interview of John Vessey, July 18, 2007.
[14] Interview of Richard Grunawalt, February 14, 2008; interview of Brian Jenkins, December 18, 2007; interview of John Lehman, February 27, 2008; interview of Lawrence Snowden, January 28, 2008.

influence, because a commission formed by Congress could not have been named and issued a report nearly as quickly as did the Long Commission, possibly allowing the window of opportunity for changing Lebanon policy to close. As discussed in Chapter 2, congressional commissions rarely get set up quickly because it can take many months to enact authorizing legislation for a commission, and the members of congressional commissions are typically appointed by several policy makers, some of whom can have an incentive to drag their feet in naming their appointments. In fact, of the twenty-five congressional commissions in my data set, none of them reported in fewer than six months – far longer than the six weeks that the Long Commission took to complete its work.[15]

Moreover, the compromises typically necessary to create a congressional commission would have probably produced a panel with more members and greater ideological diversity, complicating the task of achieving unanimity on hard-hitting findings and specific recommendations. The Long Commission's narrow mandate – limited to an examination of the rules of engagement and security measures in place before and after the Marine barracks bombing – also helped the panel work through a manageable number of issues and reach consensus in a short period of time.

The Long Commission offers little support for the alternative hypothesis that expertise, rather than political credibility, is the key source of commission influence. Certainly the panel possessed substantial expertise through its commissioners and its staff of twenty-three people, most of whom were active-duty military officers. However, the Pentagon and congressional armed services committees also possessed ample military expertise; indeed, the report of the House subcommittee included as much technical detail as did the Long Commission report. Moreover, the commission did not investigate a highly specialized issue that only a select group of military officers understood: Thousands of officers were knowledgeable about rules of engagement and force-protection measures. Further, the very short period of time available to the commission to conduct its work precluded it from accumulating a great body of specialized knowledge that the Pentagon or congressional committees did not possess.

---

[15] The issuance of the House armed services subcommittee report within two months of the Marine barracks bombing does not undermine my argument that congressional commissions cannot operate that quickly. Congressional committees, unlike independent commissions, have the ability to begin investigations almost immediately because their members and staff are already in place.

Instead, the crucial difference among the commission, the House investigations subcommittee, and the Defense Department was that the commission was independent and could produce a unanimous report with credibility on both sides of the political aisle. These factors enabled it to criticize the administration publicly, which Weinberger could not do, and allowed it to send a more powerful signal than the divided congressional subcommittee that its proposals should be acceptable to Democrats and Republicans.

The Inman Panel and Embassy Security

The bombing of the Marine barracks was not the only attack on Americans in the Middle East in the early 1980s, though it was the bloodiest. Several other bombings targeted U.S. diplomatic facilities. In April 1983, seventeen Americans, including eight Central Intelligence Agency (CIA) officers, were killed by a Hezbollah suicide bomber who exploded a van full of explosives at the entrance of the U.S. Embassy in Beirut. Eight months later, members of Hezbollah and another group backed by Iran targeted the U.S. Embassy in Kuwait with a truck bomb, killing two Palestinians, two Kuwaitis, and a Syrian, but no Americans. The February 1984 American withdrawal from Lebanon did not end the attacks. Seven months after the pullout, Hezbollah struck an annex of the U.S. Embassy in Beirut with another truck bomb, killing two U.S. military personnel and twenty-one non-Americans. After that bombing, a Hezbollah spokesman boasted, "The operation comes to prove that we will carry out our previous promise not to allow a single American to remain on Lebanese soil" (Wright 2001, 107).

These bombings naturally raised questions about the level of security at American facilities abroad. Even before the September 1984 bombing, the General Accounting Office (now the Government Accountability Office) issued a report stating that government efforts to improve embassy security were lagging, hampered by a lack of direction, bureaucratic sluggishness, and disagreements within the State Department (Farrell 1984). After the September bombing, leading Democrats lambasted the Reagan administration. Presidential candidate Mondale charged the administration with "a serious failure of security," and Speaker of the House O'Neill said security arrangements had been "an absolute disgrace" (Goshko and Hiatt 1984). These charges threatened to be particularly potent in the midst of a presidential election season.

In response to the bombings, the State Department took interim steps to bolster security, including building new barricades and tightening some security procedures. However, senior officials in the department believed that more dramatic security changes were necessary. These changes would require increased funding from Congress, which tended to be stingy in funding security upgrades, and were likely to face opposition from elements of the department's bureaucracy – particularly Foreign Service officers – who resisted prioritizing security over diplomatic openness. The difficulty of winning congressional approval for major upgrades was compounded by the weakness of the existing State Department office that covered security threats, the Office for Combating Terrorism and Emergency Planning. A Reagan administration official commented that the office "didn't have the stature to sell a large program outside the department."[16]

To help overcome these obstacles to major reform, Robert Lamb, the assistant secretary of state for administration, and John Shumate, the executive director of the Bureau of Administration, suggested to Secretary of State George Shultz that he form an independent panel. Shumate commented, "I thought a panel would help the department get more money from Congress for security and buildings. It would give the effort cosmetics and gravitas."[17] Lamb noted, "It was clear that whatever we did was not going to be popular in the Foreign Service. We needed clout to overcome their objections."[18]

Creating a commission also had the obvious benefit for the Reagan administration of defusing political pressure in the wake of the bombings by enabling it to say it was doing something to address security shortcomings. Then–Under Secretary of State for Management Ronald Spiers recalled that although the State Department did not seek White House approval to form the panel, department officials knew that President Reagan was concerned that he was politically vulnerable on the embassy security issue.[19]

Shultz charged the commission, officially called the Secretary of State's Advisory Panel on Overseas Security, with developing a plan to meet the security challenges of U.S. government operations abroad. He chose retired Navy Admiral Bobby Inman to chair the panel. Inman was an unorthodox choice because of his military, rather than diplomatic, background, but his independence from the State Department was likely to

---

[16] Interview of Reagan administration official, March 2008.
[17] Interview of John Shumate, June 15, 2007.
[18] Interview of Robert Lamb, March 18, 2008.
[19] Interview of Ronald Spiers, March 10, 2009.

enhance his already substantial credibility on Capitol Hill. Shultz also set the stage for congressional buy-in by naming two key members of Congress to the panel: Senator Warren Rudman (R-NH), who chaired the Senate appropriations subcommittee with responsibility for the State Department, and Representative Daniel Mica (D-FL), who chaired the House Foreign Affairs Subcommittee on International Operations. Former Ambassadors Anne Armstrong and Lawrence Eagleburger, retired Marine Corps General D'Wayne Gray, and former New York City Police Commissioner Robert McGuire comprised the rest of the seven-member commission. The panel was supported by a small staff of eleven people.

Reaching Consensus

The process through which the Inman Panel formulated its recommendations illustrates well how the deliberative environment of a commission can lead its members to change their positions and reach consensus on surprising recommendations. As the panel conducted its work, a staff member, Nina Stewart, developed the original idea of creating a new professional diplomatic security service within the State Department. (At the time, embassy security was handled by a security office that the panel considered to lack sufficient clout). Inman was skeptical at first that reorganizing would be effective, and some other commissioners and staff members feared it would be viewed by many people within the department as a power grab, which might create internal strife among department personnel.[20]

Ultimately, however, the panel's investigation and deliberations led the commissioners to agree unanimously that the creation of a professional security service was necessary to improve security sufficiently.[21] As the panel's report, issued on June 24, 1985, states, "The large, important, and growing security demand at home and abroad requires a competent professional organization with a sense of mission and identity legislatively defined and yet accountable to the traditional authority of management" (Secretary of State's Advisory Panel on Overseas Security 1985, 1). Based on this finding, the panel recommended establishing a diplomatic security service as the principal element of a new bureau for diplomatic security, with over 1,100 diplomatic security officers at home and abroad. (The existing security office had only 176 total employees as of 1983.[22])

---

[20] Interview of Bobby Inman, July 5, 2007; interview of panel staff member, April 2008.
[21] Testimony by Bobby Inman before the House Committee on Foreign Affairs, July 16, 1985.
[22] Interview of Robert Lamb, March 18, 2008.

The Inman Panel's eighty-two-page unanimous report included dozens of other recommendations on issues ranging from intelligence and diplomacy to building standards for embassies. The report identified a few of these proposals as particularly important ones: (1) appropriating about $3.5 billion in new funds to renovate or replace more than 100 overseas facilities that had security shortcomings; (2) transferring responsibility for counterterrorism diplomacy from the under secretary for management to the under secretary for political affairs; and (3) enacting legislation that would require the establishment of a board of inquiry after any future security incident involving the loss of life or major destruction of property.

Shultz liked some of the panel's recommendations much more than others. He naturally favored increased appropriations for embassy security upgrades, but initially resisted the proposal to establish a diplomatic security service, instead wanting to turn over security functions to the Secret Service.[23] Shultz also opposed the panel's recommendation on reassigning responsibility for counterterrorism diplomacy, opting instead to create a new ambassador at large for counterterrorism.[24] His stances on these principal panel recommendations represent strong evidence of the commission's independence, as the panel would not have proposed measures that Shultz opposed if it sought simply to do his bidding. In addition, the recommendation to require future boards of inquiry was opposed by many State Department officials, though Shultz endorsed it.[25] Inman commented, "Officials resisted it because that kind of accountability wasn't part of their culture."[26]

Congress Acts

Nevertheless, the Inman Panel had a powerful impact. Although Shultz disagreed with some of the panel's proposals, he named Robert Lamb to a new position of coordinator for diplomatic security and instructed Lamb to assess each recommendation and monitor its implementation. At the same time, Inman worked with panel members Mica and Rudman to build congressional backing for the panel's proposals.[27] In July 1985,

[23] Testimony by Bobby Inman before the House Committee on Foreign Affairs, July 16, 1985.
[24] Testimony by George Shultz before the House Committee on Foreign Affairs, July 24, 1985.
[25] Interview of John Shumate, June 15, 2007; interview of Nina Stewart, April 8, 2008.
[26] Interview of Bobby Inman, July 5, 2007.
[27] Interview of Bobby Inman, July 5, 2007; interview of Dan Mica, June 19, 2008.

Inman testified in support of the recommendations before the House Foreign Affairs Committee and Senate Foreign Relations Committee. At the House hearing, Committee Chairman Dante Fascell expressed skepticism about the diplomatic security-service proposal, echoing the resistance of Shultz and the Foreign Service.[28] But persistent advocacy by Inman, Mica, and Rudman during subsequent months boosted congressional support for the idea and established it as a focal point for the embassy security debate.

In December 1985 – six months after the Inman Panel reported – Mica introduced a bill whose principal provisions were drawn directly from the commission report.[29] They included the establishment of a bureau of diplomatic security headed by a new assistant secretary for diplomatic security, the creation of a diplomatic security service (DSS) within the new bureau, and the requirement that the secretary of state convene accountability review boards to investigate future security incidents involving serious injury or loss of life. One month later, Senate Foreign Relations Committee Chairman Richard Lugar (R-IN) introduced a nearly identical bill in the Senate.[30] Before the Inman Panel reported, none of the main provisions of these bills had been proposed by a member of Congress, providing strong evidence that their introduction resulted directly from the commission.[31] In interviews, Mica, State Department officials Lamb and Shumate, and others involved in the panel and the legislative debate agreed that the panel originated these policy ideas.[32]

The House bill was approved by an overwhelming margin in March 1986, and the Senate version was passed by voice vote three months later, leading to the legislation's enactment in August as the Diplomatic Security Act of 1986.[33] Given that Shultz and/or other top State Department officials initially resisted each of the central elements of the legislation, it is

---

[28] Comments by Dante Fascell, Hearing on Diplomatic Security, House Committee on Foreign Affairs, July 16, 1985.

[29] The bill was H.R. 3946.

[30] The bill was S. 2015.

[31] In fact, there were very few, if any, competing congressional proposals for bolstering embassy security. A systematic search of the congressional database THOMAS revealed that no other bills were introduced in 1985 or early 1986 to strengthen security at diplomatic facilities.

[32] Interview of Brian Jenkins, December 18, 2007; interview of Robert Lamb, March 18, 2008; interview of Rich McBride, June 19, 2008; interview of Dan Mica, June 19, 2008; interview of John Shumate, June 15, 2007.

[33] The act is Public Law 99–399. Dante Fascell was among the 389 House members who voted for the legislation, despite his earlier skepticism about the diplomatic security-service proposal – an indication of the effective advocacy by Mica, Rudman, and Inman.

unlikely that any of them would have been enacted into law if the panel had not recommended them. Lamb and Shumate observed that the new bureau and DSS would not have been established without the Inman Panel because there was not preexisting support for those ideas within either the State Department or Congress.[34]

More generally, congressional and administration officials agreed that the Inman Panel was primarily responsible for enactment of the legislation. Lamb said, "The legislation was a direct result of the panel. It essentially fleshed out what the panel recommended."[35] Rich McBride, then the chief of staff of Mica's House subcommittee, recalled, "The Inman Panel was the tipping point [in enacting legislation]. We recognized that it opened a window for us, and we needed to move quickly, and we did."[36]

In addition to triggering enactment of the Diplomatic Security Act, the Inman Panel influenced the development of new security standards for U.S. diplomatic facilities. The panel recommended that the State Department revise its guidelines for the construction and protection of facilities to make them less vulnerable to terrorist attack. After the commission reported, the department convened an expert committee to translate the panel's general recommendations on this topic into new embassy design specifications. The department subsequently adopted many of these guidelines, including a standard that new buildings should be set back at least 100 feet from the nearest street. Although the Inman Panel did not formulate these specifications, they continue to be known in the department as the "Inman standards," reflecting the panel's contribution to their development (Lamb 2000).

The Inman Panel also influenced the appropriation of new funds to implement the strict new standards. The panel's report called for a massive spending program of $3.5 billion over five years to bolster security at existing facilities and build new ones. To put this amount of funding in perspective, from 1979 to 1983 Congress had appropriated a total of just $140 million for embassy security upgrades. Moreover, even after the 1983 and 1984 embassy bombings, spending for this purpose was comparatively very limited. Shortly after the September 1984 bombing, Congress appropriated $110 million in supplemental diplomatic security spending, and in February 1985 the administration requested a total of $251 million for FY 1986 security upgrades (Atlas 1985). Although the

---

[34] Interview of Robert Lamb, March 18, 2008; interview of John Shumate, June 15, 2007.
[35] Interview of Robert Lamb, March 18, 2008.
[36] Interview of Rich McBride, June 19, 2008.

State Department had sought White House approval of a larger request for FY 1986, the Office of Management and Budget (OMB) – concerned with restraining overall government spending – blocked it from asking for more than $251 million.[37] The Inman Panel's proposal, issued in June 1985, therefore represented a huge increase over the existing spending level and administration request. In fact, the proposal exceeded the entire annual operating budget of the State Department, which totaled only about $2 billion at the time.

Shultz decided to seek the amount of funding proposed by the commission, and its recommendation helped him gain approval from OMB to request the full $3.5 billion over five years.[38] The State Department submitted this huge request to Congress in September 1985, labeling it "the Inman supplemental budget request" in recognition of its origins, and perhaps in a bid to borrow the panel's legitimacy. The exact match between the amount proposed by the panel and that requested by the department provides strong evidence that the request was based directly on the commission's proposal. Furthermore, according to Lamb, who became the first assistant secretary for diplomatic security, the department was not considering a request of that size before the panel reported: "It wouldn't have been considered realistic. No one would have thought it conceivable without Inman."[39]

The $3.5 billion proposal was the biggest new program request by the State Department in two decades.[40] In response, Congress appropriated $1.1 billion in funding for security upgrades and new building construction for FY 1986 and 1987 – far more than the administration had requested prior to the Inman Panel report, and more than had ever been appropriated for a State Department construction program overseas (Omang 1986).[41] Advocacy by Mica was especially important in obtaining congressional approval of this funding. According to two officials involved in the funding debate, Mica was a determined advocate for the appropriation and persuaded House Speaker O'Neill to support it.[42]

---

[37] Comment by Dante Fascell, hearing of the House Committee on Foreign Affairs, July 24, 1985.
[38] Interview of Ronald Spiers, March 10, 2009.
[39] Interview of Robert Lamb, March 18, 2008.
[40] Comment by Dan Mica, hearing of the House Committee on Foreign Affairs, July 24, 1985
[41] The funding was appropriated by Public Law 99–349.
[42] Interview of Robert Lamb, March 18, 2008; interview of Rich McBride, June 19, 2008.

Ultimately, however, Congress did not come close to appropriating the full $3.5 billion. After the appropriation of $1.1 billion in 1986, backing for more funding dried up in both Congress and OMB. This loss of support was due in part to the effort to rein in federal spending in the second half of the 1980s, and in part due to the absence of additional attacks on U.S. embassies, which reduced the pressure on policy makers to bolster diplomatic security (Epstein 2001; Lamb 2000; Risen 1999a). Ronald Spiers, then the State Department's top management official, noted, "We started out with a bang in getting support, but the support melted away when nothing else happened [to highlight the need for more funding]."[43]

The failure to appropriate the full amount recommended by the Inman Panel, the difficulty of establishing a 100-foot setback for embassies in urban areas, and continued resistance from Foreign Service officers prevented application of the Inman standards to all diplomatic facilities. Anthony Quainton, who served as assistant secretary for diplomatic security in the early 1990s, recalled: "The embassies did not want the security upgrades because they regarded them as intrusive and as undermining the diplomatic mission of the embassy, which was facilitating interaction with foreigners."[44] In fact, only fifteen existing embassies were fully upgraded to meet all of the Inman standards in the decade after enactment of the Diplomatic Security Act (Epstein 2001; Mintz 1999). However, a new round of upgrades following the 1998 bombings of U.S. embassies in Kenya and Tanzania applied the Inman standards to dozens of other facilities.

How the Panel Sparked Reform
Overall, then, what was the Inman Panel's impact? In the near term, its greatest influence was in triggering enactment of the Diplomatic Security Act. By establishing a professional diplomatic security service within a new bureau headed by an assistant secretary, that law significantly elevated the clout and capability of the State Department's security personnel. As Lamb commented, "Before the 1980s, the State Department didn't have a professional security operation. The Inman Panel turned all that upside down. Because of it we cleaned house and got money that we'd never have gotten without it."[45] Over the long term, the panel set the stage for further security upgrades by spurring the formulation of the Inman standards.

[43] Interview of Ronald Spiers, March 10, 2009.
[44] Interview of Anthony Quainton, March 10, 2010.
[45] Interview of Robert Lamb, March 18, 2008.

The panel's substantial impact stemmed principally from the crisis generated by the 1983 and 1984 bombings, which placed pressure on policy makers to change diplomatic security policies. As Inman noted, "The panel was influential because of its timing and the reality of dealing with three embassy bombings. There was a desire on the part of Secretary Shultz to take action."[46] However, major reform was not inevitable in the wake of the bombings, because of the resistance of many State Department officials to changes that would increase the authority of security personnel as well as the reluctance of congressional and White House officials to provide the funding necessary for major security improvements. Given this resistance and reluctance, Shultz needed the assistance of an independent panel to construct a focal point for reform and help develop political support for adopting ambitious proposals.

The Inman Panel's authorization by the executive and its narrow mandate facilitated its impact in several ways. First, its executive-branch origins allowed the panel to get appointed quickly, enabling it to complete its work within eight months of its authorization. Thanks to this short time frame, demand for reform ideas still existed on Capitol Hill when the panel reported.

Second, Shultz was able to appoint a relatively small group of seven panel members who represented both parties but were not extremely diverse ideologically. This allowed the group to reach consensus more easily than it could have done if it had been appointed by congressional leaders with incentives to name political partisans to the commission.

Third, the panel's narrow scope – restricted to embassy security – permitted the panel to focus intensively on a tractable number of issues, and to target its advocacy on a limited number of policy makers in the executive and Congress. In particular, the panel only needed to influence Shultz, OMB, and key members of the House and Senate committees with responsibility for State Department operations in order to advance its recommendations effectively. The latter task was further simplified by the presence of Mica and Rudman on the panel, who served, along with Inman, as very effective advocates of the panel's proposals on Capitol Hill.

Finally, there is scant support for the alternative hypothesis that expertise was the primary source of the Inman Panel's influence. The panel's staff totaled just eleven people, giving it relatively little technical capacity. Moreover, none of the panel's members was an embassy security expert, and its chairman had never served in the State Department or an embassy.

---

[46] Interview of Bobby Inman, July 5, 2007.

The most important members of the commission – Inman, Mica, and Rudman – were critical to the panel's success not because of their expertise, but because of their political credibility, which derived from their stature, bipartisanship, and independence. Whereas Mica and Rudman possessed clout on Capitol Hill, Inman was an especially effective advocate because he was well respected by Democrats and Republicans as a distinguished military officer and political independent. Spiers noted that, in addition to Inman's reputation among policy makers, the panel's independence was central to its political appeal: "[The panel members] had more legitimacy with Congress because they weren't serving their own interest. If it had been a State Department study, it wouldn't have had the same weight."[47] Nor would a panel made up of technical experts lacking in political stature have been able to generate as much support for its recommendations in the White House or Congress.

The Lockerbie Commission and Aviation Security

Stricter security measures at U.S. diplomatic facilities helped to reduce sharply the number of attacks on American embassies after the mid-1980s. Terrorist strikes on Americans and U.S. allies, however, continued in other settings, often directed or supported by Libya under the radical leadership of Muammar Qaddafi. In 1985, militant groups seeking to call attention to the plight of Palestinians killed a total of six Americans in attacks on an Italian cruise ship (the Achille Lauro) and at airports in Rome and Vienna. U.S. investigators determined that Libyan intelligence officers assisted in planning the airport attacks, which were carried out by the Abu Nidal Organization (Seale 1992, 244–260). In April 1986, Libyan agents struck again, bombing a night club in West Berlin that was often frequented by off-duty U.S. troops. That bombing killed two American soldiers and a Turkish woman, and wounded 229 others. After U.S. intelligence intercepted communications implicating Libya's government in the bombing, President Reagan ordered retaliatory air strikes on Libya, which hit one of Qaddafi's residences, among other locations, and killed Qaddafi's daughter (Erlanger 2001).

For the next two years, the U.S. air strikes seemed to have succeeded in deterring Qaddafi from engaging in anti-American terrorism, but that time represented a misleading lull during which the Libyan leader plotted his most devastating attack: the bombing of Pan Am Flight 103

---

[47] Interview of Ronald Spiers, March 10, 2009.

from London to New York. On the evening of December 21, 1988, the Boeing 747 exploded some 31,000 feet over the small town of Lockerbie, Scotland, killing all 259 people on board, as well as 11 Lockerbie residents on the ground. The plane was shredded into pieces by a small but extremely powerful plastic explosive, which had been concealed in a Toshiba radio-cassette player and packed in a suitcase loaded onto the baggage hold (President's Commission on Aviation Security and Terrorism 1990, ii). The dead included 180 Americans and citizens of twenty other countries. Investigators later determined that Libyan intelligence officers were responsible for the bombing (McNeil Jr. 2001).

At the time, the destruction of Pan Am 103 represented the largest loss of American civilians from an act of terrorism in history, and it prompted a number of responses in Washington. The FBI and Federal Aviation Administration (FAA) immediately began investigating the bombing, while the Department of Transportation established an aviation security task force. As these probes proceeded, newspapers reported that the FAA had obtained intelligence one month prior to Pan Am 103's explosion suggesting that terrorists might target airlines with an explosive hidden in a Toshiba radio-cassette player – exactly the method used in the bombing (Parker 1989). Although the FAA had advised U.S. airlines of this threat, Pan Am had not acted to prevent it, and relatives of the victims criticized the FAA for not warning the traveling public (McFadden 1989).

Congress Forces Bush's Hand

These revelations and conversations with victims' family members prompted some members of Congress to push for the establishment of an independent commission. On March 17, 1989, Senator Frank Lautenberg (D-NJ) introduced a "sense of the Senate resolution" calling on President George H. W. Bush to appoint a commission to conduct a comprehensive investigation into the bombing and to recommend measures to prevent future aviation attacks. In comments on the Senate floor, Lautenberg argued that Congress and the American people had not received the full story from the government's own investigations: "Families and friends of the Pan Am 103 victims have been frustrated in their attempts to find out how their loved ones were murdered, and why more could not have been done to try to prevent that. I share their frustration."[48] He added that a commission was necessary in part because the issue transcended departmental lines, involving the State Department and intelligence agencies,

---

[48] Statement by Frank Lautenberg on the Senate floor, March 17, 1989.

as well as the Transportation Department.[49] Lautenberg's resolution was strongly supported by relatives of the victims, many of whom believed the administration was engaging in a cover-up.

However, the nonbinding resolution was opposed by the Senate Republican leadership and was not approved by the Senate. In opposing the resolution, Senate Republicans were following the lead of the Bush administration, which claimed that the FAA and FBI investigations were sufficient and that a commission would compromise the criminal probe. In a letter to Congress, Secretary of State James Baker, Attorney General Dick Thornburgh, and Transportation Secretary Samuel Skinner wrote that "adding another layer of investigation to this issue would be unnecessary and disruptive" (Parker and Ottaway 1989). The more likely real motivation for the administration's stance was fear that an independent body might uncover executive-branch negligence.[50] As one congressional aide involved in the issue commented, "Nobody likes another branch poking around in what they've done."[51]

Nonetheless, support for the commission idea spread in Congress during the spring and summer of 1989, in large part due to advocacy by victims' relatives, which generated substantial media attention (Salant 1989). Lautenberg and Senate Majority Leader George Mitchell (D-ME) cosponsored a bill introduced by Senator Wendell Ford (D-KY) in May 1989 to establish a commission through legislation – a signal of the idea's growing popularity.[52] As the bill gained congressional backing, Bush decided in August to preempt Congress from establishing a panel by forming the Commission on Aviation Security and Terrorism (the Lockerbie Commission) through executive order. From Bush's perspective, a presidential panel was preferable to a congressional commission because Bush could write the charter and appoint all of the members of a presidential commission. Then–FAA Administrator James Busey and then–NSC Director for Counterterrorism Rand Beers commented that Bush would not have created the commission without the pressure from Congress and the victims' family members.[53]

---

[49] *Ibid.*

[50] Interview of Michael Bayer, November 20, 2007; interview of Ann Korologos, Frank Duggan, and Alan Schwartz, September 27, 2007.

[51] Interview of Caroline Gabel, November 19, 2007.

[52] The bill was introduced as the Aviation Security and Terrorism Commission Act of 1989, S. 1043.

[53] Interview of Rand Beers, October 16, 2008; interview of James Busey, October 30, 2008.

Bush appointed seven people to the commission, including four members of Congress who were named in consultation with the congressional leadership: Senators Alfonse D'Amato (R-NY) and Lautenberg, and Representatives James Oberstar (D-MN) and John Hammerschmidt (R-AR). Each of these commissioners was chosen in part because they played a key role on aviation issues. Lautenberg and D'Amato served respectively as the chairman and ranking member of the Senate appropriations subcommittee on transportation. In the House, Hammerschmidt was the senior Republican on the Public Works and Transportation Committee, whereas Oberstar was the chairman of its aviation subcommittee. Bush also appointed retired Air Force General Thomas Richards and Carter administration Navy Secretary Edward Hidalgo to the commission. As commission chair, Bush named Ann McLaughlin, a Republican who had served as secretary of labor under Ronald Reagan. As a whole, the commissioners constituted a group of hefty stature and bipartisan balance.

Bush tasked the commission with evaluating existing "practices and policy options with respect to the prevention of terrorist acts involving aviation security" – a mandate I classify as broad because it spanned many government policies, programs, and agencies.[54] Although the commission lacked subpoena power, it held five public hearings between November 1989 and April 1990 as part of its fact-finding activities, which helped to establish its credibility and build interest in its work.[55] Oberstar aviation security aide Caroline Gabel explained that the distinct deliberative environment of the commission also fostered fresh thinking: "The commission enabled cross-fertilization of ideas among the commissioners and staff. They thought things through and bounced ideas off of each other. They wouldn't have been able to do this through the normal congressional process."[56]

A Hard-Hitting Report

The commission's unanimous report, issued on May 15, 1990, harshly criticized the government's handling of aviation security. The panel concluded that the U.S. civil aviation security system was "seriously flawed," and called the FAA "a reactive agency – preoccupied with responses to

---

[54] Executive Order 12686.
[55] Interview of Michael Bayer, November 20, 2007; interview of Ann Korologos, Frank Duggan, and Alan Schwartz, September 27, 2007.
[56] Interview of Caroline Gabel, November 19, 2007.

events to the exclusion of adequate contingency planning in anticipation of future threats" (President's Commission on Aviation Security and Terrorism 1990, i). The 182-page report also argued that stricter security procedures could have prevented the destruction of Pan Am 103, and it criticized the FAA for failing to disclose key security shortcomings in the agency's own public report on the bombing. The panel further charged that, in the bombing's aftermath, the State Department failed to notify and assist victims' families in a compassionate fashion.

The report included sixty-four recommendations, covering terrorism-related military, diplomatic, and intelligence policies, as well as various aspects of aviation security. The commission recommended that the United States make state sponsors of terrorism "pay a price for their actions," arguing that the government should plan and train for preemptive or retaliatory military strikes against terrorists in countries that harbor them (President's Commission on Aviation Security and Terrorism 1990, 125). The commission also proposed reorganizing the Transportation Department and FAA by establishing a new position of assistant secretary of transportation for security and intelligence, elevating the standing of the FAA's security division so that it reports directly to the FAA administrator, and creating a system of federal security managers at major domestic airports. In addition, the panel called for the adoption of a requirement that the government inform the public of threats to aviation in certain circumstances, and it recommended deferring deployment of "thermal neutron analysis" (TNA) bomb detection machines, which it found to be of limited utility.

The recommendation on the TNA machines directly challenged a plan developed by the FAA shortly after the destruction of Pan Am 103 to install the machines at about forty international airports by the end of 1991, at a cost of $175 million. This plan, announced by the FAA in April 1989, represented the Bush administration's principal policy response to the Lockerbie bombing. Congress ratified it through legislation enacted in June 1989, and the FAA purchased six of the van-sized machines by the time the commission reported in May 1990. The commission determined, however, that the TNA devices could not detect explosives of the size used in sophisticated terrorist attacks (President's Commission on Aviation Security and Terrorism 1990, iv).

Commentators praised the commission report's hard-hitting character. Writing in the *New York Times*, columnist A. M. Rosenthal wrote, "It turned out to be a runaway commission, polite but independent. Its members told the President the truth, knowing it would not appeal to him"

(Rosenthal 1990). Similarly, an account in the *Washington Post* noted that the commission's descriptions of a lax and confused security system "stung the government" (Phillips 1990).

The commission's independence was further demonstrated by the Bush administration's opposition to some of its recommendations, particularly its proposal to defer deployment of the TNA machines. The administration continued to claim that the devices would be effective, and FAA Administrator James Busey testified to Congress that prohibiting their deployment "would seriously hamstring the FAA's ability to respond to the terrorist threat."[57]

Congress Acts

Despite the administration's resistance to important elements of the commission's report, the report triggered the enactment of a major aviation security law. On June 28, 1990 – six weeks after the commission reported – Representative Oberstar and Senators Lautenberg and D'Amato introduced companion bills in the House and Senate that were based almost entirely on the panel report and included nearly all of its recommendations.[58] Most of these proposals were not being considered in Congress before the commission recommended them.[59] Lautenberg aviation security aide Joe McGrail recalled, "The commission's work was the driver in getting these ideas into the mix."[60] The timing of the bills' introduction and their cosponsorship by three commissioners represents strong additional evidence that their introduction was a direct result of the panel's work.

Even more striking, the legislation was a departure both from the June 1989 law mandating the deployment of TNA explosive-detection machines and from a separate aviation security bill introduced by Oberstar in April 1989. The latter bill, which was approved by the House in September 1989 but never voted on in the Senate, mandated a host of security upgrades, but included none of the principal proposals that the Lockerbie Commission made one year later.[61] The many

---

[57] Testimony by James Busey before the Senate Committee on Commerce, Science, and Transportation, October 4, 1990.
[58] The bills were H.R. 5200 and S. 2822. One commission recommendation that was left out of these bills was the proposal to plan and train for military strikes against terrorist hideouts. The administration claimed that the recommendation was unnecessary because the military already conducted such planning and training (Lardner 1990).
[59] Interview of Caroline Gabel, November 19, 2007.
[60] Interview of Joe McGrail, March 30, 2009.
[61] The bill was H.R. 1659.

differences between that bill and the legislation introduced by Oberstar and his commission colleagues in 1990 show that Oberstar's service on the commission led him to change his stance on how to reform aviation security.

The Bush administration initially opposed the new legislation because it prohibited deployment of the TNA devices. But commission members and families of the Pan Am 103 victims lobbied Congress and the administration persistently to enact the legislation, helping to build congressional support for it and placing pressure on the White House to endorse it.[62] These advocacy efforts were facilitated by about fifteen commission staff members who remained on the panel's payroll for up to three months after the report's release.[63] Ultimately, Congress and the administration reached a compromise on the TNA machine provision, which was changed to prohibit the purchase or deployment of explosive-detection equipment unless the FAA certified that the equipment could reliably detect explosive material. In practice, the legislation represented the death knell of the machines, as they were not subsequently acquired or deployed.

The legislation was approved by voice vote in the House and Senate in October 1990, and was enacted as the Aviation Security Improvement Act of 1990 (the Aviation Security Act) on November 16 – six months after the commission reported.[64] In addition to the TNA machine provision, the act adopted dozens of other commission recommendations, including the following:

- Authorizing a program to accelerate and expand research and development on new explosive-detection technology
- Mandating the development of new controls over checked baggage and individuals with access to aircraft
- Establishing an FAA assistant administrator for civil aviation security
- Forming a nationwide system of airport security managers
- Requiring that all airport personnel be subject to FBI background checks
- Directing the FAA to issue guidelines for notifying the public of security threats

---

[62] Interview of James Busey, October 30, 2008; interview of Caroline Gabel, November 19, 2007; interview of Ann Korologos, Frank Duggan, and Alan Schwartz, September 27, 2007; interview of Joe McGrail, March 30, 2009.
[63] Interview of Michael Bayer, November 20, 2007.
[64] The act is Public Law 101–604.

- Ordering that intelligence agencies make terrorism reports available to the DOT and FAA
- Requiring the State Department to negotiate aviation security agreements with foreign countries
- Creating a State Department office to manage relations with the families of victims of aviation disasters

In interviews, congressional and administration officials involved in the passage of the legislation agreed that the Aviation Security Act would probably not have been enacted without the work of the Lockerbie Commission.[65] As mentioned earlier, many of the law's provisions had not been proposed in Congress before the commission reported. Moreover, Oberstar had been unable to win Senate passage of his earlier aviation security bill, suggesting that Congress might not have approved any new aviation security legislation without the impetus provided by the commission.

The administration also had not previously considered many of the Aviation Security Act's key provisions. FAA Administrator Busey noted that the FAA was not thinking of establishing a system of airport security managers or a new senior aviation security post before the commission recommended those changes.[66] In addition, Busey said that the agency was unenthusiastic about adopting a rule for notifying the public of security threats in certain circumstances and would not have done so if the commission had not proposed the idea.[67]

Although enactment of the Aviation Security Act represented a triumph for the commission, the law's implementation in subsequent years was uneven, hampered by airline industry opposition to some reforms and the receding of the memory of the Pan Am 103 bombing.[68] For instance, in 1992, the industry opposed adoption of a regulation to implement the law's requirement for FBI background checks of all airport employees, arguing that the requirement would be too onerous. This lobbying effort led the FAA and Congress to dilute the regulation by exempting personnel who were already employed by airlines from the checks (Drew 1996).

The industry's success in blocking new regulations stemmed in part from the diminishing perception of a security threat to aviation in the

---

[65] Interview of James Busey, October 30, 2008; interview of Caroline Gabel, November 19, 2007; interview of Joe McGrail, March 30, 2009; interview of O.K. Steele, June 23, 2008.
[66] Interview of James Busey, October 30, 2008.
[67] *Ibid.*
[68] Interview of Rand Beers, October 16, 2008; interview of James Busey, October 30, 2008.

early 1990s. As then–FAA Assistant Administrator for Civil Aviation Security O.K. Steele commented about those years, "There had been no further serious mishaps or breaches into the [airline security] system, and security was once again taking a back seat to other more pressing concerns."[69] It took the crash of TWA Flight 800 in July 1996 (which was initially suspected to be a result of terrorism) and the terrorist attacks of September 11, 2001, to spark new rounds of aviation security upgrades.

The failure to fully implement key elements of the Aviation Security Act – like the failure to apply the Inman standards to all U.S. embassies – demonstrates the difficulty of instituting lasting government reform, which has been well documented in other contexts by Eric Patashnik and Amy Zegart (Patashnik 2008; Zegart 2007). However, the Lockerbie Commission must still be judged as having a large impact because it sparked enactment of a major law with dozens of aviation security provisions. Ensuring that the law was fully implemented was beyond the commission's capacity.

Explaining the Commission's Influence

The commission's substantial impact was due, above all, to the window of opportunity for reform created by the Pan Am 103 tragedy, which placed pressure on policy makers to take new steps to protect the traveling public. Yet the bombing of Pan Am 103 was not sufficient to prompt the adoption of many significant reforms. The Bush administration's principal aviation policy response to the terrorist act was to pursue the deployment of TNA explosive-detection machines at airports handling international flights. Other reforms, proposed in Oberstar's 1989 bill, failed to attract sufficient Senate support to be enacted. When the Lockerbie Commission was formed in August 1989, there was little reason to expect that it would trigger not only a rejection of the TNA machine policy, but also a host of policy changes that were not under consideration in either branch of government at that point. Yet the commission established a new focal point for the debate over aviation security that prompted an array of reforms.

In one respect, the commission's influence departs from my theory's expectation: It catalyzed reform despite possessing a relatively broad mandate. This outcome occurred because, even though the commission's mandate spanned multiple agencies, most of its proposals fell within the jurisdiction of single committees in the House and Senate, facilitating

[69] Testimony by O.K. Steele before the National Commission on Terrorist Attacks upon the United States, May 23, 2003.

their adoption. In addition, the presence on the commission of four members of Congress with authorization and appropriation responsibilities concerning aviation security gave the panel powerful advocates who could shepherd its recommendations through the legislative process. Importantly, these legislators were assisted in this effort by the relatives of Pan Am 103 victims. Oberstar aide Caroline Gabel noted, "The families were our best lobbyists for the legislation."[70]

The evidence further suggests that political credibility was a more important source of the commission's appeal than was specialized expertise. Expertise was far from irrelevant: The commission's staff conducted a detailed investigation of aviation security practices and events related to the Pan Am 103 bombing, which shaped the panel's findings. But the commission's staff of thirty-three people possessed much less aviation security expertise than existing agencies, particularly the FAA and Transportation Department. Moreover, three of the seven commissioners – Ann McLaughlin, Edward Hidalgo, and Thomas Richards – lacked any previous professional experience with aviation security, whereas the four members of Congress on the commission had many responsibilities other than aviation security.

What the commission did possess in great measure were independence, stature, and bipartisanship. This combination of attributes distinguished the panel from both congressional committees and the executive branch. The commission's independence was especially important because it enabled the panel to satisfy the demands of victims' families to uncover the truth about the bombing, thereby gaining their backing for its proposals. At the same time, the panel's political clout enabled it to dominate the reform debate once it issued its report. Gabel commented: "The commissioners gave credibility, weight, and a high profile to the recommendations. A bill introduced by a member of Congress or a congressional hearing wouldn't have gotten as much attention as the release of the commission report did.... If Oberstar just said by himself, 'I, Chairman Oberstar, think we need to do this,' it wouldn't have had the same impact."[71]

Conclusion

Each of the three commissions formed in the 1980s to address terrorism influenced policy significantly. The Long Commission prompted

---

[70] Interview of Caroline Gabel, March 18, 2009.
[71] *Ibid.*

leading members of Congress to push for an immediate withdrawal from Lebanon, thereby placing heavy pressure on Ronald Reagan and hastening his decision to pull out U.S. troops. The Inman Panel and Lockerbie Commission shaped policy in other ways – by triggering the enactment of legislation that overhauled how the government managed diplomatic and aviation security.

All three commissions sparked important changes by providing a focal point when there was demand for reform but insufficient agreement among policy makers on what to do. In the wake of the Marine barracks bombing, many legislators questioned the execution of the Lebanon mission, but congressional consensus on the need for a rapid pullout only coalesced after the Long Commission reported. After the bombings of several U.S. embassies in 1983 and 1984, there was broad recognition of the need to bolster diplomatic security, but Congress and the executive did not reach agreement on how to do so until the Inman Panel offered its recommendations in the summer of 1985. Similarly, following the downing of Pan Am 103, the two political branches did not reach consensus on a wide-ranging set of aviation security changes until the Lockerbie Commission provided a reform blueprint. Although the United States probably would have withdrawn from Lebanon at some point in 1984 even without the Long Commission report, it is unlikely that major diplomatic and aviation security laws would have been enacted in 1985 and 1990 without the focal points provided by the Inman Panel and Lockerbie Commission reports. As described earlier, most of those laws' principal provisions were not even being considered in Congress or the executive branch before the panels reported.

In all three cases, the terrorist acts that precipitated the commissions provided windows of opportunity that the panels exploited by offering unanimous proposals that appealed to Republicans and Democrats alike. In addition to their bipartisanship or nonpartisanship, the commissions' political credibility derived from the significant stature of their membership, which was weighted heavily toward retired senior military officers, other former high-ranking officials, and members of Congress.

The commissions' authorization by the executive branch and the narrow scope of two of the three panels further facilitated their influence. All three panels were appointed and completed their work within nine months – thirteen months faster than the average duration of the congressional commissions in my data set. This relative speed was due to the executive's ability to name commissioners quickly, which enabled the panels to report before the windows of opportunity for reform closed.

The narrow mandates of the Long Commission and Inman Panel were also helpful, because they allowed the panels to reach consensus on specific proposals more easily and simplified the task of advancing legislation to adopt the recommendations. The Inman Panel and Lockerbie Commission benefited greatly as well from the participation of members of Congress whose leadership positions on key committees enabled them to champion such legislation effectively.[72]

Of course, the story of anti-American terrorism and the U.S. response to it did not end with the work of these commissions and the reforms they spurred. Although Hezbollah and Libya ceased to target Americans after the 1980s, Al Qaeda emerged as a new foe during the following decade. Its successful strikes against two American embassies in 1998 and against the U.S. aviation system in 2001, among other targets, revealed that major vulnerabilities in U.S. security policies and procedures remained. Those later strikes prompted the formation of new commissions and led to new reforms, which are the focus of Chapters 5 and 6.

[72] Surprisingly, however, for my full data set of fifty-one national security commissions, having members of Congress serve on panels does not generally boost their impact. Nor is the presence on commissions of executive-branch officials correlated with commission influence. These findings may reflect the fact that the service of government officials on commissions can be a double-edged sword: On the one hand, such officials may have the power to advance adoption of the panel's proposals; on the other hand, their involvement can diminish a commission's independence, and they may be unable to devote much time to the panel's work given their other responsibilities.

5

Grappling with the Rise of Al Qaeda

Chapter 4 assessed the impact of all three U.S. commissions on terrorism set up during the 1980s. This chapter picks up the story of U.S. counterterrorism policy in the following decade, when Al Qaeda replaced Libya, Iran, and Hezbollah as the preeminent terrorist threat to the United States. I focus on the period after Al Qaeda successfully perpetrated its first major attack: the nearly simultaneous bombings in 1998 of the U.S. embassies in Nairobi, Kenya and Dar es Salaam, Tanzania, which claimed 224 lives.

The chapter centers on two commissions: the National Commission on Terrorism (the Bremer Commission), and the Accountability Review Boards on the Embassy Bombings in Nairobi and Dar es Salaam on August 7, 1998 (the Crowe Panel).[1] Comparing these commissions is particularly instructive because they were both formed shortly after the African embassy bombings – making their political context similar – but they differed in their sources of authority and scope.[2] Whereas the Crowe Panel was an executive-branch commission with a narrow mandate, the Bremer Commission was a congressional commission with a broad mandate. My argument about commission influence implies that the Crowe

---

[1] I treat the Accountability Review Boards as a single panel because the boards worked in tandem under the chairmanship of William Crowe and issued a single report.

[2] A third body – the Advisory Panel to Assess Domestic Response Capabilities for Terrorism Involving Weapons of Mass Destruction, chaired by former Virginia Governor Jim Gilmore – was also established after the embassy bombings. However, the Gilmore Commission is excluded from my commission data set because it was mandated by law to issue annual reports for five years, making it resemble a permanent body more than an ad hoc commission. (My definition of an ad hoc commission, presented on page 5, requires that it be mandated to issue a final report within four years.)

Panel should have prompted more reform than the Bremer Commission, because executive-branch authorization and a narrow scope tend to make it easier for a commission to reach consensus, report quickly, and promote its proposals effectively. The case studies show that this was the case.

Toward the end of the chapter, I assess more briefly the impact of a third panel – the *USS Cole* Commission – which was established by the Clinton administration after Al Qaeda's next large-scale strike: the October 2000 bombing of a U.S. Navy destroyer. Like the Crowe Panel, the *Cole* Commission used its distinct political credibility to trigger important security reforms.

Al Qaeda's Rise

As the 1990s began, many U.S. policy makers believed that terrorism was receding as a threat (Clarke 2004, 73). Hezbollah had stopped perpetrating direct attacks against the United States after the mid-1980s, focusing its militant activities entirely on Israel. Libya ceased targeting Americans as well after George H. W. Bush ended the cycle of tit-for-tat retaliation with Muammar Qaddafi and gained enactment of strict multilateral sanctions on Libya in response to the 1988 bombing of Pan Am Flight 103. In fact, Bush's presidency was marked by the absence of a single major act of anti-American terrorism. For a time, it seemed that terrorism would not be a major U.S. concern in the post–Cold War world.

This perception was challenged early in Bill Clinton's presidency by the February 1993 World Trade Center bombing and the April 1995 Oklahoma City bombing. The former attack was executed by a cell of Islamist militants based in New York and northern New Jersey, who exploded a van full of bombs in the World Trade Center's underground parking garage, killing six people. Within weeks of the bombing, the FBI arrested several members of the cell, who were ultimately convicted in federal court for their involvement in the plot. The 9/11 Commission later noted an irony of these convictions: "An unfortunate consequence of this superb investigative and prosecutorial effort was that it created an impression that the law enforcement system was well-equipped to cope with terrorism" (National Commission on Terrorist Attacks upon the United States 2004, 72).

Interestingly, there is no evidence that either the executive branch or Congress seriously considered creating a commission to probe whether the World Trade Center attack signaled broader security shortcomings or

the emergence of a new terrorist threat. During congressional hearings on
the bombing, the idea of a commission was not broached by members of
Congress or the Clinton administration.[3] In interviews, former FBI and
World Trade Center officials said that there was not interest in a commission because the plot was uncovered quickly and most policy makers
saw the bombing as a singular event, rather than as a national problem
or continuing danger.[4] This view suggests that commissions are less likely
to be formed in response to disasters that are not perceived to be part of
a larger trend. Yet later revelations suggested that the 1993 World Trade
Center plot was probably hatched in Afghanistan or Pakistan, and that
Osama bin Laden might have helped bankroll it (National Commission
on Terrorist Attacks upon the United States 2004, 73).

Two years later, the bombing by Timothy McVeigh and two co-
conspirators of a federal building in Oklahoma City killed 168 people
and temporarily placed terrorism on the front burner of national politics.
In response, President Clinton signed a presidential decision directive
(PDD-39) in June 1995 that described terrorism as a national security
issue and assigned various counterterrorism responsibilities to federal
agencies. But the Oklahoma City bombing, like the World Trade Center
bombing, was widely viewed as an isolated attack carried out by dis-
gruntled individuals, and it did not galvanize the federal government into
making counterterrorism policy a top priority.[5] In the words of Clinton
administration NSC officials Daniel Benjamin and Steven Simon, terrorism remained for most national security policy makers a second- or
third-level concern: "It was [viewed as] a nuisance to be attended to, not
a strategic threat" (Benjamin and Simon 2002, 220).

Meanwhile, many thousands of miles away, Osama bin Laden, the
wealthy son of a Saudi construction magnate, was gradually turning

---

[3] See, for example, hearing of the House Judiciary Subcommittee on Crime and Criminal
Justice, March 9, 1993; hearing of the House Foreign Affairs Subcommittee on International
Security, International Organizations, and Human Rights, March 15, 1993.
[4] Interview of Charlie Maikish, July 9, 2008; interview of Thomas Pickard, June 16, 2008.
[5] A third important bombing occurred in June 1996, when a group named Saudi Hezbollah,
backed by Iran, blew up a fuel truck full of explosives next to a facility called Khobar
Towers that housed U.S. military personnel in Saudi Arabia. The explosion destroyed the
front of the building, killing nineteen American servicemen. The bombing showed that
Iran remained a significant terrorist threat, but this was the only attack on Americans
during the 1990s that was traced back to Iran. In response, Secretary of Defense William
Perry appointed retired General Wayne Downing to probe the facts and circumstances
surrounding the bombing. I do not consider Downing's report, issued in August 1996, to
be a commission report because a commission, in my definition, must have more than
one member.

Al Qaeda into a sophisticated organization capable of carrying out complex terrorism operations. After fighting successfully with rebel groups to expel the Soviet Union from Afghanistan, bin Laden formed Al Qaeda in 1988, with the goal of pursuing jihad elsewhere. Two years later, the government of Saudi Arabia infuriated bin Laden by inviting the United States to station troops on its territory following Iraq's invasion of Kuwait, prompting bin Laden to move Al Qaeda to Sudan and to turn the group's attention to attacking America. Aside from the 1993 World Trade Center bombing, which bin Laden might have helped finance, Al Qaeda's first opportunity to strike Americans came in Somalia, where President George H. W. Bush deployed U.S. peacekeepers in 1992. Bin Laden sent Al Qaeda operatives to Somalia to help train Somali clans that battled the U.S. troops throughout 1993. He later took credit for the killing of eighteen U.S. soldiers in a Mogadishu firefight in October of that year, but others claimed that Al Qaeda fighters did not participate in that battle (Bergen 2002, 22, 86; Wright 2006, 213–215).

By the mid-1990s, American officials were worried enough about bin Laden's funding of terrorism that the United States joined with Egypt to pressure Sudanese leaders to expel him from Sudan. In response, bin Laden moved to Afghanistan in 1996, where he released a fatwa in June of that year declaring war on America and built new terrorist training camps. Yet as late as 1997, few American policy makers focused on the growing danger presented by Al Qaeda. As journalist Lawrence Wright observes of that time, "The most frightening aspect of this new threat... was the fact that almost no one took it seriously" (Wright 2006, 7). This complacency also reflected the fact that, until 1998, as Benjamin and Simon write, "Bin Laden's fingerprints could still not be discerned definitively on any significant act against the United States or American citizens" (Benjamin and Simon 2002, 256). A stark warning sign that this would change came in February 1998, when bin Laden issued a new fatwa declaring that "to kill the Americans and their allies – civilians and military – is an individual duty for every Muslim who can do it in any country in which it is possible to do it."

Six months later, on August 7, 1998 – the eighth anniversary of the arrival of U.S. troops in Saudi Arabia – Al Qaeda acted on these words when its operatives exploded massive truck bombs next to the American embassies in Kenya and Tanzania. The first explosion was set off in the rear parking area of the Nairobi embassy at 10:35 A.M. local time by two men driving a Toyota pickup truck carrying twenty specially designed crates full of dynamite that had been ground into a powder. The second blast, from a similarly filled Nissan truck, occurred four minutes later at one of the gates of the Dar es Salaam embassy. The death toll and damage were tremendous, particularly in Nairobi. Altogether, 12 Americans, 40 Kenyan and Tanzanian U.S. government employees, and 172 other Kenyans and Tanzanians were killed – rivaling the 1983 Beirut Marine barracks bombing and the 1988 Pan Am 103 bombing as the deadliest terrorist attack targeting Americans before 9/11. In addition, more than 4,000 people were injured by the explosions, and several buildings were badly damaged or destroyed (Accountability Review Boards 1999).[6]

The 9/11 Commission report notes that these bombings were the first major attacks "planned, directed, and executed by Al Qaeda, under the direct supervision of bin Laden and his chief aides" (National Commission on Terrorist Attacks upon the United States 2004, 67). They were all the more startling because of the sophistication required to bomb, within a few minutes, two embassies located some 500 miles from each other. In their wake, the U.S. government devoted new resources and attention to combating Al Qaeda (Benjamin and Simon 2002, 256; Wright 2001, 246). On August 20, President Clinton authorized the U.S. military to launch dozens of Tomahawk cruise missiles at several Al Qaeda training camps in Afghanistan and a plant in Sudan that was believed to produce chemical weapons. The missiles killed some militants at the camps, but missed bin Laden and other Al Qaeda leaders (Bergen 2002, 123–124; Wright 2006, 323). Two months later, Congress approved a Clinton administration request for $1.5 billion in emergency funding to rebuild the Nairobi and Dar es Salaam embassies and implement other security upgrades at diplomatic facilities.[7]

The U.S. government also formed two commissions soon after the embassy bombings. On October 5, Secretary of State Madeleine Albright established the Crowe Panel. The panel's formation was mandated by the 1986 Diplomatic Security Act, which requires the secretary of state to convene an accountability review board to investigate any incident involving serious injury or loss of life. (This requirement had been recommended by the Inman Panel, discussed in Chapter 4).[8] Because the Nairobi and Dar es Salaam embassies were bombed separately, Albright

---

[6] Both embassy buildings had been built before the State Department's formulation of the "Inman standards" for constructing diplomatic facilities, which are discussed in Chapter 4.

[7] This funding was appropriated by Public Law 105–277, enacted on October 21, 1998.

[8] The requirement that the secretary of state establish the panel implies that, unlike most executive-branch commissions, the Crowe Panel's formation was not primarily motivated by political or policy goals of the administration. Nevertheless, my argument that executive commissions are more likely than congressional panels to reach consensus and report quickly should still apply to it.

formally established two boards, but the boards worked in tandem under the chairmanship of retired Navy Admiral William Crowe and issued a single report. I therefore treat them as a single panel. The commission's relatively narrow mandate was to investigate the August 7 bombings and to recommend improved diplomatic security policies and procedures.

On October 21 – just two weeks after Albright formed the Crowe Panel – Congress established the Bremer Commission, named after its chairman, Paul Bremer. Representative Frank Wolf (R-VA) had introduced the bill to form the commission in September, and it was enacted as part of the same emergency legislation that provided $1.5 billion in diplomatic security spending. The panel's charter gave it the relatively broad mandate of reviewing the effectiveness of U.S. policies related to counterterrorism, and recommending changes to those policies.

As noted earlier, my argument about commission influence implies that the Crowe Panel should have catalyzed more policy change than the Bremer Commission. In fact, it did, because, unlike the Bremer Commission, it completed its work while interest in reform remained strong; it issued a unanimous report with proposals focused on a single agency (the State Department); and its chairman possessed a sterling nonpartisan reputation and advocated intensely for adoption of its recommendations.

The Crowe Panel and a New Round of Embassy Security Reform

The Crowe Panel was made up of nine members appointed by Secretary of State Albright: former State Department ambassadors and senior officials Michael Armacost, Lynn Davis, Terrence Todman, and Philip Wilcox; former intelligence officials Arthur Donahue and Montgomery Rogers; former Senate national security aides David Busby and Janne Nolan; and Crowe, who had served during the 1980s as chairman of the Joint Chiefs of Staff. The panel members were assisted by a small staff of five people.

A Highly Critical Report

The panel's unanimous report, issued on January 8, 1999 – just three months after the commission was formed – took the State Department and the U.S. government as a whole to task for failing to fulfill their responsibility to protect against terrorist threats. In a cover letter to Albright, the panel concluded sharply, "What is most troubling is the failure of the U.S. government to take the necessary steps to prevent such tragedies through an unwillingness to give sustained priority and funding to security improvements" (Accountability Review Boards 1999).[9] The panel went on to bemoan "an institutional failure of the Department of State and embassies under its direction to recognize threats posed by transnational terrorism and vehicle bombs" (Accountability Review Boards 1999, Executive Overview). It was especially critical of the State Department for failing to act on repeated requests by the U.S. Ambassador to Kenya for emergency security upgrades in the months leading up to the bombings. These hard-hitting conclusions provide strong evidence of the panel's independence: Although the panel's members were appointed by the secretary of state, their report did not present the State Department's leadership in a positive light.

The Crowe Panel's report included twenty-four recommendations, covering ways to enhance security at diplomatic facilities, strengthen crisis-management systems and procedures, and improve the flow of relevant intelligence information. Of these recommendations, one was especially notable: to appropriate $14 billion over ten years for the building of new embassies and for needed security upgrades at existing ones. Importantly, the panel emphasized that this funding should be appropriated without taking funds away from other foreign affairs programs. The recommendation was remarkably ambitious considering that the annual operating expenses of the State Department at the time totaled less than $4 billion. Moreover, the panel's proposed funding level was far higher than any figure previously considered for diplomatic security spending by the administration or members of Congress (Shenon 1999a).

Other facts made it seem highly unlikely that this key recommendation would be adopted. In December 1998, just weeks before the panel reported, the Clinton administration decided to propose only $3 billion over five years for embassy construction and fortification – much less money than the panel recommended. Furthermore, Albright had been reluctant to dedicate even that much funding to embassy security because the administration's Office of Management and Budget (OMB), trying to limit overall spending, insisted that the money come out of other State Department programs.[10] History also suggested that the Crowe Panel's

---

[9] This statement by the panel reflects the government's failure to fully implement the security standards adopted in response to the Inman Panel's 1985 report. As described in Chapter 4, funding for security upgrades dried up just a few years after the Inman Panel reported.

[10] Interview of David Carpenter, March 5, 2009; comments by Madeleine Albright, Hearing of the House Appropriations Subcommittee on Commerce, Justice, State, and the Judiciary, March 10, 1999.

core proposal would probably not be adopted. The recommendation was reminiscent of the Inman Panel's 1985 proposal for $3.5 billion in diplomatic security spending over five years. As described in Chapter 4, Congress fell far short of appropriating that amount after the Inman Panel reported, providing just $1.1 billion in new funding.

When the Crowe Panel issued its report, Albright immediately adopted many of its recommendations and instructed Assistant Secretary of State for Diplomatic Security David Carpenter to begin implementing them.[11] Carpenter described his charge from Albright: "We needed to satisfy each of the recommendations, as much as possible."[12] But Albright did not publicly endorse the huge spending proposal, remaining constrained by OMB's unwillingness to give the department a new pot of money. By February 1999, as it became clear that the administration was not going to seek the amount of funding requested by the panel, criticism of the administration began to mount – from Admiral Crowe, the media, and Congress.

Crowe's Campaign Bears Fruit

Crowe led the charge. In a February 18 media interview, he said the administration's existing spending plan revealed "a timid approach to the problem" that would not allow the replacement of many vulnerable embassies (Shenon 1999b). In subsequent weeks, Crowe testified twice about diplomatic security before key congressional committees. In both instances, he called the administration's spending request "inadequate" and issued a strong appeal to Congress to provide the funding levels recommended by his panel.[13] At one hearing, he was particularly scathing: "We're switching off lives for budgetary reasons. And that disturbs me mightily.... We need a firm declaration by the U.S. government that this failure, this vulnerability, should be eradicated, and we should have a sustained program to correct it, supported by all the government."[14] In May, Crowe kept up the heat in a *Washington Post* op-ed: "We should

---

[11] Remarks by Secretary of State Madeleine Albright, January 8, 1999; State Department, "Report to the U.S. Congress on Actions Taken by the State Department in Response to the Program Recommendations of the Accountability Review Boards on the Embassy Bombings in Nairobi and Dar es Salaam," April 9, 1999.

[12] Interview of David Carpenter, March 5, 2009.

[13] Comments by William Crowe, hearing of the Senate Foreign Relations Committee, March 11, 1999; comments by William Crowe, hearing of the House International Relations Subcommittee on International Operations and Human Rights, March 12, 1999.

[14] Comments by William Crowe, hearing of the Senate Foreign Relations Committee, March 11, 1999.

never allow budgetary considerations to achieve greater importance than the lives of the people who serve our country with selfless dedication" (Crowe 1999). Throughout these months, Crowe also lobbied administration and congressional officials privately in an effort to gain their support for the funding proposed by his panel.[15]

Crowe's criticism was echoed by prominent newspapers and members of Congress. A February *Chicago Tribune* editorial stated, "Sadly, President Clinton's budget request for next year for embassy security falls far short of the recommendation of an independent review board [the Crowe Panel] that the U.S. spend $1.4 billion a year on new security measures" (*Chicago Tribune* 1999). Congressional Republicans also attacked the administration for failing to request the full amount proposed by the Crowe Panel. In March, Representative Christopher Smith (R-NJ), chairman of the House international relations subcommittee that oversees the State Department, called the administration's request "grossly inadequate," and Senator Chuck Hagel (R-NE) charged that the administration's budget did not reflect its rhetoric about protecting America's diplomats.[16] Senator Judd Gregg (R-NH), chairman of the Senate appropriations subcommittee responsible for the State Department, also criticized the department for underfunding security, even as he maintained, like OMB, that the money must be taken from other department programs (Risen 1999a). In making these criticisms, the congressional Republicans frequently cited the Crowe Panel's report, though some of them may have been motivated by a desire to use the report to score political points against the administration.

Ultimately, Crowe's advocacy and the pressure from Congress triggered a change in the administration's position. In June 1999, after an internal review, the White House amended its budget request, expanding it to ask for a total of $11.4 billion over ten years for embassy construction and other security improvements – a large increase over its earlier request for $3 billion over five years. The new proposal called for taking the money from other government programs, but not from State Department or foreign aid budgets – satisfying Albright's concern. Five months later, Congress enacted legislation authorizing a total of $4.5 billion in security spending for fiscal years 2000–2004 – the amount

---

[15] Interview of Kenneth McKune, October 6, 2007.
[16] Hearing of the House International Relations Subcommittee on International Operations and Human Rights, March 12, 1999; hearing of the Senate Foreign Relations Committee March 11, 1999.

requested by the administration for the first half of its ten-year plan.[17] As part of the same legislation, Congress appropriated the first installment of that plan: $600 million for FY 2000 (double the administration's initial FY 2000 proposal).

Despite this significant funding increase, the administration's revised spending plan remained $2.6 billion short of the Crowe Panel's recommendation. As a result, Crowe and other advocates continued to press for the full $14 billion in funding. Crowe served on another State Department commission, called the Overseas Presence Advisory Panel, which endorsed the Crowe Panel's spending proposal in its November 1999 report (Overseas Presence Advisory Panel 1999, 6). The American Foreign Service Association also pushed for adopting the Crowe Panel's recommendation (Moose 1999).

This continued advocacy by Crowe and others paid off. In February 2000, President Clinton announced a request for $1.1 billion for FY 2001 and $14 billion over the next ten years for new embassy construction and security upgrades at existing facilities.[18] This ten-year request represented the exact amount proposed a year earlier by the Crowe Panel – strongly suggesting that it was based on the panel's recommendation. Although Congress did not then authorize the revised ten-year plan, it did approve the $1.1 billion for FY 2001 – a hefty increase from the $600 million appropriated the previous year. A year later, Congress approved the new Bush administration's request for $1.3 billion for FY 2002 (Epstein 2001, 7–8).

Funding levels for security upgrades and new construction increased still further in subsequent years: $1.5 billion for FY 2003, $1.5 billion for FY 2004, and $1.6 billion for FY 2005 (Nakamura 2004). These funding levels corresponded very closely to the Crowe Panel's recommendation, although they might not have been as high without the new impetus for security spending provided by the 9/11 terrorist attack. Ultimately, more than $14 billion in new embassy security spending was appropriated in the ten years following the Crowe Panel report.[19] In addition to funding

---

[17] This legislation is Public Law 106–113, the omnibus appropriations act for FY 2000, enacted on November 29, 1999.

[18] Statement by President William Jefferson Clinton, February 10, 2000.

[19] After 2005, the State Department categorized security spending somewhat differently, making it difficult to generate equivalent annual figures for the later years of this period. However, a State Department official with responsibility for diplomatic security confirmed in an interview in October 2008 that over $14 billion had been spent on construction and upgrades since the Crowe Panel reported.

upgrades at existing facilities, this spending allowed the construction of about eight to ten new diplomatic buildings per year – most of them replacing facilities that were considered to be insecure. That building pace represented a sharp increase from the pace of the 1990s, when only one new building was constructed annually.[20]

This funding history provides powerful evidence of the Crowe Panel's impact. As described earlier, when the Crowe Panel reported, the administration was only seeking $3 billion over five years. After the panel's recommendation and Crowe's determined advocacy placed new political pressure on the administration, the Clinton White House boosted its funding request dramatically – first to $11.4 billion over ten years and then to $14 billion over ten years. The final funding levels for FY 2000 ($600 million), FY 2001 ($1.1 billion), and FY 2002 ($1.3 billion) more than doubled the Clinton administration's initial spending proposal for those three years. Furthermore, funding remained at or above the levels recommended by the panel in subsequent years.

Although the African embassy bombings provided the impetus for this funding boost, its huge scale cannot be attributed to the bombings themselves, because the administration's initial spending plan – calling for a much more modest increase – was itself formulated and proposed several months *after* the bombings. In other words, that initial spending plan already took into account the security vulnerabilities revealed by the terrorist attack. No additional embassy attacks occurred between the announcement of that initial plan and its two upward revisions, followed by the big jumps in approved appropriations in 1999 and 2000. The most relevant intervening event was the Crowe Panel's report and the political pressure it generated.

Indeed, knowledgeable sources give substantial credit to the Crowe Panel for triggering the funding boost. One State Department official commented, "The [Accountability Review] Boards had an enormous impact.... They started to create political will in both the executive and Congress to fund embassy security. The White House wasn't going to be outdone by Congress on this, and Congress wasn't going to be outdone by the White House."[21] Media coverage also highlighted the Crowe Panel's impact, emphasizing the importance of the political pressure generated by Crowe and Congress through their denunciations of the administration's original spending plan as inadequate (Lippman 1999; Risen

---

[20] Interview of State Department official, October 2008.
[21] *Ibid.*

1999b). A *New York Times* article anonymously quoted an administration official as saying, "Admiral Crowe did a service by bringing so much attention to this" (Risen 1999b).

In addition to the funding increase, most of the Crowe Panel's other recommendations were adopted before the end of 1999. For instance, the State Department acted quickly to broaden perimeters around embassies, deploy plainclothes surveillance teams to look out for dangers, modify its criteria for classifying threat levels at embassies, and provide more counterterrorism and crisis-management training to security officers and Foreign Service personnel – all panel proposals.[22] In congressional testimony, David Carpenter, the State Department's top diplomatic security official, gave some of the credit for these and other reforms to the Crowe Panel: "Some of these actions have been based solely on DS [Diplomatic Security Bureau] initiatives; others were suggested by the Accountability Review Boards chaired by retired Admiral William J. Crowe."[23]

Additional Crowe Panel proposals were adopted through the Secure Embassy Construction and Counterterrorism Act of 1999, enacted in November of that year.[24] That law adopted the panel's recommendations to formulate new State Department emergency action procedures, develop new State Department rapid reaction capabilities, and require embassies to store emergency supplies and documents at secure off-site facilities. The legislation cited the Crowe Panel in explaining the importance of its provisions: "Unless the vulnerabilities identified by the Crowe panels are addressed in a sustained and financially realistic manner, the lives and safety of United States employees in diplomatic facilities will continue to be at risk from further terrorist attacks."[25]

Why the Panel Was Successful

The Crowe Panel's significant impact stemmed from the crisis generated by the embassy bombings, which caused the largest loss of life from a

---

[22] Testimony by Madeleine Albright, hearing of the Senate Appropriations Subcommittee on Commerce, Justice, and State, the Judiciary, and Related Agencies, February 4, 1999; testimony by David Carpenter, hearing of the House International Relations Committee, May 17, 2000.

[23] Testimony by David Carpenter, hearing of the House International Relations Committee, May 17, 2000.

[24] This measure was introduced by Senator Rod Grams (R-MN), chairman of the Senate subcommittee with oversight responsibilities for embassy security. It was initially included in the Foreign Relations Authorization Act for fiscal year 2000 and 2001, but was ultimately signed into law as part of the FY 2000 omnibus appropriations act, Public Law 106–113.

[25] Public Law 106–113.

terrorist attack targeting Americans since the 1988 bombing of Pan Am 103. This crisis underscored that the status quo in embassy security policy was not sufficient to protect U.S. facilities, creating a window of opportunity for the panel to spark policy change. In the wake of the bombings, most policy makers agreed on the need to boost security funding, but they lacked consensus on how large that boost should be.

The Crowe Panel's recommendation of $14 billion over ten years provided a focal point for this debate. Once the panel made this proposal, it became the key reference point for all discussions of embassy security funding. Without it, the Clinton administration would have probably faced much less pressure to revise its initial spending plan, because critics would have been unable to cite a politically credible alternative proposal. In addition, the panel's other recommendations shaped deliberations on how to update specific security policies and procedures. Representative Christopher Smith commented, "This report, I think, is the catalyst that will make the difference in helping all of us. It is the blueprint."[26]

The existence of a crisis, however, did not ensure that the Crowe Panel would be influential. The panel's design and membership were also critical to its ability to provide a focal point. Its authorization by the executive branch allowed its members to be appointed quickly because they were all named by a single policy maker: Albright. The panel's relatively narrow mandate – limited to investigating the embassy bombings and recommending improved security policies for overseas facilities – generated three additional benefits: (1) It allowed the commission to complete its work quickly. (2) It facilitated the task of reaching consensus by limiting the number of issues to be considered. (3) It simplified Admiral Crowe's campaign to win adoption of the proposals, because they primarily concerned only the State Department and a small number of congressional committees.

The evidence further suggests that the Crowe Panel's political credibility, rather than specialized expertise, accounted for its ability to shape policy. In Chapter 2, I argue that a commission's distinct appeal stems from its political credibility, which is based on its independence, stature, and ideological diversity. An alternative hypothesis asserts instead that commissions exert influence because of their expertise. If political credibility is in fact the key commission attribute, one should find that successful panels are unique among political institutions in their combination

---

[26] Hearing of the House International Relations Subcommittee on International Operations and Human Rights, March 12, 1999.

of independence, stature, and ideological diversity, and that they are highly praised for their possession of these qualities and for their bipartisan cohesion. If expertise is most important, however, successful panels should possess technical knowledge that other political institutions lack, and should be lauded for this expertise.

The Crowe Panel's political credibility distinguished it from other institutions far more than its expertise. The panel demonstrated its bipartisanship and independence by issuing a unanimous report that sharply criticized the State Department. In addition, it was led by someone possessing a nonpartisan reputation and great stature as a former chairman of the Joint Chiefs of Staff. A State Department official observed, "Admiral Crowe was respected by both parties and by the White House and Congress. He had the respect and clout to get it done."[27] Importantly, Crowe's stature amplified the impact of his persistent advocacy on behalf of the panel, which was critical to the panel's success. David Carpenter commented that Crowe's advocacy was "extremely helpful" in building political support for the embassy security funding increases.[28]

On the other hand, Crowe was far from an expert on embassy security, with a background primarily in military affairs. Nor did the Crowe Panel as a whole have great expertise on the issue it addressed. Although several of its members had worked in embassies or the State Department, none of them were diplomatic security specialists, and they were assisted by a staff of just five people, three of whom performed clerical duties. Moreover, the panel lacked resources to hire consultants. As a whole, therefore, it possessed much less embassy security expertise than the State Department, whose Bureau of Diplomatic Security includes more than 1,000 specialists.

In fact, Crowe had no qualms about referring to his panel's limited expertise during his congressional appearances. When discussing at one hearing his panel's recommendation for $14 billion in spending over ten years, he noted, "Now, I am not contending that we were really equipped to analyze as an accountant some of these figures, but this was our best estimate, and we think that it is in the neighborhood if it is not exactly correct."[29] At another hearing, he commented about the same proposal, "Now, when we submitted that figure we were aware, first of all, that that

[27] Interview of State Department official, October 2008.
[28] Interview of David Carpenter, March 5, 2009.
[29] Hearing of the House International Relations Subcommittee on International Operations and Human Rights, March 12, 1999.

figure is an estimate made by some people [the panel members] who are not in this business.... Those figures of course must now be honed and refined by people who are expert in this regard."[30] If expertise is the key source of a commission's influence, a panel chairman would not so readily tell policy makers that his commission lacked expertise when advocating on behalf of its proposals. The fact that the Crowe Panel's spending proposal nevertheless became the focal point for the debate on this issue strongly suggests that the commission's political credibility, rather than expertise, was its most important attribute.

Indeed, Carpenter identified the panel's independence and Crowe's political reputation as the main reasons for the commission's impact: "There was nothing in the [panel's] findings that really surprised us, but it helped tremendously to have an independent group make these findings because what the State Department says is often considered self-serving.... Crowe was a respected person in Washington, DC, and a familiar face. That's why he was an outstanding spokesperson on this."[31]

The Bremer Commission and Counterterrorism Policy

As noted earlier, the Crowe Panel was not the only commission formed soon after the African embassy bombings. The Bremer Commission was established based on a bill introduced by Representative Frank Wolf (R-VA), which was enacted into law on October 21, 1998.[32] Wolf said of the legislation, "My goal was to educate Americans about the problem of terrorism, and to make changes to ensure that the country is safe and secure."[33]

Some congressional Republicans, however, probably backed creating the Bremer Commission as part of an effort to show that the Clinton administration was not doing enough to protect America from terrorism. Speaker of the House Newt Gingrich (R-GA) had pushed to create a commission on terrorism as early as 1996, after a bombing in Atlanta and a plane crash initially suspected to be a terrorist act.[34] At the time, Gingrich charged that forming a commission was necessary because "the administration's effort on terrorism has been, frankly, sophomoric and

---

[30] Hearing of the Senate Foreign Relations Committee, March 11, 1999.
[31] Interview of David Carpenter, March 5, 2009.
[32] This legislation is Public Law 105–277.
[33] Interview of Frank Wolf, October 2, 2007.
[34] The plane crash was the July 1996 destruction of TWA Flight 800 over Long Island, which was later determined to be an accident.

remarkably tactical" (Gray 1996). Gingrich's bill to create the commission also included a political swipe at the administration, stating that the panel shall examine "the failure to expend and utilize resources and authority previously provided by Congress for the implementation of enhanced counterterrorism activities."[35] The proposal passed the House in August 1996, but it was never approved by the Senate.

Wolf's introduction of a similar bill after the African embassy bombings might have been influenced by the earlier Gingrich measure – or even encouraged by Gingrich – though Wolf claims that the bill originated with him.[36] Wolf's bill did not include any language criticizing the Clinton administration, but it still gave the Bremer Commission a partisan slant by stipulating that six of the panel's ten members would be appointed by Republican congressional leaders, with the remainder appointed by Democratic congressional leaders, ensuring a Republican majority. (Congressional Republicans also appointed the chairman.) This commission structure, combined with the Clinton administration's pre-existing mistrust of congressional Republican motives, led administration officials to be wary of the commission from the outset. Then–NSC counterterrorism coordinator Richard Clarke commented, "The commission was viewed in the White House as unnecessary and partisan.... The Republicans were trying to make terrorism their issue."[37]

The Bremer Commission's charter stipulated that the panel members must be appointed within three months. Yet eight months passed before the four legislators with appointment power – the Speaker of the House, the Senate Majority Leader, and the House and Senate Minority Leaders – named all of their appointees, suggesting that the panel was not a priority for some of these policy makers. (The congressional Democrats may have intentionally delayed their appointments because they viewed the commission as a Republican project.) Even after all of the commissioners were named, several more months passed before the commission began meeting in late 1999. These delays and the administration's perception that the panel was a partisan tool illustrate some of the obstacles congressional commissions frequently face in trying to influence policy.

Aside from Bremer, a former ambassador at large for counterterrorism in the Reagan administration, the commissioners included political scientist Richard Betts; retired Army General Wayne Downing; Representative

---

[35] The bill was H.R. 3953.
[36] Interview of Frank Wolf, October 2, 2007.
[37] E-mail exchange with Richard Clarke, October 20, 2008.

Jane Harman (D-CA), who was not serving in Congress at the time; former Arms Control and Disarmament Agency Director Fred Iklé; former Justice Department official Juliette Kayyem; former FBI official John Lewis; former NSC official Gardner Peckham; former Director of Central Intelligence James Woolsey; and investment banker Maurice Sonnenberg, whom Bremer named vice chairman.[38] The commission was assisted by a staff of eleven people.

An Alarm about the New Threat

The commission's sixty-four-page report, issued on June 5, 2000, sounded the alarm about the evolution of the terrorist danger, emphasizing that Al Qaeda and other transnational groups sought to kill civilians on a large scale – unlike earlier terrorist groups – and were attempting to do so both overseas and on American soil. The report criticized many parts of the executive branch, from law enforcement and intelligence agencies to the State Department, for not acting more vigorously to address this growing threat, calling the executive's implementation of existing laws "seriously deficient" (National Commission on Terrorism 2000, ii). It concluded:

The government must immediately take steps to reinvigorate the collection of intelligence about terrorists' plans, use all available legal avenues to disrupt and prosecute terrorist activities and private sources of support, convince other nations to cease all support for terrorists, and ensure that federal, state, and local officials are prepared for attacks that may result in mass casualties. (National Commission on Terrorism 2000, iv)

On one important issue, the commission was unable to achieve consensus. Nine of the ten commissioners endorsed a section of the commission's report that criticized how the Department of Justice applied the Foreign Intelligence Surveillance Act (FISA), calling the department's interpretation of that law "cumbersome and overly cautious" (National Commission on Terrorism 2000, 10). The majority recommended that the attorney general loosen rules on the information required to conduct wiretaps and searches, and expand cooperation between the government's FISA lawyers and the FBI. Juliette Kayyem, who had served in the Clinton administration's Justice Department and was appointed to the commission by House Minority Leader Richard Gephardt (D-MO), dissented from this part of the report.

---

[38] Several people involved with the commission commented that Sonnenberg did not play a major role leading the panel, suggesting that Bremer made him vice chairman only to make the panel appear to be more bipartisan.

Aside from these FISA proposals, the commission issued thirty-five other proposals unanimously, including the following key recommendations:

- The director of central intelligence (DCI) should direct that guidelines for recruiting informants that were issued in 1995 will no longer apply to terrorist informants. (Those guidelines required the DCI's approval for the recruitment of informants with criminal records or a history of human rights abuses.)
- The FBI should develop a cadre of reports officers to distill its terrorism-related intelligence and disseminate that information to other intelligence agencies.
- The secretary of state should consider imposing sanctions on Greece and Pakistan for not cooperating with U.S. counterterrorism efforts.
- The government should develop contingency plans for giving the Defense Department the authority to direct the government's response to a catastrophic attack on American soil.
- The government should create a system for monitoring the status of foreign students nationwide.

A Dismissive Response

The Clinton administration's response to the report was generally dismissive. National Security Advisor Sandy Berger declined to be briefed on it, and the administration publicly opposed several of the commission's principal recommendations.[39] For instance, administration officials criticized the proposal to stop requiring the DCI's approval for recruiting terrorist informants with troubling backgrounds. One administration spokesperson commented, "An ax murderer may be a good agent. But you need the bureaucracy to evaluate it and say, 'We're willing to live with it because the intelligence take is good'" (Loeb 2000a).

The administration also opposed the proposals to consider sanctioning Greece and Pakistan, to disseminate terrorism information gathered by the FBI to other intelligence agencies, and to give the Defense Department authority to serve as the lead federal agency in the event of a catastrophic attack in the United States. On the sanctions proposal, Albright said the State Department was pressing the two countries to cooperate on counterterrorism, but would not put sanctions on the table (*Washington Post* 2000). On the FBI recommendation, the Justice Department claimed that allowing the FBI to share its information with

---

[39] Interview of Paul Bremer, September 26, 2007.

other agencies would violate the principle of separating law enforcement and intelligence activities (Best 2007, 8; Loeb 2000b). And on the Defense Department proposal, administration officials said there was no need to change existing law, which allowed civilian agencies to call on the military for assistance during a catastrophe.[40]

In Congress, reaction to the report was mixed, but divided largely along partisan lines. At congressional hearings on the report, some Republicans praised it highly for pointing out administration shortcomings. Senate Foreign Relations Committee Chairman Jesse Helms (R-NC), frequently a fierce critic of the administration, crowed, "The Commission exposes a pattern in the administration of appeasing terrorist states and coddling governments that are AWOL in the fight against terrorism."[41] Some leading Republicans, including Helms and Senate Intelligence Committee Chairman Richard Shelby (R-AL), also endorsed several of the commission's recommendations, such as the proposals on sanctioning Greece and Pakistan and changing the CIA guidelines on recruiting informants.[42]

Most congressional Democrats, for their part, sided with the Clinton administration in opposing the commission's principal recommendations. Several Democrats, including Senate Foreign Relations Committee members Christopher Dodd (D-CT), Paul Sarbanes (D-MD), and Robert Torricelli (D-NJ), argued that it would be counterproductive to sanction Greece and Pakistan, that it was unnecessary to make contingency plans for the military to have lead authority during a domestic attack, and that it would be inappropriate to monitor foreign students. On the student monitoring issue, Dodd said sharply, "This [proposal], to me, seems to contradict the rights set forth in the Constitution and Bill of Rights, and constitutes a dangerous violation of the personal liberties we take for granted."[43]

In two of the hearings on the Bremer Commission's report, members of Congress spent a significant amount of time discussing the commission's recommendation to ease regulations governing wiretaps and searches. On this topic, the discussion focused on the disagreement between Juliette Kayyem and the commission majority. Although Kayyem emphasized that she endorsed the rest of the panel's report, she did not

---

[40] Comments by Dale Watson and James Reynolds, hearing of the Senate Foreign Relations Committee, June 15, 2000.
[41] Hearing of the Senate Foreign Relations Committee, June 15, 2000.
[42] Hearing of the Senate Select Committee on Intelligence, June 8, 2000; hearing of the Senate Foreign Relations Committee, June 15, 2000.
[43] Hearing of the Senate Foreign Relations Committee, June 15, 2000.

hesitate to explain her dissent from the report's section on FISA. In a published letter to Senator Jon Kyl (R-AZ), chairman of the Senate Judiciary Subcommittee on Technology, Terrorism, and Government Information, Kayyem argued there was no need to change the Justice Department's existing standards for applying FISA.[44] She and fellow commission member John Lewis then debated their differences on this issue at a hearing of Kyl's subcommittee.[45] At a separate hearing of the Senate Intelligence Committee, Kayyem and Bremer had a similar exchange, which became somewhat contentious:

Bremer: "The problem we found…was that while the FISA statute establishes hurdles that have to be overcome in order for a court to issue a FISA wiretap, in the process of reviewing FBI requests for such wiretaps, which go through the [Department of Justice's] Office of Intelligence and Policy Review, OIPR was setting up still higher barriers."

Kayyem: "The argument that the FBI is somehow handcuffed is belied by the numbers, and there was no specific showing before the Commission of a need to expand its capacities…. I think it would be a really terrible mistake to permit the FBI to wiretap any American who was at one time, no matter how long ago, a member of an organization that we now have deemed as terrorists, as the [commission's] report apparently recommends."[46]

Kayyem's dissent and these discussions of it probably eroded some of the commission's bipartisan credibility. Bremer acknowledged, "When reports are footnoted [as with a dissent], that dilutes their impact."[47] Indeed, for my set of fifty-one national security commissions, panels issuing unanimous reports were much more influential than those issuing divided reports, according to both measures of impact employed in Chapter 3.

The Clinton administration's dismissal of the report and the mixed reaction to it in Congress resulted in little action to adopt any of its proposals. The only related action was the introduction of a bill by Senators Kyl and Dianne Feinstein (D-CA) in October 2000 that would have required the administration to report to Congress on possible changes to guidelines for recruiting informants and to authorities governing the sharing of information between law enforcement and intelligence agencies.[48]

---

[44] Letter from Juliette Kayyem to Senator Jon Kyl, June 27, 2000.
[45] Hearing of the Senate Judiciary Subcommittee on Technology, Terrorism, and Government Information, June 28, 2000.
[46] Hearing of the Senate Select Committee on Intelligence, June 8, 2000.
[47] Interview of Paul Bremer, September 26, 2007.
[48] This bill was S. 3205, the Kyl-Feinstein Counterterrorism Act of 2000.

Even though this bill only mandated reports, it was opposed by the administration and did not win congressional approval (Best 2007, 7–9). All told, none of the commission's principal recommendations was adopted in full or in part during the year and a half that followed its June 2000 report.

Why the Commission Didn't Catalyze Reform

This minimal impact reflected, above all, the timing of the commission report's publication. The commission reported between crises – nearly two years after the African embassy bombings, but before the October 2000 bombing of the *USS Cole* and the 9/11 attack. If the commission had been appointed by the executive branch, it could have been set up and completed its work more quickly, enabling it to report while policy makers still faced pressure to make reforms because of the embassy bombings. But the long delays in appointing commissioners enabled the window of opportunity opened by those bombings to close. Then–U.S. Ambassador at Large for Counterterrorism Michael Sheehan has observed that the crisis atmosphere generated by the African embassy bombings did not last long: "[O]ver time the embassy bombings faded from public memory, and counterterrorism once again fell several notches on the government's agenda. America simply shook off the nightmare of August 7 and went back to sleep" (Sheehan 2008, 18).

By the time the commission reported, even some counterterrorism experts were arguing that terrorism was no longer a serious threat. In a *Wall Street Journal* op-ed, former CIA and State Department officials Milt Bearden and Larry Johnson criticized the Bremer Commission for being alarmist: "The reality is that terrorism is on the decline.... The state sponsors of terrorism have been replaced by a few loosely organized groups that have plenty of grievances but lack the ability to launch the doomsday attacks we fear" (Bearden and Johnson 2000). Although Bearden and Johnson did not represent the prevailing opinion of counterterrorism experts, their critique reflected the commission's distinct disadvantage in reporting at a moment when counterterrorism policy was not a major concern of the public or a top priority of much of the government. Bremer Commission member James Woolsey colorfully described the tenor of the times: "It was the 1920s again. We'd won the Cold War. The stock market was up. People said, 'What are you causing trouble for? Let's relax. Let's party.'"[49]

---

[49] Interview of James Woolsey, November 8, 2007.

The commission's broad scope – covering all aspects of counterterrorism policy – further complicated its task. Whereas the Crowe Panel's proposals primarily concerned only the State Department and the few congressional committees with responsibility for that department, the Bremer Commission's recommendations spanned every major national security agency, from the CIA to the Defense, State, and Justice Departments. Gaining support for its proposals therefore would have required a Herculean advocacy effort directed at each of those agencies and the many congressional committees that oversee them. Moreover, with jurisdiction for the commission's proposals spread across so many agencies and committees, it would have been very difficult for any single policy maker to shepherd through legislation adopting many of the recommendations.

The commission's impact was also diminished by its inability to project a fully bipartisan image, which weakened its political credibility. As mentioned earlier, even before the commission began operating, the Clinton administration viewed it as a Republican tool to score political points.[50] The commission's design, with six Republican and four Democratic appointees – none of whom was named by the executive branch – fueled this perception. The appointment to the chairmanship of Bremer, who was generally known as a conservative protégé of Henry Kissinger, added to it. As Bremer Commission advisor William Wise commented, "Bremer wasn't viewed as a nonpartisan figure. He was viewed as a Republican."[51] The commission's inability to achieve complete unanimity further tarnished its bipartisan veneer.

For a congressional commission addressing national security policy, gaining buy-in from the administration is especially important because of the executive branch's dominance of that policy area. Few major changes to national security policy are enacted without the executive's support. The White House's perception that the Bremer Commission was biased therefore represented a major liability for the panel.

Although the Bremer Commission's deficit in political credibility diminished its impact, there is little evidence that inadequate expertise significantly limited its influence. Bremer possessed ample expertise himself, having served as the Reagan administration's top counterterrorism official for three years. Several other commissioners, including Richard Betts, Wayne Downing, Juliette Kayyem, and John Lewis, had also studied

[50] E-mail exchange with Richard Clarke, October 20, 2008.
[51] Interview of William Wise, March 26, 2009.

or worked on counterterrorism policy. Moreover, the commission's staff and budget were larger than that of the Crowe Panel, implying that the Crowe Panel's greater influence was not due to a difference between the levels of expertise at the commissions' disposal.

Postscript

Eventually, the government did adopt some of the Bremer Commission's recommendations in the wake of the 9/11 attack. In December 2001, Congress enacted legislation that required the director of central intelligence to rescind the 1995 restrictions on the recruitment of informants.[52] Five months later, Congress enacted a law directing the Justice Department to develop an electronic means of tracking the visa and enrollment status of international students in the United States.[53] And in August 2002, the FBI set up an office to disseminate terrorism-related information to other intelligence agencies.[54]

These post-9/11 changes suggest that, in the end, the commission may have had an impact on policy, but that its recommendations required a new, and bigger, crisis to gain momentum. Bremer commented, "Before 9/11, the report was ignored.... A lot of what we recommended seemed more commendable to people in the blue light of dawn of 9/12."[55] Commission staff director Suzanne Spaulding similarly observed, "The report was destined to gather dust on the shelf until 9/11, at which point it became a very useful set of practical recommendations that people in position to make policies were able to implement."[56] The role of 9/11 in sparking the adoption of the commission's proposals underscores the importance of a crisis in prompting reforms.

Indeed, the adoption of these recommendations mainly resulted from the 9/11 attack, not the commission report. Considering that none of the commission's principal proposals was endorsed by Congress or the executive branch prior to 9/11, it is unlikely that any of them would have been adopted without the shock of the World Trade Center's destruction by Al Qaeda. Moreover, in the post-9/11 political climate, which generally favored looser intelligence restrictions and tighter border controls, these policy changes would probably have been made even if the commission had not recommended them. As Bremer recognized, "Some of

---

[52] This legislation is Public Law 107–108.
[53] This act is Public Law 107–173.
[54] E-mail exchange with FBI official, February 2008.
[55] Interview of Paul Bremer, September 26, 2007.
[56] Interview of Suzanne Spaulding, June 26, 2007.

our proposals were adopted after 9/11, but it's hard to draw a causal line from the commission to those changes."[57]

In the end, the Bremer Commission's greatest effect was in provoking public discussion of some controversial ideas, thereby helping to set the stage for their adoption at a later date. Although the political environment was not ripe for approving those proposals in 2000, congressional consideration of the panel's report that year introduced legislators to the ideas – perhaps making policy makers more likely to consider them again after 9/11.

The *USS Cole* Commission and Military Force Protection

On the morning of October 12, 2000, barely more than two years after the African embassy bombings, Al Qaeda struck again. The *USS Cole*, a Navy destroyer, was docked for refueling in the harbor of Aden, off the coast of Yemen, when two men approached the warship in a small motorized dinghy packed with more than 500 pounds of explosives. After calmly waving at the American sailors on board the ship, the men detonated their cargo, blowing a gaping forty-by-forty-foot hole in the *Cole*'s steel hull. The blast killed the two boatmen and seventeen U.S. sailors, injured thirty-nine others, and caused $250 million worth of damage to the destroyer. The explosion's shock wave was so powerful that it toppled cars onshore (Bergen 2002, 171–172; Wright 2006, 360–361).

Like the embassy bombings, the *Cole* attack was directed by Al Qaeda from start to finish (National Commission on Terrorist Attacks upon the United States 2004, 190). For the terrorist group, the *Cole* bombing was a success that gave it worldwide publicity and drew new recruits to its training camps in Afghanistan (Wright 2006, 374). For the United States, the disaster offered new evidence of Al Qaeda's determination to kill Americans.

In the bombing's immediate aftermath, U.S. intelligence and law enforcement officials could not definitively tie Al Qaeda's leadership to the attack, and President Clinton refrained from retaliating against Al Qaeda militarily. Still, political pressure grew on the administration to remedy the security deficiencies revealed by the bombing. At a Senate Armed Services Committee hearing one week after the bombing, the committee's chairman, Senator John Warner (R-VA), suggested that the Defense Department might have ignored red flags about the security of

[57] Interview of Paul Bremer, September 26, 2007.

Aden's harbor, and other senators called for holding military officers or Defense Department officials accountable.[58]

The FBI quickly began an investigation into who perpetrated the bombing, and the Navy started an internal investigation of the performance of the *Cole*'s crew. On November 2, Secretary of Defense William Cohen established an additional probe by forming the *USS Cole* Commission, which Cohen instructed to review the force-protection policies and practices of military units in transit. Cohen probably had two motivations in forming the commission: first, to defuse the congressional criticism that followed the bombing; and second, to examine issues that the Navy investigation would not address, particularly the conduct of the chain of command above the *Cole*'s officers and vulnerabilities of transiting units in all of the military services.[59] Cohen appointed just two commissioners, who served as cochairs: retired Army General William Crouch and retired Navy Admiral Harold Gehman.

The Commission's Call for Reform

The commission worked quickly, and submitted its report to Cohen on January 9, 2001.[60] The report argued that protecting U.S. ships, aircraft, and troops when they are in transit required improved policies for deterring, anticipating, and disrupting terrorist attacks (DoD *USS Cole* Commission 2001). Its fifty-three recommendations included the following key proposals:

- The military services should make antiterrorism and force-protection training part of the pre-deployment regimen for all units.
- Commanders in the field should take proactive steps to deter terrorists.
- Commanders in the field should be given full-time force-protection officers and staffs.
- The secretary of defense should reprioritize intelligence collection and analysis so that sufficient resources are devoted to combating terrorism.
- The secretary of defense should reprioritize intelligence production to ensure that transiting units are given tailored, focused intelligence on threats.

---

[58] Hearing of the Senate Armed Services Committee, October 19, 2000.
[59] Interview of William Crouch, June 7, 2007; interview of Harold Gehman, January 17, 2008; interview of Defense Department official, June 2008.
[60] Much of the commission's report was classified, but the commission released an unclassified executive summary, on which my discussion of the report is based.

The Defense Department Acts

Even though the *Cole* Commission reported less than two weeks before
the end of the Clinton administration, its recommendations influenced
defense policy significantly. Secretary Cohen immediately ordered adoption of the proposals and formed a working group consisting of representatives from his own office and the military services to direct the
implementation effort. This working group was led by Robert Newberry,
the principal deputy assistant secretary for special operations and low-
intensity conflict, and it continued operating for six months after the
changeover in administrations. Newberry explained that he and his staff
worked systematically to implement each of the commission's proposals
within certain timelines: "The report was like a checklist. We walked down
that list and found ways to make the recommendations happen."[61]

The effort of Newberry's working group and staff led to the publication of updated Defense Department regulations in June 2001 that incorporated twenty-eight of the commission's recommendations.[62] Among
these changes, the revised regulations required that antiterrorism training be incorporated into unit-level training regimens and be treated as
seriously as combat training; mandated that commanders at all levels
identify ways to detect and deter terrorists; ordered that full-time force-
protection officers be assigned to all commanders in the field; and directed
that transiting units be provided with tailored terrorist-threat information. Another key commission proposal was adopted separately when the
Defense Intelligence Agency established a task force to enhance its terrorist
warning and analysis capabilities.[63]

Newberry observed that some of these reforms would not have
occurred without the *Cole* Commission's report: "The commission had
a direct and major impact [on those changes]."[64] In congressional testimony, Joint Chiefs of Staff Chairman Henry Shelton also implied that the
commission influenced the department's actions: "With the assistance of
the Crouch-Gehman Commission report, we are now reducing vulnerabilities associated with in-transit units."[65]

[61] Interview of Robert Newberry, February 12, 2008.
[62] Department of Defense Instruction, Number 2000.16, June 14, 2001; comments by
    Robert Newberry, hearing of the House Armed Services Committee Special Oversight
    Panel on Terrorism, June 14, 2001.
[63] Testimony by Eleanor Hill, Congressional Joint Inquiry into Intelligence Community
    Activities before and after the Terrorist Attacks of September 11, 2001, October 1, 2002.
[64] Interview of Robert Newberry, February 12, 2008.
[65] Hearing of the Senate Armed Services Committee, May 3, 2001.

Explaining the Commission's Impact

These policy changes were driven primarily by the dramatic nature of the *Cole* bombing. Newberry noted, "The *Cole* incident was something different, totally new – a maritime attack. So there was a need for a fresh look and lots of changes."[66] This need was magnified by pressure from Congress to remedy security shortcomings. When the *Cole* Commission reported in January 2001, it provided classified briefings to members of Congress. Then, in May and June 2001, the House and Senate armed services committees held public hearings on the Defense Department's response to the bombing and the commission's recommendations.[67] This congressional interest surely added to the department's motivation to implement the commission's proposals quickly.

Like the Crowe Panel, the *Cole* Commission's influence was facilitated by its executive-branch authorization and relatively limited scope, which enabled it to complete its work in less than ten weeks. Although I classify the commission as a panel of broad scope in my statistical analysis because its mandate spanned multiple military services, its mandate's restriction to a highly specific issue – force-protection policies of transiting units – enabled a single Defense Department official to take charge of implementing most of the proposals.[68] The executive branch's response to a commission with a broader mandate would have probably been much more diffuse, most likely resulting in less action to adopt its proposals.

The *Cole* Commission provides further evidence that political credibility tends to be a greater source of commission influence than expertise. The commission did possess ample expertise: Its cochairs, General Crouch and Admiral Gehman, had both commanded military units, and they were assisted by a staff of about thirty people, consisting largely of active-duty officers from the military services. But the fact that the staff came from the services reveals that the Defense Department did not lack sufficient expertise to investigate force-protection practices. If Secretary Cohen only sought expertise, he could have charged the same set of active-duty officers with conducting an internal investigation instead.

---

[66] Interview of Robert Newberry, February 12, 2008.
[67] Hearing of the Senate Armed Services Committee, May 3, 2001; hearing of the House Armed Services Committee Special Oversight Panel on Terrorism, June 14, 2001.
[68] In Chapter 3, I define a commission of narrow scope as one whose mandate concerns a single issue, challenge, or event, *and* is focused on a single agency, program, or policy. In applying this definition, I treat the Army, Navy, and Air Force as separate agencies. However, as a robustness check in Chapter 3's statistical analysis I treat the Defense Department as a whole as a single agency.

The key attribute of the commission was not expertise, but independence. In the face of congressional criticism following the *Cole* bombing, Cohen needed to demonstrate that acts of negligence or security vulnerabilities were not being covered up. An investigation conducted by retired officers was likely to send a stronger signal of independence than a probe led by active-duty officers. Moreover, the commission's independence bolstered its ability to catalyze reform by enabling it to make proposals that the services might oppose. Newberry explained, "An outside group has no command pressure and feels freer to voice its views. There are a lot of pressures on the services, and when something costs money, they may not want to do it because they need to cut something else to do it. Someone from outside doesn't have to worry about money, and doesn't worry about turf battles."[69] Newberry added that the commission's report strengthened the ability of the office of the secretary of defense to overcome service resistance to some changes.[70]

As far as the other two components of political credibility – stature and political diversity – the commission's cochairs possessed significant stature as retired four-star officers, but were a nonpartisan, rather than bipartisan, pair. (The political affiliations of Crouch and Gehman are not widely known). The commission's diversity derived instead from the fact that Crouch and Gehman had served in different military services. This type of diversity might not be as impressive to elected officials as political diversity, but it was appropriate for a commission seeking to influence military regulations that generally did not require legislative changes.

Conclusion

This chapter's case studies illustrate well how a commission can drive reform if it takes advantage of a window of opportunity for policy change. The Crowe Panel and *Cole* Commission were influential for one primary reason: Each was formed and reported within months of a major disaster that dramatically highlighted the need to address security vulnerabilities. In the wake of both the African embassy bombings and the *Cole* attack, policy makers faced pressure to bolster or change security policies. The Crowe Panel and *Cole* Commission helped officials respond to this pressure by providing them with politically credible blueprints for reform. In each case, the commission's ability to establish a focal point

---

[69] Interview of Robert Newberry, March 10, 2009.
[70] *Ibid.*

was enhanced by its executive-branch authorization and relatively limited mandate, which enabled it to complete its work quickly, simplified its task of reaching consensus, and placed the burden of implementing its proposals on a relatively small number of policy makers. The Crowe Panel's impact was also greatly aided by Admiral Crowe's nonpartisan reputation, impressive stature, and persistent advocacy.

By contrast, the Bremer Commission exerted less influence in part because its connection to a disaster was more distant, thanks to the delays associated with its congressional authorization. In addition, the very broad scope of the commission's report made it difficult for a single member of Congress to champion it effectively. Perhaps most important, the Bremer Commission's impact was constrained by the Clinton administration's perception that the commission was designed to advance a partisan Republican agenda. Given the executive branch's dominance of national security policy, a congressional commission is unlikely to influence policy if it is greatly mistrusted by the White House.

This chapter demonstrates that, in response to Al Qaeda's first major attacks on the United States, commissions prompted significant reforms concerning diplomatic security and military force protection. Those reforms may have helped deter additional attacks on U.S. embassies and military units, but they did not prevent Al Qaeda from planning and executing its most devastating strike: the launching of four hijacked planes into the World Trade Center and Pentagon on 9/11. In this respect, the Bremer Commission's minimal impact may have been costly, because its expansive mandate gave it the potential to influence counterterrorism policy more broadly.

Chapter 6 continues the story of terrorism commissions by focusing on two panels that reported during the first term of President George W. Bush: the Hart-Rudman Commission and the 9/11 Commission. The chapter shows that the Hart-Rudman Commission, an agenda commission, was initially ignored despite an eerily prescient prediction, and it explains how the two panels catalyzed major homeland security and intelligence overhauls in the wake of the Twin Towers' destruction.

6

Reforming Homeland Security and Intelligence after 9/11

On January 31, 2001 – eleven days after the presidential inauguration of George W. Bush – the U.S. Commission on National Security/21st Century (the Hart-Rudman Commission) issued a dire warning and a related recommendation on the first page of its final report's executive summary:

> The combination of unconventional weapons proliferation with the persistence of international terrorism will end the relative invulnerability of the U.S. homeland to catastrophic attack. A direct attack against American citizens on American soil is likely over the next quarter century. The risk is not only death and destruction but also a demoralization that could undermine U.S. global leadership. In the face of this threat, our nation has no coherent or integrated governmental structures.
>
> We therefore recommend the creation of an independent National Homeland Security Agency (NHSA) with responsibility for planning, coordinating, and integrating various U.S. government activities involved in homeland security. (U.S. Commission on National Security 2001, xiii)

The commission's report, produced by a star-studded group led by former Senators Gary Hart (D-CO) and Warren Rudman (R-NH), was the culmination of the most comprehensive review of U.S. national security in more than fifty years (Zegart 2007, 5). Yet the commission's doomsday forecast was barely noticed by the national media – the *New York Times* did not publish a single article on the report – and received little attention in Washington. President Bush and Vice President Dick Cheney declined to be briefed on it.[1] Neither Congress nor the Bush administration moved quickly to adopt any of the commission's fifty recommendations.

---

[1] Interview of Gary Hart, June 11, 2007.

Less than eight months after the report's release, Al Qaeda fulfilled the commission's prophecy when it executed the deadliest terrorist attack in world history, killing nearly 3,000 people aboard four planes and in the World Trade Center and Pentagon. The 9/11 attack brought new attention to the Hart-Rudman Commission's report, leading Senator Joseph Lieberman (D-CT) to introduce a bill based on its proposal to establish a homeland security agency. As Lieberman's bill gained congressional support, it prompted the Bush administration to reverse its previous opposition to reorganization and issue its own proposal for a department of homeland security (DHS), which was enacted into law in November 2002.[2] The establishment of DHS, merging 170,000 employees from twenty-two agencies, represented the largest government reorganization since the creation of the Defense Department in 1947 (Stevenson 2002). Yet it might not have occurred without the Hart-Rudman Commission's recommendation.

Two years after the establishment of DHS, Congress and President Bush reached agreement on another massive reorganization – this time of the intelligence community. The Intelligence Reform and Terrorism Prevention Act of 2004 placed the government's fifteen intelligence agencies under the leadership of a new director of national intelligence (DNI) and mandated a host of other changes in intelligence management and counterterrorism policy.[3] The enactment of this legislation was especially remarkable because just six months before its passage there existed little congressional support for intelligence reorganization, and President Bush opposed the notion of establishing a DNI. This political landscape changed primarily because of the July 2004 report of the National Commission on Terrorist Attacks upon the United States (the 9/11 Commission), which recommended creating a DNI, among many other reforms. The commission's broad public support and intensive advocacy prompted Congress to act and forced Bush to change his stance. It is almost certain that the DNI post would not have been established if the 9/11 Commission had not proposed it.

In this chapter, I explain how the Hart-Rudman Commission and 9/11 Commission spurred these two landmark reforms. To preview the argument, in both cases, a window of opportunity for reform was opened by the 9/11 disaster, but the disaster was not sufficient to forge

---

[2] This law is the Homeland Security Act of 2002, Public Law 107–296, enacted on November 25, 2002.
[3] This act is Public Law 108–458, enacted on December 17, 2004.

political agreement on organizational change. The commissions' proposals sparked such agreement by providing a focal point for the policy debate, which enabled reformers to overcome resistance to changing the status quo. I further show that the influence of the panels stemmed from their impressive political credibility, which was bolstered by their ability – thanks to the unique deliberative environment of commissions – to issue unanimous reports with highly specific proposals. In addition, the Hart-Rudman Commission's minimal impact before 9/11 demonstrates how difficult it is for a commission to trigger reform without the interest in change generated by a crisis.

The Hart-Rudman Commission and Homeland Security Reorganization

In 1997, Speaker of the House Newt Gingrich (R-GA) sought to establish a congressionally chartered commission on U.S. national security strategy, with the goal of building a national consensus on America's role in the world.[4] Gingrich achieved the enactment of legislation authorizing the commission in October 1997, but congressional Democrats – fearful that the panel would have a Republican slant – blocked it from getting established by tying its formation to a complex set of conditions.[5] Realizing that the law would not be implemented, Gingrich asked President Clinton to form the commission through the Defense Department instead. Clinton agreed – possibly in return for a favor from Gingrich.[6] Defense Secretary William Cohen then chartered the panel, which I label an agenda commission, in October 1998, funding it out of the Defense Department's budget.

Cohen gave the commission a breathtakingly ambitious charge: to "define America's role and purpose in the first quarter of the 21st century," and to "identify the national security strategy in political, economic, military, societal, and technological terms that must be implemented for America to fulfill that role and achieve its purpose" (U.S. Commission on National Security 2001, 136). He instructed the commission to issue three reports: one describing the likely international security environment of the early 21st century, a second outlining a national security strategy,

---

[4] Interview of Charles Boyd, July 24, 2007; interview of Warren Rudman, June 14, 2007.
[5] Interview of Charles Boyd, July 24, 2007. The statute is the Department of Defense Appropriations Act of 1998, Public Law 105–56, enacted on October 8, 1997.
[6] Interview of Charles Boyd, July 24, 2007; interview of Clinton administration official, April 2008.

and a third providing recommendations on the government's national security apparatus (U.S. Commission on National Security 2001, 137–138). The commission's very broad scope and its establishment in the absence of a crisis suggest, according to my theory, that it was unlikely to be influential.

Cohen appointed seven Republicans and seven Democrats to the panel. In addition to Hart and Rudman, the commissioners included former Counselor to the President Anne Armstrong, Lockheed Martin Chairman Norman Augustine, journalist John Dancy, former Supreme Allied Commander John Galvin, Council on Foreign Relations President Leslie Gelb, former Representative Lee Hamilton (D-IN), former Under Secretary of Commerce Lionel Olmer, former Air Force Secretary Donald Rice, former Secretary of Defense James Schlesinger, retired Navy Admiral Harry Train, and former U.S. Ambassador to the United Nations Andrew Young. Lynne Cheney, former Chairwoman of the National Endowment for the Humanities, also initially served on the commission. She resigned from it in 1999, and Cohen appointed Gingrich, who had left Congress by that point, to replace her. The commissioners were supported by a staff of twenty-nine people and several dozen consultants, directed by retired Air Force General Charles Boyd, a longtime advisor to Gingrich.

Reaching Consensus

The Hart-Rudman Commission's deliberative process illustrates well the type of learning and compromise that can occur on commissions, and the special ability of panels to foster consensus among people who would not otherwise tend to agree. The commission was very diverse ideologically. As commissioner Norman Augustine noted, "We went all the way from Andy Young to Newt Gingrich, which is about as far as you can go in either direction."[7] Indeed, the left-leaning Young was a former civil rights activist who had antagonized conservatives while serving as President Jimmy Carter's UN Ambassador by criticizing white racism, meeting secretly with the Palestine Liberation Organization, and calling Cuban troops a "stabilizing" force in Angola (Schram 1979). Gingrich, on the other hand, was a fiery conservative who spearheaded the Republican Party's takeover of Congress in 1994 and was reviled by most Democrats.

In fact, my quantitative data (described in Chapter 3) suggest that the commission was more diverse ideologically than most panels. When

---

[7] Interview of Norman Augustine, February 7, 2008.

asked to rate the Hart-Rudman Commission's ideological diversity on a scale of one to five, with one representing a commission of like-minded people and five representing a panel with a very broad spectrum of opinion, commission members and staff gave it an average rating of 4.67 – compared to a mean score of 3.69 for all of the panels in my data set. Given this wide diversity of views, it is remarkable that the commission issued three unanimous reports and dozens of highly specific proposals.

Equally noteworthy is the evolution in the commission's focus during its work. At the outset, Hart and Rudman expected that the panel would emphasize Defense Department reorganization.[8] Instead, the commission spent more time on the growing danger of international terrorism. Gary Hart observed, "I don't think any of us walked into the room in 1998 thinking terrorism was the biggest threat. We didn't think that until we began speaking to experts."[9] The commission's emerging consensus on this was expressed in its first report, issued in September 1999, which concluded, "America will become increasingly vulnerable to hostile attack on our homeland.... States, terrorists, and other disaffected groups will acquire weapons of mass destruction and mass disruption, and some will use them. Americans will likely die on American soil, possibly in large numbers" (U.S. Commission on National Security 1999, 141). However, Lynne Cheney believed the commission should focus more on the threat posed by a rising China. She resigned out of frustration with its direction.[10]

Still, reaching consensus on how to address the terrorist threat organizationally was challenging. As the commissioners began to consider recommendations, they debated a draft proposal to form a new department that would merge various government agencies and offices with domestic security responsibilities. Several commissioners were initially skeptical of such a major reorganization – either because they were reluctant to expand government or because they thought a large new department would be unmanageable.[11]

Over time, though, all of the commissioners were convinced to endorse a large-scale reorganization. Lee Hamilton remembered, "We came to

---

[8] Interview of Gary Hart, June 11, 2007; interview of Warren Rudman, June 14, 2007.

[9] Interview of Gary Hart, June 11, 2007.

[10] Cheney also was reportedly frustrated by the way Chuck Boyd directed the commission's work. Interview of Patti Benner, October 10, 2007; interview of James Schlesinger, November 29, 2007.

[11] Interview of Norman Augustine, February 7, 2008; interview of James Schlesinger, November 29, 2007.

it slowly. I had some reluctance on it. I've always been cautious about the idea of creating a new department. Finally, what persuaded us was the disparate scattering of all of these agencies dealing with homeland security across all of the government. We saw we needed more unity of effort."[12] The achievement of consensus was facilitated by a concession to those who were skeptical of forming a new department: The commission's report calls for forming a new "agency," rather than a new "department," even though it specifies that the director of the homeland security agency should have cabinet status, like heads of government departments.

The unique environment of commissions, which allows private deliberations in a setting that is relatively removed from political pressures, helped the panel achieve unanimity. Gary Hart commented, "Whatever predisposition members might have had to take a hard line was discarded at the outset. They felt they were working as Americans, not as partisans."[13] The task of reaching consensus was further eased by the fact that many commissioners were not specialists in national security policy. Although most of them had some background in foreign policy or defense matters, few of them joined the commission with set views about how the government should improve the national security policy-making process. Hart recalled, "We all went in pretty much with a tabula rasa."[14] In particular, it was helpful that commissioners had not previously taken public positions on issues such as homeland security reorganization, because that allowed them to reach compromises without contradicting such public stances.

The Commission's Reports

The commission's first and second reports did not include policy recommendations, and predictably received little public attention. The first report outlined likely changes in the international security environment over the next quarter century and emphasized that an array of new threats, including terrorism, was making Americans "less secure than they believe themselves to be" (U.S. Commission on National Security 1999, 2). The second report argued that America's security strategy must aim to strike a balance between benefiting from a more integrated world and dampening forces of global instability (U.S. Commission on National Security 2000).

---

[12] Interview of Lee Hamilton, January 24, 2008.
[13] Interview of Gary Hart, June 11, 2007.
[14] *Ibid.*

In addition to reiterating the first report's forecast of a catastrophic attack on American soil and recommending the formation of a homeland security agency, the commission's final report, released on January 31, 2001, proposed a wide range of changes intended to strengthen the U.S. national security apparatus (U.S. Commission on National Security 2001). These proposals included:

- Making homeland security a primary mission of the National Guard
- Doubling America's investment in science and technology research and development by 2010
- Providing financial incentives for students to pursue degrees in science, math, and engineering
- Putting the national security advisor in charge of a governmentwide strategic-planning process
- Reorganizing the State Department under five new regional under secretaries
- Establishing a national security service corps to enhance civilian government career paths
- Merging congressional authorizing and appropriations subcommittees that deal with national security issues

A Meager Initial Response

The commission held a press conference to publicize its final report and conducted media interviews to promote it. Yet the commission's dramatic prediction and wide-ranging recommendations failed to attract much public or governmental interest. Out of four major newspapers I consulted as a sample of media coverage – the *Chicago Tribune, New York Times, Wall Street Journal,* and *Washington Post* – only the *Tribune* and *Post* covered the report at all, each devoting a single article to it (Kempster 2001; Mufson 2001). The commission briefed Secretary of State Colin Powell, Secretary of Defense Donald Rumsfeld, and National Security Advisor Condoleezza Rice on its findings, but President Bush declined repeated requests from Rudman for a meeting (Shenon 2008, 55–56). In subsequent months, the Bush administration did not attempt to adopt any of the commission's proposals.

There are several plausible explanations of the Bush administration's inaction in response to the report. Top administration officials, including Vice President Cheney, Rumsfeld, and Rice, entered the administration primarily concerned with issues such as China and ballistic missile defense, rather than Al Qaeda (Clarke 2004, 227–238). Like Lynne Cheney, they may have believed the panel was misguided in focusing on the terrorist threat, and they faced little pressure to make combating terrorism a high priority in the absence of a crisis. In addition, the commission's proposals to form a large new agency and pour government resources into science and education clashed with the "small government" orthodoxy of many Bush administration officials.

More pointedly, some commission participants suggested the administration might not have been receptive to its ideas because of a general lack of openness to outside input in the Bush White House, which journalists have documented in other contexts (Draper 2007; Woodward 2006). Rudman stated, "It was typical administration arrogance. They didn't want to take ideas from outsiders."[15] Commission staff director Charles Boyd noted that the panel's origins in the Clinton administration might also have eroded its standing with the Bush administration: "The administration came into town believing that they knew exactly what needed to be done, and that they didn't need help from a commission chartered by a Democratic president."[16] It is also possible that sour personal relationships tarnished the commission's standing with the new administration: Lynne Cheney, who had resigned in frustration, was Vice President Cheney's wife, and Rudman had campaigned for John McCain in his 2000 Republican primary campaign against Bush (Preble 2005, 31–35). Most likely, a combination of these factors accounted for the White House's coolness toward the commission.

Some members of Congress showed more interest in the commission's report. Three congressional committees held hearings on it in March and April 2001.[17] Separately, on March 21, Representative Mac Thornberry (R-TX) introduced a bill based on the commission's homeland security agency proposal. This measure, entitled the "National Homeland Security Agency Act," copied the panel's recommendation almost precisely.[18] The bill mandated the same merger proposed by the commission: transferring the Federal Emergency Management Agency (FEMA), the Customs Service, the Border Patrol, the Coast Guard, and several other offices to a new agency, headed by a cabinet-level director. It also organized

---

[15] Interview of Warren Rudman, June 14, 2007.
[16] Interview of Charles Boyd, July 24, 2007.
[17] Hearing of the House Budget Committee, March 15, 2001; hearing of the House Government Reform Subcommittee on National Security, Veterans Affairs, and International Relations, March 27, 2001; hearing of the Senate Judiciary Subcommittee on Technology, Terrorism, and Government Information, April 3, 2001.
[18] The bill was H.R. 1158.

the new agency in the same way as the commission recommended – in three directorates responsible for prevention, protection, and emergency preparedness and response. Notably, the Thornberry bill was the first measure introduced in Congress to establish a domestic security agency.[19] It was also the first legislative proposal of any kind that contained the phrase "homeland security," reflecting the Hart-Rudman Commission's introduction of this term, which has since become ubiquitous, into American political discourse.[20]

Two House subcommittees considered Thornberry's bill and a pair of competing proposals for addressing terrorism at a joint hearing on April 24, 2001.[21] The alternative proposals were introduced by Representatives Wayne Gilchrest (R-MD) and Ike Skelton (D-MO). Gilchrest's bill mandated the formation of a presidential council that would draft a strategy for defending America against terrorist attacks.[22] Skelton's proposal required that the president designate a single official to be responsible for combating terrorism – the so-called czar approach.[23] The comments of legislators at the hearing did not clearly indicate whether one of the three House proposals had the most support among representatives, indicating that a focal point had not yet been established for the debate on how to organize the government to counter the terrorist threat.[24]

Before 9/11, Thornberry gained only one cosponsor of his bill, and the House did not take any action on it. Nor did the House act on the Gilchrest and Skelton measures. The Thornberry bill's failure to advance reflected the absence of a crisis to pressure policy makers to adopt such a large-scale reform. Even if Thornberry had attracted many

---

[19] I determined this through a systematic search of THOMAS, the congressional database.

[20] I determined this through a systematic search of THOMAS, the congressional database. A systematic search of LexisNexis provided further evidence that the commission is responsible for popularizing the term "homeland security" in the American political context. In all articles in "Major U.S. and World Publications" before January 2001, this phrase was only used once in reference to American domestic security, and that was in a 1981 *Washington Post* op-ed on the Cold War (Rosenfeld 1981).

[21] Joint hearing of the House Transportation and Infrastructure Subcommittee on Economic Development, Public Buildings, and Emergency Management, and the House Government Reform Subcommittee on National Security, Veterans Affairs and International Relations, April 24, 2001.

[22] The bill was H.R. 525.

[23] The bill was H.R. 1292.

[24] In Chapter 2, I define a focal point as "a proposal or idea around which political debate revolves in a given policy area." A focal point is therefore only formed when a single proposal or idea dominates the debate.

more cosponsors, achieving passage of his bill would have been very difficult, because it stretched over the jurisdictions of at least seven congressional authorizing committees, and it proposed to siphon off parts of several existing government departments, which could be expected, along with their oversight committees, to protect their turf jealously.[25] The bill's already dim prospects of enactment further darkened in May 2001, when the Bush administration sought to preempt any congressional action on reorganization by announcing that Vice President Cheney would oversee the development of a plan for responding to terrorist acts (Loeb 2001).

The commission's other recommendations did not fare any better. Its proposal to make homeland security a primary mission of the National Guard was resisted by the Guard's leadership and the Pentagon, which feared diminishing the Guard's preparation for fighting overseas.[26] The panel's recommendations to double federal investment in science and technology, provide new financial incentives for students to study math and engineering, and develop a civilian career path for national security professionals also gained little traction.[27] Out of the commission's eleven recommendations directed at the Defense Department and five proposals concerning the State Department, only one of them was fully adopted during the remainder of the Bush presidency.

Aside from the absence of a crisis before 9/11, the very small impact of most of the commission's proposals was due in part to the panel's extremely broad scope. Rudman, Hart, and several other commissioners and staff members promoted the report in a variety of fora, but it was not possible for the commission to lobby intensively the dozens of agencies and congressional committees that its proposals affected. Moreover, there was no single policy maker, short of the president, who could direct or shepherd through the legislative process the adoption of a large number of the recommendations. One of the commission's staff members lamented, "The longer and bigger a commission is, the harder it is to have impact. If we just looked at DoD [the Defense Department] or the State Department, we could have had more focus."[28]

---

[25] Interview of Mac Thornberry, April 3, 2009; comments by Warren Rudman, hearing of the House Government Reform Subcommittee on National Security, Veterans Affairs and International Relations, March 27, 2001.

[26] Interview of Arnold Punaro, December 19, 2007; interview of James Schlesinger, November 29, 2007.

[27] Interview of Norman Augustine, February 7, 2008.

[28] Interview of commission staff member, November 2007.

New Interest after 9/11

Although the vast majority of the Hart-Rudman Commission's proposals
triggered no action before or after 9/11, the terrorist attack of that day
generated new interest in the homeland security agency recommendation.
In the immediate wake of the attack, journalists dug up the commission's
report and noted its widely ignored prediction of a catastrophic terrorist strike in articles with titles such as "Now Will We Pay Attention?"
and "Back from the Brink of Obscurity" (Broder 2001; Kamen 2001).
One of these articles, published on September 14 in the *Washington Post*,
began, "Tuesday's terrorist attacks had people in Washington dusting off
their copies of a prescient – if little read – report in February by the U.S.
Commission on National Security/21st Century" (Kamen 2001). In subsequent days, Hart and Rudman noted that their phones were ringing
off the hook with calls from journalists and others (Fritz 2001; McPhee
2001).

The influential members of Congress also showed new interest in the
report, particularly its recommendation to establish a homeland security agency. One congressional aide recalled, "The 9/11 attacks gave new
attention and credibility to the Hart-Rudman report based on its prediction that there'd be an attack of mass destruction or mass disruption."[29]
On September 21, Senate Governmental Affairs Committee Chairman
Joseph Lieberman held a hearing on whether the government was ade-
quately organized to address threats within the United States.[30] The first
witnesses were Hart and Rudman, who presented the commission's case
for forming a new agency. In response to their testimony, Lieberman said
he was inclined to agree with them that creating a White House coordinator for homeland security, as the Bush administration had just announced
it would do, was insufficient: "If you want to get a job done, there's no
substitute for having an organization with a budget in line, as opposed
to advisory authority, because in such a context, real people are responsible and accountable for making decisions and taking the necessary and
appropriate action."[31]

The hearing persuaded Lieberman to draft a bill based on the commission's proposal, and his staff worked with Thornberry's staff, as well
as Hart, Rudman, and Boyd, in crafting the measure. On October 11,
Lieberman introduced the bill, which mirrored the commission's

[29] Interview of congressional staff member, October 2008.
[30] Hearing of the Senate Governmental Affairs Committee, September 21, 2001.
[31] *Ibid.*

recommendation (and the Thornberry bill) almost entirely.[32] It mandated the formation of a cabinet-level department of national homeland security incorporating the same agencies and offices, and organized around the same three functional directorates, as the commission's recommendation. The only significant difference between the Lieberman bill and the commission's proposal was that the bill called the new entity a department, rather than an agency, and called its head a cabinet secretary, instead of a cabinet-level director. On the Senate floor, Lieberman said his bill was "based largely on the [Hart-Rudman] Commission's recommendation."[33]

In the meantime, on October 8, President Bush had established by executive order the White House Office of Homeland Security to coordinate domestic security efforts, and had appointed Tom Ridge as head of the office.[34] Four days after the release of this executive order and one day after introducing his bill, Lieberman held a second hearing on options for responding to terrorist threats. At the hearing, Lieberman restated his concern that Ridge would not be effective because he lacked sufficient authority over the agencies he was meant to oversee, and Lee Hamilton and Charles Boyd testified in support of Lieberman's bill.[35] But Lieberman's measure was not the only bill considered at the hearing. Senator Bob Graham (D-FL) described a measure he had introduced with Senator Dianne Feinstein (D-CA) that embodied the White House czar model promoted by Representative Skelton in the House.[36] This bill made the White House homeland security director subject to Senate confirmation and gave that official the authority to certify whether agencies' budgets were consistent with the government's homeland security strategy. The committee's consideration of these competing proposals revealed that a focal point for the legislative debate had still not been established. Most senators attending the hearing did not indicate whether they favored one measure over the other.

At the same time, some Republican senators argued that Congress should let Ridge's office operate for a while before judging it or pursuing an institutional overhaul.[37] Their comments revealed the preemptive effect

---

[32] The bill was S. 1534.

[33] Comments by Joseph Lieberman on the Senate floor, October 11, 2001.

[34] Executive Order 13228, issued October 8, 2001.

[35] Hearing of the Senate Governmental Affairs Committee, October 12, 2001.

[36] Comments by Bob Graham, hearing of the Senate Governmental Affairs Committee, October 12, 2001. The Graham-Feinstein bill was S. 1449.

[37] Comments by Robert Bennett and George Voinovich, hearing of the Senate Governmental Affairs Committee, October 12, 2001.

of Bush's decision to form a White House office: It reduced Congress' inclination to push for reorganization (Lewis 2003, 77–78). In fact, the White House lobbied members of Congress directly to discourage them from pursuing legislative change, asking for time to show that Ridge's position could work (Koffler 2001).

By the new year, however, many observers concluded that Ridge was not coordinating homeland security policy effectively. A February 2002 *New York Times* article began, "Four months into his tenure as director of homeland security, Tom Ridge is facing significant doubts about his authority and ability to do his job" (Brinkley and Shenon 2002). In addition, influential members of Congress from both parties became increasingly frustrated by the Bush administration's refusal to allow Ridge to testify before Congress (Mitchell 2002b).

With congressional discontent growing, Lieberman held a new hearing on homeland security organization on April 11, 2002, at which he reiterated his concern that Ridge lacked "the necessary authority to overcome the bureaucratic obstacles that always get in the way of major change."[38] Lieberman also announced at the hearing that he intended to reintroduce his bill in a modified form that would include Senator Graham's proposal to establish a White House position resembling a czar. Lieberman stated he was making this revision because a strong White House coordinator would be needed to oversee the homeland security activities of agencies that would not be folded into the new department. He also probably made the change to gain Graham's support for his bill.[39]

This revised measure was introduced by Lieberman on May 2 and was approved by the Governmental Affairs Committee on May 22 by a 9–7 vote along party lines.[40] With the Democrats controlling the Senate, this vote signaled that the bill would probably have enough support to win Senate approval, particularly because one Republican – Senator Arlen Specter (R-PA) – was an original cosponsor of it.[41] In the House, Thornberry introduced the same revised bill on May 2 and gained thirty-five cosponsors of it by the end of May, including thirteen Republicans – a level of bipartisan support that suggested the bill might also be approved in that chamber if the House Republican leadership allowed it to come up

---

[38] Comments by Joseph Lieberman, hearing of the Senate Governmental Affairs Committee, April 11, 2002.
[39] Interview of senior congressional aide, March 2009.
[40] The bill was S. 2452.
[41] Interview of senior congressional aide, March 2009.

for a vote.[42] The extent of the bill's support showed that it had become, after incorporating the Graham provision, the focal point for debate on homeland security reorganization.

Bush's About-Face and the Enactment of Reform

As congressional approval of the bill became more likely, the Bush administration made a remarkable about-face and thereby regained the initiative on counterterrorism policy going into the 2002 elections. On June 6, President Bush unveiled his own proposal to establish a department of homeland security. This proposal dramatically reversed the administration's previous opposition to the idea of forming a new department, which had been stated repeatedly by the White House press secretary between October 2001 and March 2002 (Cohen, Cuellar, and Weingast 2006, 685). Then–White House counterterrorism advisor Richard Clarke, who opposed forming a new department, asserts that the reversal was motivated by the goal of preempting passage of Lieberman's bill:

The White House legislative affairs office began to take a head count on Capitol Hill. The Lieberman Bill would pass both houses, creating two disasters for President Bush: first, an unmanageable new department created just at the time its agencies and staff needed to be working on increasing domestic security, and second, the major new piece of legislation in response to September 11 would be named after the man whom the majority of voters had wanted to be Vice President just twenty months earlier. For the political analysts in the Bush White House, it was better to have one of those two outcomes than both. Thus, President Bush completely changed his position and announced the urgent need for the Lieberman Bill, except he did not call it that. He called it the Homeland Security Act. (Clarke 2004, 250)

Clarke is generally a harsh critic of the Bush administration, but other informed observers also concluded that the administration's decision was motivated by a desire to get out in front of the Lieberman bill. A senior Bush administration official involved in the issue said, "The White House concluded that an agency was coming their way, and that it would be better if the administration designed it, rather than being peripheral [to the debate]."[43] Similarly, Larry Halloran, staff director of the government reform subcommittee that considered the House version of the bill, commented, "They [the Bush administration] saw the inevitability of

[42] In the House, the bill was H.R. 4660.
[43] Interview of senior Bush administration official, May 2009.

something happening in Congress, and they decided it was better to control the game than to be beaten by it."[44]

Indeed, momentum was building on Capitol Hill on behalf of the Lieberman bill in the spring of 2002, not only because of dissatisfaction with Ridge's performance, but also because of a drumbeat of startling revelations of government lapses in the months leading up to 9/11. A *Washington Post* article noted: "New details hit the news almost daily of failure to anticipate the Sept. 11 attacks. This had two effects: it raised the pressure for a serious response and it built support for Lieberman's bill, leading to fears in the White House that he would preempt the administration" (Von Drehle and Allen 2002). The timing of internal administration deliberations on reorganization provides additional evidence that they were heavily influenced by the threat presented by Lieberman's bill. President Bush had first ordered a group of advisers to consider reorganization options on April 23 – shortly after the April hearing where Lieberman announced his intention to reintroduce his bill (Relyea 2003, 617).

Bush's reorganization proposal differed significantly from Lieberman's, encompassing more agencies and offices. Most notably, Bush's proposal transferred the entire Immigration and Naturalization Service and the Transportation Security Administration to the proposed new department, whereas Lieberman's bill did not.[45] The Republican leadership of the House introduced a measure based directly on Bush's proposal on June 24, which was approved by the chamber on July 26 by a vote of 295–132.[46] In the Democratic-controlled Senate, Lieberman's bill remained the legislative vehicle for reorganization, and tortuous negotiations over it dragged on through the summer, until they bogged down because of a partisan dispute over whether the new department's employees should have civil-service protections (Relyea 2003, 621–622).

This dispute was only resolved after the November 2002 elections, in which the Republicans gained control of the Senate in part by arguing that Democrats were blocking the department's establishment because of their fidelity to labor unions. In the wake of this Republican victory, the outgoing Democratic leadership of the Senate gave up the fight

---

[44] Interview of Larry Halloran, March 24, 2009.
[45] Dara Cohen, Mariano-Florentino Cuellar, and Barry Weingast argue that Bush pushed for a larger reorganization to force other agencies to take on homeland security responsibilities without giving them extra funding, thereby draining resources from their other programs (Cohen, Cuellar, and Weingast 2006, 678).
[46] The bill was H.R. 5005.

and brought the House's version of the legislation to the floor, where it was approved on November 19 by a vote of ninety to nine. Six days later, President Bush signed the legislation, creating the Department of Homeland Security largely as outlined in his June proposal.[47] In a matter of six months, Bush had successfully moved from defense to offense on homeland security, winning political rewards and the policy debate over the department's design.

Assessing the Commission's Impact

Although the structure of DHS differs from that of the Hart-Rudman Commission's proposal, the sequence of events strongly suggests that the department might not have been formed without the commission's recommendation. Before the commission reported, no member of Congress had introduced a measure of any kind to create a domestic security agency. If the commission had not recommended establishing a homeland security agency, Thornberry would probably not have introduced a reorganization bill, and Lieberman, in the powerful position of Senate Governmental Affairs Committee chairman, might have advanced a different approach after 9/11.[48] Further, without the threat of Lieberman's bill achieving congressional passage, the administration would probably not have issued its own reorganization proposal.[49] One congressional aide involved in the legislative process on the issue said simply, "If the commission hadn't existed, the Department [of Homeland Security] wouldn't exist."[50]

The commission's significant influence on the establishment of DHS was made possible by the 9/11 attack, which created a window of opportunity for reform. As a Bush administration official commented about the formation of DHS, "Changes like this in government require a huge catalyst."[51] Yet the disaster alone did not force large-scale reorganization. The Bush administration remained opposed to a government overhaul in the months after 9/11, and Congress did not quickly reach consensus on a reorganization plan. The commission's recommendation for a homeland security agency was important because it helped Lieberman and Thornberry construct a focal point for the congressional debate, thereby pressuring the Bush administration to change its position.

---

[47] The Homeland Security Act, Public Law 107–296, enacted on November 25, 2002.
[48] Interview of Mac Thornberry, April 3, 2009; interview of senior congressional aide, March 2009.
[49] Interview of senior Bush administration official, May 2009.
[50] Interview of congressional aide, October 2008.
[51] Interview of Bush administration official, September 2008.

The commission's impact on the creation of DHS challenges my hypothesis that panels are less likely to influence policy when their scope is relatively broad. In Chapter 2, I argue that a broad mandate makes it harder for a commission to achieve unanimity and promote its proposals effectively. There are four reasons why the commission overcame these disadvantages. First, the panel reached consensus despite its very broad scope. Second, the commission highlighted – both in its report and in its public advocacy – a single primary recommendation: the proposal to establish a homeland security agency. This emphasis on a single proposal meant that the commission's other forty-nine recommendations were largely ignored, but it helped bring the principal recommendation to the attention of Thornberry, Lieberman, and other legislators.

Third, the 9/11 attack was of such great magnitude that it created an especially large window of opportunity for reform, enabling Lieberman and Thornberry to gain substantial congressional support for their bills despite the threat they posed to powerful committees and bureaucracies. Fourth, Lieberman had the power to move his bill through the legislative process because of his position as chairman of the committee primarily responsible for government reorganization. Without Lieberman's backing, the proposal would have had little chance of being approved by Congress.

The final ingredient of the commission's influence was its political credibility. This credibility derived from the commission's independence, stature, and ideological diversity, and was enhanced by its unanimity. The ability of the panel's seven Republicans and seven Democrats to reach consensus sent a powerful signal to policy makers that the commission's proposals were ones that members of both parties could support. In addition, it was important that both commission cochairs were widely respected on both sides of the aisle.[52] The commission's bipartisan appeal was reflected in the fact that Thornberry, a conservative Republican, introduced the first bill based on its homeland security agency proposal, yet he and Lieberman ultimately gained more Democratic than Republican cosponsors for their bills.

In fact, Thornberry explained that he found the commission's report compelling because of the panel's stature, political diversity, and unanimity. At an April 2001 hearing in the House, he noted, "[The] Commission

---

[52] Comments by John Sununu, hearing of the House Budget Committee, March 15, 2001; comments by Dianne Feinstein, hearing of the Senate Judiciary Subcommittee on Technology, Terrorism, and Government Information, April 3, 2001.

was unique in the exceptional background, experience – and I would say gravitas – of its members. Their political philosophies ranged from the left to the right. But they unanimously agreed on the nature of the threats we face and on a lack of adequate preparation, and most amazingly, they agreed on what we should do."[53] In an interview, Thornberry elaborated on the commission's appeal:

> You have this ready-to-go idea, backed by very well respected people on both sides of the aisle. That made it easier for people to cosponsor or push it, rather than having to formulate a proposal from scratch when the crisis hit. Having Rudman, Hamilton, and everyone else on the commission who were real heavy-weights gave credibility to the idea and made the advocacy easier.[54]

Whereas the commission's political credibility distinguished it from permanent government institutions – none of which possesses the same combination of independence, bipartisanship, and stature – there is less evidence that the panel influenced the establishment of DHS because it possessed distinctive expertise. One of the alternative hypotheses investigated in this book asserts that commissions tend to be more influential when they possess greater expertise. By contrast, my own expectation is that a panel's expertise is less important than its political credibility because policy makers can obtain expertise from many other sources.

Indeed, the Hart-Rudman Commission did not possess more expertise than existing government agencies. The panel's staff of twenty-nine people included at most a few experts on each of the national security agencies that the commission examined. Those agencies – from the State and Defense Departments to the National Security Council, CIA, and FEMA – therefore possessed far more expertise on their own management and operations than did the commission. Nor did the commission possess more expertise on each of these agencies than the congressional committees that oversee them.

However, expertise – or the perception of it – was very important in one respect: The fact that the commission predicted that there would be a catastrophic terrorist attack on American soil made it seem particularly intelligent. In the end, it was this combination of prescience and the commission's political credibility that made its homeland security

---

[53] Joint hearing of the House Transportation and Infrastructure Subcommittee on Economic Development, Public Buildings, and Emergency Management, and the House Government Reform Subcommittee on National Security, Veterans Affairs, and International Relations, April 24, 2001.

[54] Interview of Mac Thornberry, April 3, 2009.

agency proposal so politically appealing after 9/11. As one congressional aide recalled: "The fact that the commission had prophesied that something [like 9/11] would happen and had a proposal at the ready resonated because there was a lot of confusion about how to respond to 9/11. Here was this very well respected bipartisan group of people that seemed awfully wise, and they were being interviewed on TV shows and quoted in the press.... Having the template [for reorganization] drawn up with the moral authority of the commission gave it tremendous credibility."[55]

The 9/11 Commission and Intelligence Reform

On November 27, 2002, just two days after President Bush signed into law the Homeland Security Act creating DHS, he signed a separate measure establishing the 9/11 Commission. The circumstances surrounding the commission's authorization suggested the panel was unlikely to be effective in influencing policy:

- Its establishment had been opposed by the Bush administration for over a year, raising doubts about whether the administration would cooperate with it.
- Its members were to be named by Republican and Democratic leaders with incentives to appoint partisan loyalists – a recipe for commission disunity.
- Its charge to investigate the 9/11 attack threatened to embroil the commission in disputes over Clinton and Bush administration errors prior to the attack.
- Its mandate to propose measures to prevent terrorism was relatively broad, further complicating the achievement of unanimity.
- Its final report was not due until May 2004, when the window of opportunity for post-9/11 reforms might no longer be open and the pressures of a presidential election campaign could further politicize the report.

As Michael Bayer, who was not involved in the panel but served as counselor to the Lockerbie Commission (discussed in Chapter 4), commented, "The 9/11 Commission had every impossible condition at the outset setting it up to fail."[56]

---

[55] Interview of congressional aide, October 2008.
[56] Interview of Michael Bayer, November 20, 2007.

Yet the commission sparked the biggest intelligence overhaul since 1947 and prompted numerous other reforms in counterterrorism policy. This very large impact was primarily due to three important factors that enabled the commission to overcome the long odds that it initially faced: (1) the huge scale of the 9/11 attack, which extended the window of opportunity for reform; (2) the unanimity of the commission's report; and (3) the innovative and persistent advocacy campaign waged by the commission and the relatives of 9/11 victims (the "9/11 families").

The Joint Inquiry and the Commission's Creation

The 9/11 Commission was not the first high-profile investigation of the 9/11 disaster. In February 2002, the House and Senate intelligence committees began a joint probe of the U.S. intelligence community's activities related to the attack. This investigation, called the Joint Inquiry, was conducted by all thirty-seven members of the two congressional committees, supported by a staff of twenty-four people hired just for the probe.[57] (Because the Joint Inquiry's members were all government officials, I do not consider it to be a commission.)

The Joint Inquiry held nine hearings and uncovered many government mistakes before 9/11, such as the CIA's failure to share information with the FBI about Al Qaeda operatives who entered the United States, and the FBI's failure to respond to warnings by one of its agents that terrorists might be training at American flight schools. The inquiry's 858-page report, released in a classified form on December 10, 2002 and in an unclassified version on July 24, 2003, recounted these lapses and offered nineteen recommendations for intelligence reforms. Its principal proposal was to establish a director of national intelligence (DNI) with full budgetary and personnel powers to manage all fifteen intelligence agencies (Joint Inquiry 2002, Recommendations).

But media coverage of the Joint Inquiry report focused on the Bush administration's refusal to declassify a section on Saudi Arabia and on a 137-page minority opinion by Senator Richard Shelby (R-AL) (Priest and Schmidt 2002; Risen 2002). Shelby's blistering dissent, which was excerpted in the *New York Times*, argued that the report should have held six senior intelligence officials, whom Shelby named, personally accountable for their agencies' failures (Joint Inquiry 2002, Additional Views). The report also included seven other minority statements, totaling

---

[57] The probe was formally called the Joint Inquiry into Intelligence Community Activities before and after the Terrorist Attacks of September 11, 2001.

fifty-six pages. Some of these statements, such as those by Senators Mike DeWine (R-OH), Jon Kyl (R-AZ), and Pat Roberts (R-KS), were sharply critical of the majority report and argued against establishing a DNI. Kyl and Roberts even slammed the way the inquiry was conducted, complaining that the inquiry's leaders and staff frequently withheld information from other inquiry members and did not allow time to debate the report. They concluded, "These inadequacies in the process resulted in a Report that falls well short of addressing the core problems that led to 9/11" (Joint Inquiry 2002, Additional Views).

Although the Joint Inquiry report added greatly to the public record of the events leading up to 9/11, its influence on policy was quite small (Zegart 2007, 175). The Bush administration opposed the DNI proposal, making its approval by a Republican-led Congress highly unlikely (Fessenden 2005, 107). Senator Feinstein introduced a bill to establish a DNI in January 2003, but she obtained no cosponsors of the bill until June 2004, when the release of the 9/11 Commission report was imminent.[58] In the House, nobody introduced a similar bill before April 2004.

The inquiry's minimal impact on policy stemmed primarily from its disunity and the partisan approach of some of its members. From the beginning of the inquiry's work, many members, according to a journalist's account, were "looking for headlines and scapegoats in either the Bush or Clinton administration" (Davies 2002). The scathing dissents by Shelby, Kyl, and Roberts were cases in point. The partisan loyalty of some Republican members to the Bush administration also prevented the inquiry from pressing the White House in a united fashion for access to key witnesses and documents that were withheld by the administration, thereby reducing its credibility in the eyes of many observers (Mitchell 2002a). The lack of genuine deliberation among the members – a result of the very large size of the group (thirty-seven members) and the many other demands on the members' time – contributed to the inquiry's inability to bridge congressional divides.[59] These shortcomings reveal a general limitation in the ability of congressional probes to conduct politically credible investigations and overcome partisanship.

The Joint Inquiry's deficiencies were part of the reason why other members of Congress sought to establish an independent commission to investigate the 9/11 attack. The formation of an independent commission

---

[58] The bill was S. 190.
[59] Interview of Daniel Byman, October 1, 2008; interview of Michael Jacobson, March 26, 2009.

was suggested as early as September 12, 2001 by Senator Robert Torricelli (D-NJ), and Representative Nancy Pelosi (D-CA) introduced the first legislative proposal to create a commission on September 26.[60] That proposal failed to gain approval, but Senators Lieberman and John McCain (R-AZ) introduced a similar measure in the Senate on December 20.[61] In promoting it, McCain argued that independence and nonpartisanship were essential ingredients to a credible probe. On the Senate floor, he said, "Neither the administration nor Congress is alone capable of conducting a thorough nonpartisan independent inquiry into what happened on September 11."[62] In a *Washington Post* op-ed, he emphasized the need to form "an independent commission of trustworthy, experienced statesmen who, if not entirely devoid of partisan loyalties, are sufficiently removed by time and wisdom from the appeal of such loyalties to know when they conflict with the national interest" (McCain 2002).

The Lieberman-McCain bill was approved unanimously by the Senate Governmental Affairs Committee on March 21, 2002. The committee's report on the bill stated that, compared to a congressional investigation, a commission would be more independent, less subject to partisan pressures, and better able to probe comprehensively issues that span many agencies and committees.[63] In May 2002, Representative Timothy Roemer (D-IN) introduced a similar bill in the House, and the measures were approved by the full House and Senate in July and August.[64] But the commission's prospects for being established remained clouded that summer by the Bush administration's opposition to the legislation. The White House publicly claimed that a commission would interfere with the government's counterterrorism efforts, but privately feared that a panel might charge the Bush administration with acting negligently before 9/11 (Shenon 2008, 25).

Ultimately, though, public advocacy on behalf of the legislation by the 9/11 families made it difficult politically for the Bush administration to remain opposed to the commission's formation. In the fall of 2002, the administration accepted the premise of forming a commission and negotiated the details of the panel's charter with congressional leaders. In one key compromise, President Bush was given the

[60] Comments by Robert Torricelli on the Senate floor, September 12, 2008. Pelosi's proposal was part of H.R. 2883, a broader intelligence bill.
[61] The measure was S. 1867.
[62] Comments by John McCain on the Senate floor, December 20, 2001.
[63] Senate Report 107–150, issued May 14, 2002.
[64] The House bill was H.R. 4777.

power to appoint the chairman, whereas the Democratic leader of the Senate was given the authority to appoint the vice chairman. The Speaker of the House, House Minority Leader, Senate Majority Leader, and Senate Minority Leader each were charged with appointing two of the commission's other eight members. Bush signed legislation forming the commission on November 27, 2002 – two weeks before the Joint Inquiry reported.[65]

The commission's charter required it to examine and report upon the facts and circumstances surrounding the 9/11 attack, and to recommend measures to prevent acts of terrorism. After their first choices to lead the commission – Henry Kissinger and George Mitchell – withdrew from the panel due to concerns about potential conflicts of interest, Bush and Senate Democratic leader Thomas Daschle (D-SD) named former New Jersey Governor Thomas Kean and Lee Hamilton to the positions of chairman and vice chairman, respectively. The commission's other members included former Watergate prosecutor Richard Ben-Veniste, former White House Counsel Fred Fielding, former Deputy Attorney General Jamie Gorelick, former Senator Slade Gorton (R-WA), former Navy Secretary John Lehman, Timothy Roemer (who was no longer serving in Congress), and former Illinois Governor James Thompson. Former Senator Max Cleland (D-GA) initially served as the tenth commissioner, but was replaced in 2003 by former Senator Bob Kerrey (D-NE). The panel was supported by a large staff of eighty-one people, directed by scholar and former National Security Council official Philip Zelikow.

Reaching Consensus

As the commission began to meet, expectations for its impact were generally low. Philip Shenon, who covered the commission for the *New York Times*, recalls that he did not initially covet the assignment: "It is odd to think of it now, but it was not clear to anyone at the time that the 9/11 commission would be much of a story" (Shenon 2008, 419). It was also reasonable to expect that the commission would fall victim to some of the same partisan pressures that embroiled the Joint Inquiry. In fact, serious tensions did exist within the commission during the first months of its work. The commission's deputy executive director, Christopher Kojm, recalled, "In the early days of the commission there was a lot of partisanship, a lot of suspicion" (Lundberg 2005, 15).

---

[65] This act is Public Law 107–306.

However, the deeply bipartisan leadership style of Kean and Hamilton and the distinct deliberative environment of commissions enabled the panel to grow unified and reach consensus over time. To foster a tone of bipartisanship, Kean decided that he and Hamilton would serve effectively as cochairs, and they agreed to speak to the media only in tandem (Kean and Hamilton 2006, 23–24). At the commission's second meeting, Kean further announced that during the panel's meetings Republicans would not be allowed to sit next to Republicans, and Democrats would not be permitted to sit next to Democrats (Kean and Hamilton 2006, 41). Hamilton and Kean also facilitated a sense of unity early in the commission's work by orchestrating the replacement of Max Cleland, who insisted that the panel investigate the Bush administration's handling of the Iraq War, with Bob Kerrey, a moderate (Shenon 2008, 160–162). One person involved in the commission said starkly, "Consensus wouldn't have been possible if Cleland didn't leave the commission."[66]

Over time, new friendships formed across party lines and partisan tensions diminished. A commission staff member noted that "commissioners learned to be less skeptical of each other's motivations."[67] Slade Gorton commented that eventually "the associations inside the group became more important than those outside" (Lundberg 2005, 53). This growing unity was put to the test when Attorney General John Ashcroft sharply criticized Jamie Gorelick at a commission hearing in April 2004, charging that she had been responsible for failed Clinton administration counterterrorism policies. Following Ashcroft's testimony, some Republican House members and editorial writers called on Gorelick to resign from the commission. But commissioners from both parties, and especially the panel's Republicans, passionately came to Gorelick's defense (Shenon 2008, 337).

Still, reaching consensus on many issues, from the use of subpoenas to report wording, was difficult. As the commission began debating recommendations, it was divided on whether to propose the establishment of a national intelligence director, as the Joint Inquiry had done. Hamilton and Roemer had publicly endorsed the idea before serving on the commission, but other commissioners, including Gorton and John Lehman, were skeptical of it.[68] Lehman said, "When I came on to the commission,

---

[66] Interview, January 2008.
[67] Interview of commission staff member, September 2008.
[68] Interview of commission staff member, January 2008. Hamilton had endorsed the idea in testimony before the Joint Inquiry on October 3, 2002. Roemer had endorsed the idea in his minority statement appended to the Joint Inquiry report.

I was totally opposed to it and thought the DNI would just become another layer of bureaucracy."[69] However, the commissioners eventually coalesced around the idea. Hamilton remembered, "We had a lot of debate and discussion on it, and what led us to it was that the only way you get sharing of information is if you have someone at the top of the [intelligence] community who enforces it."[70] Gorelick added, "You couldn't have listened to the story that we heard over 18 to 20 months and thought the intelligence community should have remained structured the same way."[71]

Even as consensus emerged on the DNI proposal, several commissioners planned until the commission's final deliberations to write dissenting statements on issues of concern to them (Lundberg 2005, 62). Avoiding that outcome required many hours of discussions and numerous compromises. Kean and Hamilton write, "How did we reach a unanimous result? We talked. And talked. And then talked some more..." (Kean and Hamilton 2006, 321). Similarly, Lehman recalled, "We got to consensus through the rigor of dialogue. It was a bottom-up, not a top-down, consensus."[72] This dialogue was smoothed by the nonpartisan approach of Hamilton and Kean and by the close personal ties that had formed among the commissioners. Gorton observed that he and other commissioners ultimately decided not to write minority opinions out of "this immense feeling of satisfaction and respect for one another after a year and a half" (Lundberg 2005, 62). These comments show how the distinct environment of commissions, which facilitates lengthy private conversations and compromises, can foster unanimity among people who would not otherwise agree.

Self-interest played a role also. Shenon writes of the commissioners, "By the end of the investigation, they knew that their own legacies were tied up in the commission and its final report.... Unanimity would cement their place in history" (Shenon 2008, 402). Recognizing this, commissioners resisted the temptation to try to use the report to cast blame principally on the Clinton or Bush administration. Their collective compromise in refraining from singling out one administration for criticism was an essential ingredient of unanimity.[73]

[69] Interview of John Lehman, February 27, 2008.
[70] Interview of Lee Hamilton, January 24, 2008.
[71] Interview of Jamie Gorelick, May 7, 2008.
[72] Interview of John Lehman, February 27, 2008.
[73] Interview of Philip Zelikow, October 22, 2007.

The Commission's Report

The commission's 567-page report, released on July 22, 2004 – twenty months after its establishment – was written in a gripping yet dispassionate style that garnered widespread praise (National Commission on Terrorist Attacks upon the United States 2004).[74] In one especially enthusiastic comment, John Updike wrote in the *New Yorker* that the King James Bible was "our language's lone masterpiece produced by committee, at least until this year's '9/11 Commission Report'" (Updike 2004).

After telling the story of 9/11 and the events leading up to it – highlighting a number of missed opportunities for countering Al Qaeda – the report drew conclusions and presented forty-one recommendations. The conclusions described four kinds of failures – of imagination, policy, capabilities, and management – that blocked the U.S. government from preventing the 9/11 attack. The recommendations spanned foreign policy, homeland security, management of the intelligence community, and the protection of civil liberties.

Media coverage focused heavily on the proposal to establish a national intelligence director to manage the national intelligence program and oversee the government's fifteen intelligence agencies. Other key recommendations included:

- Forming a national counterterrorism center (NCTC) that would conduct joint operational planning and joint intelligence activities related to counterterrorism
- Declassifying the overall budget of intelligence agencies
- Reforming congressional oversight by creating standing homeland security committees and reorganizing intelligence committees
- Distributing federal homeland security grants based strictly on an assessment of risks and vulnerabilities (rather than as pork-barrel spending)
- Establishing a board within the executive branch to monitor the protection of civil liberties
- Conveying a positive vision of America's ideals to the Muslim world

Pressure for Reform Builds

The report, which was presented by Hamilton and Kean to President Bush on national television and put on sale in bookstores on the same day by

---

[74] The report was a finalist for the 2004 National Book Award in nonfiction – surely a first for a government-sponsored publication. Another sure first occurred in 2006 when two illustrators published an adaptation of the commission's report as a graphic novel (Jacobson and Colon 2006).

a private publisher, immediately topped best-seller lists and became the focal point of national politics. Democratic presidential candidate John Kerry called right away for implementation of the commission's recommendations (Nagourney 2004). Congressional leaders announced plans to hold hearings on the report in August, when Congress would otherwise have been in recess (Eggen and Dewar 2004).

This remarkable immediate reaction reflected the fact that the 9/11 Commission had already established a strong public following and substantial political credibility by the time it reported. Between March 2003 and June 2004, it had held twelve public hearings, and some of these, such as those featuring testimony by Richard Clarke and Condoleezza Rice, had received very heavy media coverage. In addition, the commission had issued seventeen interim staff reports on aspects of the panel's investigation, which were written in a politically neutral style and read aloud by the staff at the beginning of commission hearings. These hearings and interim reports had built the commission's credibility as an impartial and authoritative body (Drew 2004). The strength of its growing political clout had been demonstrated before it reported by its success in convincing a reluctant Bush administration to give the commission access to key documents and witnesses that the administration had withheld from the Joint Inquiry.

Public interest in intelligence issues had also been elevated by the release two weeks before the 9/11 Commission reported of a separate study by the Senate Intelligence Committee on errors in intelligence assessments of Iraqi weapons of mass destruction programs before the Iraq War. The Senate Intelligence Committee report charged that many of the U.S. intelligence community's prewar judgments were "either overstated, or were not supported by, the underlying intelligence reporting" (United States Senate Select Committee on Intelligence 2004). But that report did not include policy recommendations and did not discuss the notion of creating a DNI – an idea that some Senate Intelligence Committee members, including Chairman Pat Roberts (R-KS), opposed.

Indeed, the conventional wisdom when the 9/11 Commission reported was that the prospects for adopting its national intelligence director proposal were poor. A *New York Times* article stated, "The partisan wrangling of a presidential election and the capital's entrenched resistance to change make swift action unlikely.... The Pentagon and the C.I.A., Secretary of Homeland Security Tom Ridge and some in Congress already oppose the commission's call for a new national intelligence director" (Purdum 2004). The congressional opponents of the DNI idea included not just Roberts, but other powerful, turf-conscious committee chairmen, particularly House and Senate Armed Services Committee Chairmen Duncan Hunter (R-CA) and John Warner (R-VA). Seeing this political landscape, a *Washington Post* article bluntly described the odds of establishing a DNI: "Ain't gonna happen" (Milbank 2004).

But the commission's strong public support gave Congress and the Bush administration a strong incentive to act on the panel's proposals. An opinion poll conducted by Pew just before the commission reported found that Americans approved of the panel's work by a margin of 61 percent to 24 percent, with nearly identical levels of support among Democrats, Republicans, and independents (Pew Research Center for the People & the Press 2004). A separate poll by FOX News, conducted ten days after the commission reported, found that 52 percent of Americans thought the 9/11 attack would have been prevented if the government had possessed a national intelligence director, implying that at least that proportion of Americans favored the panel's recommendation (Blanton 2004). This public support was reflected in media editorial opinion. During the ninety days following publication of the commission's report, the *Chicago Tribune, New York Times, Wall Street Journal,* and *Washington Post* – a sample of four ideologically diverse newspapers – ran sixty-one editorials and op-eds endorsing some or all of the commission's recommendations, and just ten columns criticizing some or all of the panel's proposals.

The heat of the presidential campaign placed added pressure on President Bush to endorse the commission's recommendations. In the weeks after the commission reported, John Kerry signaled that he intended to make his call to implement the proposals a major campaign message (VandeHei 2004). Kerry's national security advisor Rand Beers explained, "We were looking for a way to differentiate John Kerry from George Bush. It was an opportunity to remind Americans that there was a failure of focus at the beginning of the Bush administration. The idea was to seize the commission report and force Bush to say, 'Me too,' or to have to differentiate himself from the report."[75] By using the commission's report in this way, former Bush administration counterterrorism official Richard Falkenrath argues, Kerry and other Democrats threatened to erode Bush's political advantage on national security issues: "The 9/11 commission broke President Bush's monopoly on the political windfall generated by the September 11 attacks. No other entity in post-9/11 American life was capable of mounting a

---

[75] Interview of Rand Beers, October 16, 2008.

credible challenge to the president's leadership in the war on terror, including the U.S. Congress" (Falkenrath 2004/05, 190).

Another Bush Reversal

In response to this political pressure, Bush announced on August 2 that he supported the establishment of a DNI, and would act through his own authority to create a national counterterrorism center to coordinate the government's counterterrorism activities.[76] His endorsement of the commission's DNI proposal was only partial, though, because his statement did not call for granting the DNI authority over intelligence agency budgets, as the panel recommended. The NCTC he established was also more limited than that envisioned by the commission: Its mission did not include the planning of counterterrorism operations. Five weeks later, on September 8, Bush modified his DNI position to conform more closely to the commission's recommendation, stating that he now supported giving a DNI "full budgetary authority" (Bumiller and Shenon 2004).

These announcements by Bush represented a striking turnaround for a president who had opposed creating a DNI until the 9/11 Commission reported. Bush administration officials attributed the change, which was opposed by the heads of the CIA and the Defense and Homeland Security Departments, primarily to the pressure from the commission and Kerry. Richard Falkenrath, who served in the Bush White House until May 2004, observed, "Bush wasn't going to allow Kerry to have a talking point saying that Kerry was for implementation of the 9/11 Commission recommendations and Bush was not."[77] Then–Acting Director of Central Intelligence John McLaughlin commented similarly, "The White House felt defensive because Kerry endorsed all of the recommendations."[78] Another Bush administration official added, "Political pressure led the president to agree to the DNI."[79] This outcome vindicated an argument that Kean had made within the commission that reporting during the presidential campaign would set off a bidding war between Republicans and Democrats to embrace the panel's proposals (Kean and Hamilton 2006, 145).

Congress Acts

As the Bush administration's position evolved, attention shifted to Congress, where at least twenty-seven committee hearings were held on

---

[76] Remarks by George W. Bush on intelligence reform, August 2, 2004.
[77] Interview of Richard Falkenrath, July 14, 2008.
[78] Interview of John McLaughlin, April 3, 2008.
[79] Interview of Bush administration official, May 2008.

the commission's report in August and September. One congressional aide recalled the atmosphere on Capitol Hill: "People were carrying the commission report around, tabbing it, and drawing up legislation literally based on sentences of the report. It was like they were walking around with bibles."[80] In the Senate, Majority Leader Bill Frist (R-TN) assigned jurisdiction for drafting implementing legislation to the Governmental Affairs Committee, whose chair and ranking member were Senator Susan Collins (R-ME) and Lieberman, respectively.[81] To assist them in writing the legislation, Collins and Lieberman hired three aides who had served as commission staff members. In the House, the office of Speaker Dennis Hastert (R-IL) took charge of the drafting process.

Collins and Lieberman introduced their bill, which included most of the commission's proposals – including the DNI recommendation – on September 23, and it was approved by the Senate on October 6.[82] Two days later, the House approved a bill introduced by Hastert, which differed in a number of respects from the Senate bill, including in granting weaker budgetary and personnel powers to the DNI.[83] A House-Senate conference committee then reconciled the bills during two months of contentious negotiations. On the DNI provision, a compromise gave the DNI the authority to develop intelligence agency budgets and direct their allocation, as well as the power to concur in the nominations of agency heads and to transfer some personnel and funds from one agency to another. On December 7, the House approved the legislation, called the Intelligence Reform and Terrorism Prevention Act of 2004 (the Intelligence Reform Act), by a vote of 336–75. The Senate approved it the next day by a vote of 89–2. President Bush signed the legislation into law on December 17 – less than five months after the 9/11 Commission reported.[84]

In addition to establishing the DNI post, the Intelligence Reform Act adopted many other commission recommendations. These reforms included:

- Creating the National Counterterrorism Center to integrate intelligence on terrorism and conduct strategic operational planning for

---

[80] Interview of congressional aide, July 2008.
[81] Lieberman and John McCain initially worked together to draft legislation to implement the commission's recommendations, but their bill was folded into the Collins-Lieberman legislation in September. The Lieberman-McCain bill was S. 2774.
[82] The bill was S. 2845.
[83] The bill was H.R. 10.
[84] The act is Public Law 108–458.

counterterrorism activities (these missions matched the commission's proposal more closely than Bush's August announcement did)

- Forming the Privacy and Civil Liberties Oversight Board within the executive branch to ensure that privacy and civil liberties concerns are appropriately considered in the development and implementation of laws and regulations
- Mandating new requirements for sharing information among agencies
- Establishing new procedures for expediting the appointment of national security officials during presidential transitions

In interviews and public comments, numerous officials involved in the enactment of the Intelligence Reform Act agreed that it was prompted by the 9/11 Commission. One Senate staffer commented, "The legislation would never have been introduced, much less enacted, had it not been for the commission report."[85] Another congressional aide noted that the legislation's drafting and enactment "was entirely driven by the report."[86] A third staffer asserted, "Without the commission there probably would've been some effort in Congress to make changes, but they wouldn't have been nearly as cataclysmic or seismic, and they wouldn't have been in the same direction."[87] Many members of Congress, including Collins and Lieberman, also publicly identified the commission as the catalyst for the legislation.[88]

Indeed, before the commission report's publication became imminent in June 2004, Senator Feinstein could not obtain a single cosponsor of her bill to establish a DNI.[89] Moreover, key committee leaders with jurisdiction over intelligence agencies, including Senator Roberts and Representative Hunter, shared the Bush administration's opposition to creating a DNI before the commission reported. In the Senate, Majority Leader Frist only gave Collins and Lieberman jurisdiction to advance intelligence reform proposals – and thereby circumvent Roberts' resistance to creating a DNI – because of his desire to enact legislation to implement the 9/11 Commission's proposals.[90]

---

[85] Interview of congressional aide, October 2008.
[86] Interview of congressional aide, July 2008.
[87] Interview of congressional aide, June 2008.
[88] Comments by Senators Susan Collins (R-ME), Kent Conrad (D-ND), Richard Durbin (D-IL), Joseph Lieberman (D-CT), John McCain (R-AZ), Jay Rockefeller (D-WV), and Arlen Specter (R-PA) on the Senate floor, December 8, 2004; comments by Representatives Nancy Pelosi (D-CA) and Sylvester Reyes (D-TX) on the House floor, December 7, 2004.
[89] This bill was S. 190.
[90] Interviews of congressional aides, June 2008, July 2008, and October 2008.

The DNI's establishment was not the only Intelligence Reform Act provision that would probably not have been enacted without the commission. A senior Bush administration official commented, "The White House was under intense political pressure to agree with the commission's recommendations and ultimately did enact a number of recommendations that it otherwise wouldn't have agreed to."[91] One of these reforms was the creation of the Privacy and Civil Liberties Oversight Board.[92] Many congressional and administration officials believe the NCTC also would not have been established at the time if the commission had not proposed it, though an agency like it might have been formed eventually.[93] Bush's initial decision to give the NCTC a mandate that did not include operational planning further suggests that the administration would not have given such a role to a counterterrorism center without the pressure generated by the commission.[94]

A Second Round of Reforms

Although the Intelligence Reform Act adopted many 9/11 Commission proposals, some important panel recommendations were left out of the legislation due to opposition from the Bush administration, special interest groups, or powerful factions within Congress (Paltrow 2005). For instance, the legislation did not adopt the commission's recommendations to mandate public disclosure of the overall intelligence budget, distribute federal antiterrorism grants based solely on assessments of risks and vulnerabilities, or reorganize congressional intelligence committees.

Some of the 9/11 Commission's members and staff maintained public pressure on Congress and the Bush administration to act on the remaining recommendations through the 9/11 Public Discourse Project, a nonprofit organization established with nearly $1 million in private funding raised by the commissioners after the panel completed its work. The project, which was headed by 9/11 Commission Deputy Executive Director Christopher Kojm, helped commissioners prepare congressional testimony and organized speeches and other public events on commission-related issues. In December 2005, nearly a year and a half after the

---

[91] Interview of Bush administration official, May 2008.
[92] Interview of Carolyn Maloney, June 10, 2008; interview of Bush administration official, May 2008.
[93] Interview of John McLaughlin, April 3, 2008; interview of Sheryl Walter, November 16, 2007; interviews of Bush administration officials, March 2008 and May 2008; interviews of congressional aides, June 2008, March 2009, and March 2009.
[94] Interview of Michael Jacobson, March 26, 2009.

release of the 9/11 Commission report, the project issued a final report card on government action with respect to each of the panel's proposals. The publication of the report card, which included many D's and F's, was covered on the front page of many newspapers and sparked renewed political interest in the commission – particularly among Democrats, who saw an opportunity to score political points. House Democratic leader Pelosi commented that the report card was "an indictment of the continued failure by the Bush administration and the Republican Congress to meet the security needs of our nation and make Americans safer" (Epstein 2005).

In 2006, Pelosi continued to press this argument publicly, and announced that if the Democrats gained control of Congress in that year's elections, implementation of all of the 9/11 Commission recommendations would be one of the Democrats' top six legislative priorities (DeBose 2006; Romano 2006). On January 5, 2007, House Democrats acted on this promise by making the Implementing Recommendations of the 9/11 Commission Act the first bill introduced in the 110th Congress.[95] This bill included nearly all of the commission's recommendations that had not been part of the Intelligence Reform Act, as well as other homeland security provisions. It was passed by the House on January 9, and a similar measure was approved by the Senate in early July. After the bills were reconciled in conference negotiations, the Senate passed the legislation by a vote of 85–8, and the House did so by a vote of 371–40. The legislation, commonly known as the 9/11 Commission Implementation Act, was signed into law by President Bush on August 3, 2007.[96]

Among other reforms, this legislation fully or partially adopted commission proposals by cutting in half the proportion of federal antiterrorism grants provided to states without regard to risks and vulnerabilities, declassifying the total amount of the annual intelligence budget, and authorizing the establishment of an International Arab and Muslim Youth Opportunity Fund to support educational programs in predominantly Muslim countries. The legislation also gave new authorities to the Privacy and Civil Liberties Oversight Board that had been created by the Intelligence Reform Act.

House and Senate staffers who were involved in drafting the 9/11 Commission Implementation Act agreed that the Public Discourse Project report card provided some of the spark for it, and that some of the act's

---

[95] The bill was H.R. 1.
[96] This act is Public Law 110–053.

provisions, including the change in the formula for federal antiterrorism grants, would not have been enacted if the commission had not called for those reforms.[97] Even though many Republicans, including President Bush, opposed portions of the legislation, the imprimatur of the 9/11 Commission made it difficult for them to vote against it. One House aide involved in drafting the legislation commented, "The president couldn't veto a bill named after the 9/11 Commission."[98]

With the enactment of the 9/11 Commission Implementation Act, nearly all of the commission's specific proposals were fully or partially adopted. (Some of the panel's recommendations were vague, making it impossible to determine definitively whether they were adopted.) However, the commission's proposals for reorganizing congressional intelligence and homeland security committees remain largely unaddressed. Efforts to advance them have consistently been stymied by the age-old congressional practice of turf protection.[99] As Michael Munson, a senior staff member on two national security commissions, observed, "The hardest institution to change in Washington is Congress."[100]

Why the Commission Was So Influential

Still, in triggering a major reorganization of the intelligence community and the enactment of many other reforms, the 9/11 Commission had greater legislative impact than any other national security panel of recent decades. Its influence was due, in large part, to the magnitude of the 9/11 attack. Even though the commission reported nearly three years after the attack, public interest in its findings was exceptionally high because the public wanted to understand how Al Qaeda was able to kill nearly 3,000 people on American soil, and wanted the government to ensure that such a disaster never happened again. Indeed, Amy Zegart has found that the commission received more television news coverage than the Iraq War

---

[97] Interviews of congressional aides, June 2008, September 2008, and October 2008.

[98] Interview of House aide, September 2008.

[99] Interviews of congressional aides, June 2008, July 2008, and October 2008. The commission proposed reforming congressional intelligence oversight by creating a joint House-Senate intelligence committee or combining authorizing and appropriating authorities in a single committee in each house of Congress. This proposal has not been acted on. The commission also recommended creating a single committee in the House and Senate with exclusive homeland security oversight authority. Although each house does now have a committee with primary responsibility for homeland security, jurisdiction over many homeland security programs is still spread among numerous committees in both the House and Senate.

[100] Interview of Michael Munson, February 18, 2008.

between July and December 2004 (Zegart 2007, 179). Equally remarkably, two million copies of the commission's report were purchased during the eight months that followed its publication (May 2005). This tremendous public interest signaled to policy makers that the American people wanted them to enact the panel's proposals, and the heat of the 2004 election campaign only added to this political pressure.[101] As one Bush administration official commented, "Everyone wanted to be seen as doing something that would fix the problem."[102]

But the magnitude of the 9/11 attack does not sufficiently explain the government's enactment of commission-proposed reforms. The Joint Inquiry had described government lapses related to 9/11 and proposed establishing a DNI in December 2002, yet its recommendations were largely ignored. The commission was able to achieve what the Joint Inquiry could not because of its distinctive political credibility, which derived from its stature, independence, and bipartisanship. Although the Joint Inquiry possessed stature, it was deficient in the other two attributes. The Joint Inquiry was far from independent because the congressional intelligence committees bore some of the responsibility for the government's miscues before 9/11. In addition, the inquiry could not reach consensus, and partisan loyalties prevented it from pressing the Bush administration in a unified manner to provide access to documents and witnesses.

By contrast, the 9/11 Commission bolstered its credibility by gaining access to documents and witnesses, and it sent a powerful signal that its proposals should be acceptable to a broad cross-section of Americans and legislators by issuing a unanimous report. As one senior congressional aide involved in enacting the Intelligence Reform Act commented, "The key to the commission's success was unanimity. You had people from a broad spectrum coming together and producing a compelling report in a unified fashion and speaking with one voice."[103]

---

[101] The July 2004 Senate Intelligence Committee report on prewar intelligence assessments regarding Iraqi weapons of mass destruction programs also contributed to the public pressure to overhaul the intelligence community. However, that report was not likely to spur major reorganization on its own because it did not include recommendations and the committee's chairman, Pat Roberts, opposed the establishment of a DNI. Moreover, the Senate Intelligence Committee report received much less public attention than the 9/11 Commission report. During the ninety days after the publication of each of the two reports, there were 360 articles in the *Chicago Tribune*, *New York Times*, *Wall Street Journal*, and *Washington Post* about the 9/11 Commission report, and just 62 articles in those newspapers about the Senate Intelligence Committee report.

[102] Interview of Bush administration official, March 2008.

[103] Interview of congressional aide, March 2009.

The reactions of legislators to the commission report illustrated that political credibility was the key source of its appeal. Six days after the commission reported, Senate Majority Whip Mitch McConnell (R-KY) commented, "This Commission report has a lot of credibility because it was unanimous; there were no minority views."[104] Similarly, at the first congressional hearing on the report, Senator Richard Durbin (D-IL) said to Hamilton and Kean: "You have done an excellent job, and it is painful to concede, but I must concede, I think you did a better job than a congressional committee could have done. Yours was truly a bipartisan effort."[105] The strength of the commission's political credibility was demonstrated by the fact that even many Republicans who voted against the Intelligence Reform Act said they were doing so because the legislation did not adopt all of the commission's proposals.[106]

There is also strong evidence that political credibility was a more important contributor to the commission's impact than expertise. Kean was a university president and former governor who lacked any background in counterterrorism or intelligence issues. However, he did not view this as a shortcoming: "I conceived of my role as building consensus rather than being an expert."[107] Several other commissioners, including Richard Ben-Veniste, Fred Fielding, and Jim Thompson, also did not have any significant background in counterterrorism or intelligence policy. What these commissioners did possess were stature and ideological diversity, which helped the commission appeal to different political constituencies. Whereas Ben-Veniste was highly regarded by congressional liberals, Fielding and Thompson had close ties to powerful conservatives. A comparison with the Joint Inquiry is again illuminating. The Joint Inquiry's thirty-seven members – all of whom served on the congressional intelligence committees – had much more collective expertise on counterterrorism and intelligence policy than the commission's ten members, yet the inquiry's report was less influential.

[104] Comments by Mitch McConnell, NewsHour with Jim Lehrer, PBS, July 28, 2004. Accessible at http://www.pbs.org/newshour/bb/terrorism/july-dec04/9–11_7–28.html.
[105] Comments by Richard Durbin, hearing of the Senate Governmental Affairs Committee, July 30, 2004.
[106] For instance, see comments by Representatives Virginia Brown-Waite (R-FL), Darrell Issa (R-CA), Gary Miller (R-CA), James Sensenbrenner (R-WI), and Thomas Tancredo (R-CO) on the House floor, December 7, 2004. These representatives argued that the Intelligence Reform Act should have created strict standards for the issuance of driver's licenses and other identification documents that would make it difficult for illegal aliens to obtain the documents. Such standards were later mandated by the Real ID Act of 2005, Public Law 109–13.
[107] Interview of Thomas Kean, June 2, 2007.

There is one respect in which the commission did possess distinctive expertise. The commission's investigation of the 9/11 attack was more comprehensive than that of the Joint Inquiry, thanks to the commission's broader mandate, larger staff, and access to more information. As a result, the commission's members and staff knew more about the attack than any other body by the time the panel reported. This expertise certainly contributed substantially to the commission's influence. However, the Joint Inquiry's members and staff also possessed more expertise about the attack than any other body when the inquiry reported in December 2002, and that expertise was insufficient to spark major reforms. Moreover, the inquiry generated more revelations about pre-9/11 government lapses than did the commission, and many of the commission's findings and recommendations, including the DNI proposal, mirrored those of the inquiry.[108] These facts suggest that the provision of new information was not the principal source of the commission's appeal.

In addition to the commission's political credibility and the magnitude of the 9/11 attack, a third factor contributed greatly to the panel's impact: persistent advocacy by the commission, its follow-on Public Discourse Project, and the 9/11 families. The commission's lobbying effort included numerous private meetings with legislators and administration officials, over two dozen appearances before congressional committees, and some 500 speaking engagements throughout the country by commissioners and panel staff (Kean and Hamilton 2006, 327–328).[109] Senior congressional aides involved in enacting the Intelligence Reform Act agreed that this advocacy campaign helped pass the legislation, noting that Kean and Hamilton repeatedly influenced votes on portions of the act by stating publicly which provisions or amendments the commission supported.[110] Larry Halloran, then–staff director of the House Government Reform Subcommittee on National Security, Veterans

---

[108] Interview of Daniel Byman, October 1, 2008; interview of Michael Jacobson, March 26, 2009.

[109] According to another measure, the 9/11 Commission engaged in more advocacy than any other national security commission of recent decades. When asked to what extent the commission promoted its proposals on a scale of one to five, with one representing no promotion and five representing very extensive promotion, 9/11 Commission members and staff gave the panel an average rating of 4.9, the highest in my data set.

[110] Interview of Larry Halloran, March 24, 2009; interviews of congressional aides, June 2008 and March 2009.

Affairs, and International Relations, recalled, "Their interventions helped keep the cats from straying too far."[111]

The success of the commission's advocacy was closely linked to its ability to maintain its bipartisan credibility. All ten commissioners agreed, despite their political affiliations, not to be involved in the 2004 presidential campaign on commission-related issues and to focus instead on getting the panel's proposals enacted (Kean and Hamilton 2006, 298). The Public Discourse Project also played an important role by giving commissioners institutional support during their advocacy efforts and issuing the December 2005 report card.

The commission was significantly assisted in this advocacy effort by the 9/11 families, who testified before Congress themselves and conducted many media interviews to press for adoption of the commission's proposals.[112] The families' lobbying was influential in part because legislators and Bush administration officials feared being publicly criticized by them for inaction.[113] The families' role meant that, unlike most panels, the 9/11 Commission had the support of an influential interest group. Kean noted, "The families were extraordinarily important to us. They were the wind in our sails."[114]

These key factors – the magnitude of 9/11, the commission's unanimity, and the intensive advocacy campaign waged by the panel and the families – enabled the commission to trigger major reforms despite its congressional origins and relatively broad mandate. My theory of commission influence contends that congressional commissions are less likely than executive-branch panels to spark policy change, because they are more likely to be riven by partisanship and they take longer to be established, enabling a window of opportunity for reform to close. In addition, I argue that broad mandates are undesirable for commissions, because they complicate the achievement of consensus and the conduct of effective advocacy. The 9/11 Commission overcame these disadvantages by producing a unanimous report despite its congressional origins and broad scope, and by promoting its proposals widely and persistently. This outcome demonstrates that the conditions of a commission's creation do

[111] Interview of Larry Halloran, March 24, 2009.
[112] A hearing of the Senate Governmental Affairs Committee on August 17, 2004 was dedicated entirely to testimony by relatives of 9/11 victims.
[113] Interview of congressional aide, March 2009.
[114] Comments by Thomas Kean, Panel on "The Role and Impact of National Security Commissions," Woodrow Wilson School of Public and International Affairs, Princeton University, June 2, 2007.

not dictate its impact; much also depends on how the panel carries out its charge.

Conclusion

This chapter's case studies illustrate how commissions can trigger landmark reforms. The Department of Homeland Security might not have been established without the Hart-Rudman Commission, and the post of director of national intelligence would almost certainly not have been created if the 9/11 Commission had not proposed it. In both instances, the window of opportunity for reform was created by the 9/11 attack, but that disaster did not ensure that bureaucratic and congressional obstacles to changing the status quo would be overcome. Even after 9/11, the Bush administration and powerful members of Congress opposed creating a homeland security department and establishing a DNI. However, the political credibility of the Hart-Rudman and 9/11 commissions led influential legislators, such as Lieberman and Collins, to advance the panels' principal proposals and made it politically perilous for opponents to stand in their way. The comments of numerous policy makers involved in the enactment of the Homeland Security Act and Intelligence Reform Act, as well as a comparison between the 9/11 Commission and the Joint Inquiry, further reveal that political credibility drove the influence of these commissions more than expertise.

The history of these panels also supports other elements of my argument about commissions. The Hart-Rudman Commission's minimal impact before 9/11 illustrates that panels are unlikely to spark reforms in the absence of a crisis. The ability of the 9/11 and Hart-Rudman commissions to reach consensus on highly specific proposals, despite their political diversity, demonstrates the tendency of the commission environment to facilitate unanimity. Furthermore, the powerful effect of persistent advocacy by the 9/11 Commission shows that intensive promotion can be a critical ingredient of commission influence.

In Chapters 4–6, I have analyzed the impact of eight commissions that probed terrorism between the presidencies of Ronald Reagan and George W. Bush. These case studies have shown that commissions played critical roles in the U.S. response to the most deadly anti-American terrorist attacks of recent decades. In many instances, an attack created a window of opportunity for policy change, but Congress and the president required the prodding of a unanimous commission report to reach agreement on major reforms.

Taken together, the case studies reveal that crisis commissions do not just help policy makers defuse political pressure, delay action, avoid blame, or preempt an unwanted initiative. Although commissions are often created for those purposes, they can use their distinct political credibility to catalyze important policy changes that would not otherwise occur.

PART THREE

CONCLUSION

7

Implications and the Effort to End the Iraq War

The conventional wisdom is that commissions rarely lead to changes in government policies. I have found that the conventional wisdom is correct concerning one set of panels, but wrong with respect to another. Commissions formed to advance an agenda in the absence of a crisis tend not to trigger change because the status quo in Washington is very difficult to overturn. In the wake of a crisis, however, commissions often use their distinctive political credibility to induce the adoption of important reforms. Crisis commissions, it turns out, are not just devices used by elected officials to deflect political pressure or avoid unwanted action; they are also underappreciated and powerful tools for making public policy.

In the preceding chapters, I tested my theory of commission influence by investigating the impact of all fifty-one national security panels that reported between 1981 and 2006. The results of statistical tests supported my hypotheses that panels are more likely to influence policy if they are formed in response to a crisis; established by the executive branch, instead of Congress; or given a relatively narrow mandate.

I supplemented that statistical analysis with case studies of commissions that examined instances and threats of terrorism. These case studies revealed that commissions have frequently driven key elements of the U.S. response to terrorism, sparking or influencing major policy changes by providing a focal point for reform.

- Following the 1983 Marine barracks bombing in Beirut, the Long Commission's stinging report sharply increased congressional opposition to the U.S. deployment in Lebanon, and hastened President Reagan's decision to pull out American troops.

- After several attacks on U.S. embassies in the early 1980s, the Inman Panel prompted an overhaul of the State Department's diplomatic security apparatus and standards.
- In the wake of the 1988 downing of Pan Am Flight 103 by Libyan agents, the Lockerbie Commission induced the enactment of a major aviation security law.
- Following the 1998 African embassy bombings, the Crowe Panel catalyzed a sharp increase in funding for diplomatic security.
- After the 2000 bombing of a Navy destroyer, the *USS Cole* Commission sparked a variety of changes to military force-protection policies.
- Following the 2001 attack on the World Trade Center and Pentagon, the Hart-Rudman Commission spurred the establishment of the Department of Homeland Security, and the 9/11 Commission triggered the creation of the post of director of national intelligence and a host of other counterterrorism reforms.

The catalytic effect of these panels shows that crisis commissions are often directly responsible for important reforms, refuting this book's alternative hypothesis that commissions rarely cause policy change to occur.

What My Findings Tell Us about the Politics of Reform

The influence of these commissions also has a broader implication, revealing a chronic deficiency in the ability of the president and Congress to forge consensus on critical issues on their own – even when a crisis makes the status quo unpopular. This deficiency stems from the extreme polarization, poisonous partisanship, and intense parochial pressures that are now prevalent in Washington.

As recently as the 1960s, there existed significant ideological overlap between some congressional Republicans and Democrats, and many members of Congress frequently voted with their colleagues from the other party. Now, nearly every Republican in Congress is more conservative than every Democrat in Congress, and cross-party voting is rare. This increased polarization is exacerbated by growing partisanship: Instead of seeking to forge the compromises necessary to enact legislation, both parties often now prefer to use issues as electoral tools for distinguishing their positions. Issue activists and party donors fuel this reluctance to compromise by pressuring politicians to remain wedded to ideologically pure stances. Such pressure is one important reason why the minority party in the Senate has increasingly used filibusters to prevent the passage of legislation (Binder 2003; Bond and Fleisher 2000; Mann and Ornstein 2006; Pfiffner 2009a).

Even in times of less partisanship and polarization, it is difficult to enact laws in the United States because of the need for the president and two houses of Congress to approve them. But the trends of recent decades have made gridlock the norm in Washington, and have made commissions increasingly useful policy-making tools. Representative Frank Wolf (R-VA), who has introduced bills to create commissions on many issues, commented, "Overall, Congress is dysfunctional, partisan, and polarized, and it isn't getting anything done. We need commissions to break out of divisive partisanship."[1]

Indeed, policy making by commission can be seen as a valuable alternative to what one might call policy making by partisanship. Commentators and activists on both ends of the American political spectrum – from Paul Krugman to Rush Limbaugh – tend to favor attempts to push their party's agenda through Congress without making significant concessions to gain broader support. However, such efforts usually fail. Sarah Binder has found that bills are much more likely to be enacted into law when they are cosponsored by an ideologically broad coalition in the Senate (Binder 2003, 94–98). The forging of such coalitions is the stock-in-trade of commissions.

Equally important, commissions are sometimes necessary to enable reformers to overcome opposition to change from agencies and congressional committees seeking to protect their turf. This book's case studies include many instances of this phenomenon, from the Inman Panel triggering the formation of a diplomatic security service whose creation was resisted by the Foreign Service, to the Hart-Rudman and 9/11 commissions spurring homeland security and intelligence overhauls that were opposed by powerful cabinet secretaries and members of Congress. These examples show how difficult it generally is to institute change that threatens the power of influential officials.

Commissions can overcome these various obstacles to reform because of the political credibility derived from their independence, stature, and ability to generate unanimous bipartisan reports. The independence of commissions is bolstered by the fact that commission members are often retired from politics or government service, enabling them to focus on the national interest rather than the parochial interests of political parties,

---

[1] Interview of Frank Wolf, October 2, 2007.

executive-branch agencies, or congressional committees. At the same time, the relatively depoliticized deliberative environment of commissions usually allows them to reach consensus on findings and recommendations despite their ideological diversity. When they do issue unanimous reports and then engage in dogged advocacy on behalf of their proposals, they can place heavy pressure on elected officials to adopt the recommendations, thereby helping reformers carry the day.

Whereas this book's empirical analysis generated strong support for my argument about the political credibility of commissions, it provided little backing for the book's alternative hypothesis asserting that the possession of expertise is the primary source of a commission's appeal. This finding implies that the formation of commissions is not typically motivated by a quest for specialized information, and it suggests that a shortage of expertise is not usually the primary obstacle to the adoption of reforms.[2] Instead, the political credibility of reform proposals generally dictates the success or failure of efforts to cobble together bipartisan agreement.

The Iraq Study Group and the Challenge of Ending a War

In some instances, however, the political system is so polarized that commissions cannot bridge partisan divides even if they possess great political credibility. The initial response to the 2006 Iraq Study Group's report illustrates this situation: Its impact was heavily constrained by the difficulty of overcoming partisanship on an issue as divisive as the Iraq War. Yet the study group ended up having a large impact nevertheless through its underappreciated influence on the Iraq stance of then-Senator Barack Obama (D-IL) during the 2008 presidential campaign. I briefly tell the study group's story here to reinforce key elements of my argument about commissions, and to illustrate both the difficulty of overcoming polarization and the ability of commissions to shape policy in unexpected ways.[3]

Established in March 2006, the study group was the brainchild of Representative Wolf, who gained congressional approval for a $1 million earmark to fund the commission under the auspices of the U.S. Institute of Peace.[4] As a moderate Republican representing a northern Virginia district

---

[2] However, commissions investigating complex accidents generally do need extensive technical expertise, as Christopher Kirchhoff has demonstrated in his case study of the board that investigated the Columbia Space Shuttle's crash (Kirchhoff 2009).

[3] I have published elsewhere a more detailed study of the study group (Tama 2011).

[4] The funding was appropriated by Public Law 109–234, enacted on June 15, 2006. (The study group was formed before Congress appropriated the funding.)

that was trending Democratic, Wolf hoped the commission would forge consensus on an alternative to the Bush administration's Iraq policy, which seemed unable in 2006 to control escalating violence in Iraq and threatened to be an albatross around Republicans' necks in future elections.

Wolf said that he created the panel, which lacked a statutory charter, through the U.S. Institute of Peace because doing so was faster than establishing a typical congressional commission, whose charter is often subject to lengthy negotiations.[5] This rationale implicitly supports my argument that the impact of congressional panels is generally hindered by the long delays associated with their formation. Wolf also established the panel in this way because the Bush White House might have blocked the formation of an Iraq commission with a statutory charter, out of concern that the charter could give the panel more legitimacy.[6]

U.S. Institute of Peace President Richard Solomon decided, in consultation with the heads of two other think tanks that supported the Iraq Study Group, to ask former Secretary of State James Baker and former Representative Lee Hamilton (D-IN) to cochair the commission.[7] Baker and Hamilton, in turn, chose the eight other panel members, who included four Democrats and four Republicans. Notably, some of the commissioners, including attorney and business executive Vernon Jordan and former Supreme Court Justice Sandra Day O'Connor, possessed little experience with national security issues. Hamilton said that he and Baker chose people they thought would appeal to important constituencies and be able to reach consensus – an acknowledgment that political credibility would likely drive the group's influence.[8] In this respect also, the commission's unusual setup proved beneficial to it: If congressional leaders had appointed the members, they would have had an incentive to appoint partisan loyalists who would be unable to agree. The achievement of unanimity was further facilitated by the fact that few of the commissioners had previously staked out public stances on the war.

A Call for a Change of Course

The study group's unanimous and sharply critical report was presented to President Bush and described to the public in a nationally televised

---

[5] Interview of Frank Wolf, October 2, 2007.
[6] Interview of Iraq Study Group staff members, December 2006.
[7] The other think tank heads were David Abshire, president of the Center for the Study of the Presidency, and John Hamre, president of the Center for Strategic and International Studies.
[8] Interview of Lee Hamilton, December 14, 2006.

news conference on December 6, 2006. This scene's drama was so great
that a television critic later named it one of the ten most compelling
television moments of the year (Stanley 2006). The study group offered
a pessimistic assessment of conditions in Iraq, captured by its report's
stark opening sentence: "The situation in Iraq is grave and deteriorating"
(Iraq Study Group 2006, xiii). The report went on to make seventy-nine
recommendations, including the following key proposals:

• The United States should change the primary mission of U.S. forces in
  Iraq from combat to training Iraqi forces and conducting counterterrorism operations.
• The United States should launch a diplomatic offensive in the Middle
  East, including direct engagement with Iran and Syria and renewed
  pursuit of Arab-Israeli peace.
• The United States should condition assistance to Iraq on the Iraqi government's progress toward the achievement of milestones on national
  reconciliation, security, and governance.

In addition to these principal proposals, the report included the following sentence, which was generally interpreted as an endorsement of
withdrawal: "By the first quarter of 2008, subject to unexpected developments in the security situation on the ground, all combat brigades not
necessary for force protection could be out of Iraq" (Iraq Study Group
2006, xvi).

When the study group reported, it was reasonable to expect that its
proposals would provide the foundation for bipartisan agreement on a
policy shift. Violence in Iraq was at its peak, the Democrats' takeover
of Congress in the November 2006 elections was widely viewed as a
rejection of Bush's Iraq policy, and the study group's recommendations
enjoyed broad public support. Opinion polls conducted shortly after the
panel reported found that 66 percent of Americans trusted it a great deal
or a fair amount to recommend the right policy in Iraq, and that its primary proposals were each backed by more than six in ten Americans
(Baker and Cohen 2006; Page 2006; Reynolds 2006). These remarkable
approval ratings show the tremendous appeal of a unanimous report by
a distinguished bipartisan group.

Bush and Democratic Leaders Offer a Cold Shoulder
Yet neither Bush nor Democratic leaders in Congress embraced the report.
In a speech on January 10, 2007, Bush announced that he would send over
20,000 more troops to Iraq to execute a new counterinsurgency strategy

aimed at protecting Iraqi civilians.[9] Although the study group had indicated in its report that it could support a short-term surge, Bush's new policy did not encompass changing the primary mission of American troops to training and fighting Al Qaeda in Iraq, as the commission proposed.

In Congress, House and Senate Majority Leaders Nancy Pelosi (D-CA) and Harry Reid (D-NV) also distanced themselves from the report. In the summer of 2007, they blocked efforts by a bipartisan group of centrist legislators to advance a bill to adopt nearly all of the panel's proposals, including its recommendation to change the primary mission of U.S. troops.[10] This legislation, which was drafted by Senator Ken Salazar (D-CO) and cosponsored by fifteen other senators and sixty-two representatives, might have passed both houses if Reid and Pelosi allowed it to come up for a vote, but the Democratic leaders believed that it would reduce political pressure on Republicans without forcing a withdrawal.[11] The legislation was also opposed by Bush because it challenged his own policy. In frustration, Senator Lamar Alexander (R-TN), one of its cosponsors, commented, "The president and the Senate Democratic leader are working against it. One says it is toothless, the other says it has too many teeth" (Zeleny 2007).

These responses by Bush, Pelosi, and Reid reflected the disadvantage the study group faced in addressing an issue as politically polarizing and publicly salient as Iraq policy. The war was the signature foreign policy decision of Bush's presidency and also promised to be, for good or ill, at the center of his legacy. Doubling down on the U.S. military commitment in Iraq, in the hope that a surge could salvage the war, therefore presumably held more appeal to Bush than a gradual pullout that would be viewed as an acknowledgment of failure (Broder and Stolberg 2006). For Reid and Pelosi, on the other hand, there was little to gain politically from compromising with Bush, because the Democratic Party held a strong political advantage on the Iraq issue and the liberal base of the party was pressing for a rapid withdrawal. Moreover, Pelosi had already called publicly for pulling out troops faster than the pace suggested by the study group, making it even more politically difficult for her to endorse the commission's approach (Broder 2006).

---

[9] Remarks by President George W. Bush, "President's Address to the Nation," January 10, 2007.
[10] This legislation was the Iraq Study Group Implementation Act of 2007, H.R. 2574 and S. 1545.
[11] Interview of Frank Wolf, October 2, 2007; interviews of congressional aides, June 2007, October 2007, November 2007, and March 2008.

In other words, the positions of national leaders on Iraq policy were already too polarized for the Iraq Study Group to carve out enough political space to induce the president and Congress to reach consensus. On an issue of less public salience and weaker polarization, these leaders might have been more flexible, because they probably would have been less wedded to existing stances and less likely to suffer large political costs from compromising.

It would be wrong, however, to conclude that the Iraq Study Group's impact was minimal. A Bush administration official commented that the imminent release of the commission's report was part of the catalyst for the White House to start its own Iraq policy review in October 2006.[12] Once the study group declared, on December 6, that conditions in Iraq were "grave and deteriorating," the need for Bush to change course became even more apparent. A poll taken in the days after the commission reported found that just 28 percent of Americans approved of Bush's handling of Iraq – his lowest-ever rating on that issue (Baker and Cohen 2006). Bush's decision one month later to execute a new counterinsurgency strategy was surely informed by the recognition that staying the course was no longer a politically viable option.

The study group also contributed significantly to new legislation. One of its principal recommendations was adopted with the enactment of a law in May 2007 establishing eighteen benchmarks for the Iraqi government to meet as a condition of receiving further U.S. reconstruction aid.[13] Congressional aides involved in Iraq policy said that the commission influenced the benchmarks' establishment.[14] The study group's benchmark proposal may have been more palatable to Pelosi, Reid, and Bush than its recommendations concerning the American military deployment because the issue of reconstruction assistance was not as publicly salient or politically polarizing. Congress also approved large increases in funding for training Iraqi security forces, in accord with the study group's call for a greater emphasis on such training (Kirchhoff 2009, 157).

Influencing a Future President
In addition, the Iraq Study Group shaped the platform of Barack Obama as he began his presidential campaign. Although Obama had vocally

---

[12] Interview of Bush administration official, April 2007.
[13] This act is Public Law 110–28, enacted on May 25, 2007.
[14] Interviews of congressional aides, May 2008 and July 2008. The benchmarks measure allowed the president to waive the requirement that assistance be withheld if the Iraqi government failed to meet the benchmarks. Bush subsequently exercised that waiver.

opposed the 2003 U.S. invasion of Iraq, after being elected to the Senate in 2004 he refrained for two years from articulating a detailed position about how the United States should seek to end the Iraq War. Then, on November 20, 2006, as Obama prepared to enter the presidential race and the study group's main proposals began to be leaked to the press, he delivered a speech on Iraq that generally tracked the commission's ideas, including calls for a phased redeployment, increased training of Iraqi security forces, and diplomatic engagement with Iraq's neighbors.[15]

When the study group published its report two weeks later, Obama decided to introduce legislation based largely on the report. This bill was drafted by Obama Senate aide Mark Lippert, in conjunction with Obama foreign policy advisers Tony Lake, Susan Rice, Denis McDonough, and Ben Rhodes. Rhodes' role was particularly important because he had been a key staff member on the study group and had written much of its report. Obama's foreign policy team asked him to incorporate the report's key ideas into the Iraq bill.[16]

On January 30, 2007, Obama introduced this legislation, which mirrored the commission's main proposals.[17] The measure mandated a gradual troop pullout from Iraq, leading to the withdrawal of all combat brigades by March 31, 2008 (the date suggested by the study group); authorized the retention of troops in Iraq after that withdrawal to train Iraqi forces, conduct counterterrorism operations, and protect other American personnel (the three missions proposed by the study group); required that further economic aid to Iraq be conditioned on Iraqi progress in meeting certain benchmarks; and mandated that the United States undertake regional diplomatic initiatives in the Middle East.[18] These provisions were intentionally patterned on the study group's recommendations. Rhodes recalled, "It was intended to incorporate the study group report pretty clearly."[19] The measure even stated explicitly that it aimed to implement "key recommendations of the Iraq Study Group."

In subsequent months, Obama's presidential campaign literature continued to note that his Iraq plan was "consistent with the goals of the bipartisan Iraq Study Group."[20] These references to the study group suggest

[15] Remarks of Senator Barack Obama, "A New Way Forward in Iraq," Chicago Council on Global Affairs, November 20, 2006.
[16] Interview of Ben Rhodes, July 7, 2007.
[17] The bill was S. 433.
[18] Congress had not yet passed benchmarks legislation when Obama introduced his bill.
[19] Interview of Ben Rhodes, July 7, 2010.
[20] Undated Obama for America campaign flyers possessed by the author.

that Obama believed his Iraq stance would have greater public appeal if it was tied to the commission's political credibility. Indeed, Rhodes noted that the link to the study group helped give Obama's Iraq proposals "a bipartisan seal of approval."[21] Another senior Obama campaign aide commented that the commission's bipartisanship appealed greatly to Obama, and that the study group's impact on him was facilitated by his relationships with Lee Hamilton, who was a trusted foreign policy advisor, and Rhodes, who became his foreign policy speechwriter.[22]

Although Obama's bill did not advance in Congress, it was the foundation for his Iraq policy throughout the presidential campaign and during his first two years as president. One month into his presidency, Obama adopted the central provisions of the bill and the study group report, though on a later timeline. In a February 2009 speech, which was written by Rhodes, Obama announced that he would soon shift the U.S. mission in Iraq from combat to supporting the Iraqi government, would withdraw all combat brigades from Iraq by August 2010, and would retain a transitional force in Iraq after that date to train Iraqis, fight terrorists, and protect American personnel. Obama also emphasized that he would directly engage all the nations in the Middle East on Iraq, including Iran and Syria.[23]

In the end, then, the Iraq Study Group's impact was substantial, despite its cool initial reception by Bush, Reid, and Pelosi. Although its influence was initially limited by the severe polarization of the Iraq debate, the panel's political credibility made its unanimous recommendations very appealing not only to centrist legislators, but also to America's next president. Through its underappreciated impact on Obama, the study group crafted the plan that wound down the Iraq War.

Extensions

Before concluding, it is worth considering a few issues that merit further exploration as extensions of my findings in this book.

Other Types of Advisory Bodies

My definition of a commission (presented in Chapter 2) excludes some kinds of government advisory groups, including permanent boards, such

---

[21] Interview of Ben Rhodes, July 7, 2010.
[22] Interview of senior Obama presidential campaign aide, May 2009.
[23] Remarks of President Barack Obama, "Responsibly Ending the War in Iraq," February 27, 2009.

as the National Research Council; bodies with formal policy-making power, such as Base Realignment and Closure (BRAC) commissions; and groups that only issue a classified report. In addition, my definition of a *national security* commission (presented in Chapter 3) excludes panels that only examine administrative issues, such as the 1989 Department of Defense Advisory Committee on Uncompensated Overtime. It is possible that these other kinds of advisory bodies influence policy in a different way than the national security commissions that I examine. For instance, expertise might be more important than political credibility for panels that only produce a classified report or address administrative matters. Future research could investigate whether this is the case.

Commissions on Domestic Policy

In addition, commissions examining domestic policy issues might have different patterns of influence than national security panels. I outline here three ways in which domestic policy and national security commissions might differ, and explain why I expect my theory nonetheless explains the impact of commissions probing all policy areas.

First, crisis commissions might consist of a much smaller proportion of domestic policy commissions than of national security panels. Whereas terrorist attacks and wars spur the formation of many national security commissions, I doubt that disasters trigger the establishment of domestic policy panels as frequently. If, in fact, most domestic policy panels are agenda commissions, they might be less influential than national security panels, on average. Nevertheless, the heart of my argument should apply equally well to commissions on domestic affairs: Domestic crises, just like national security crises, make the status quo unpopular, creating windows of opportunity for reform that commissions can exploit. I therefore expect that crisis commissions on domestic issues, just like their national security counterparts, can drive policy change by providing a focal point for reform.

Second, the disparity between the impact of executive-branch panels and that of congressional commissions might not be as great on domestic issues, because the president does not dominate domestic policy making as much as national security affairs. This difference means that domestic policy commissions can rarely spur reform simply by gaining the president's backing for their proposals, as executive commissions can sometimes do. But executive commissions should still be more influential than congressional panels in domestic affairs because they share the other advantages that executive panels on national security possess: They can be appointed quickly and filled with moderate commissioners, bolstering their ability to report while a window of opportunity for reform remains open and to issue unanimous proposals.

Third, interest groups probably play a more important role with respect to domestic policy commissions because interest groups are generally more active on domestic issues than in national security affairs (Zegart 2004, 378). In particular, I expect that domestic policy panels are more often filled with interest-group representatives, and that their impact is more frequently shaped by interest-group advocacy efforts. These differences could cut two ways: (1) Interest-group representation on a commission could make it harder for the panel to reach consensus, because the commissioners might be less willing to compromise on issues relevant to their constituencies, or (2) the involvement of interest groups in advocating on behalf of a commission's proposals could boost its impact. Nevertheless, the influence of such commissions, like that of national security commissions, should be primarily driven by the existence or absence of a crisis: Interest groups are far more likely to agree on changes to the status quo when the status quo is deeply unpopular.

Is Implementation Successful or Beneficial?

I also did not focus in this book on two important issues related to commission-inspired reforms: (1) whether the reforms are fully implemented after they are adopted, and (2) whether they improve public policy or government effectiveness.

In many cases, I expect that reforms are not fully implemented because bureaucracies often resist change, shirking new programmatic responsibilities or refusing to cooperate with a new agency or office (Patashnik 2008; Zegart 2007). As George Ellard, a longtime national security official, commented, "An organizational chart and reality are different things."[24]

This distinction has been evident in the director of national intelligence's ongoing struggle to exercise the authority given to him by the 2004 Intelligence Reform Act. Although that act makes the DNI the leader of the intelligence community, intelligence agencies have fought tooth and nail to protect their traditional turf and prerogatives. For instance, after DNI Dennis Blair announced in May 2009 that his office would appoint the top U.S. intelligence official in every country, taking away a long-standing CIA responsibility, CIA Director Leon Panetta told

---

[24] Interview of George Ellard, April 16, 2008.

his agency's employees to ignore Blair's announcement (Mazzetti 2009). The Obama White House ultimately sided with Panetta and overturned Blair's decision (Pincus 2009). Such continuing turf battles suggest that the government has still not fully adapted to the six-year-old intelligence reorganization. The battles have also prompted influential members of Congress, including Senate Intelligence Committee Chairwoman Dianne Feinstein, to propose the enactment of new legislation that would strengthen the DNI's authorities.

However, I chose in this book not to focus on the implementation of proposals after they are adopted because the implementation process usually occurs well after a commission has disbanded, and a panel therefore has little capacity to shape it. Moreover, if a commission induces the government to adopt its recommendations, it has been quite influential, whether or not those changes are fully implemented.

At the same time, I have avoided assessing whether reforms improve policy or government effectiveness because that is difficult to do objectively. Consider the diplomatic security reforms adopted in response to the Inman and Crowe panels. The security upgrades carried out at U.S. embassies in accord with the proposals of those commissions surely made it more difficult for terrorists to kill American diplomats and other personnel at those facilities. In fact, there have been no American deaths from terrorism at embassies that have been built to the Inman standards. But many people believe that U.S. interests have not been well served by turning American embassies into fortress-like complexes that send an unwelcoming signal to foreigners. As Senator John Kerry (D-MA) commented in May 2009, "We're separating ourselves from people in these countries. I cringe when I see what we're doing" (Kennicott 2009).

To take other examples, opinion is divided on whether the establishment of the Department of Homeland Security and the creation of the DNI post have improved the government's handling of homeland security and intelligence issues. Whereas some experts argue that the reorganizations improved coordination and information sharing, others claim they created unnecessary layers of bureaucracy (Fenster 2008; Fessenden 2005; Fingar and Graham 2010; Posner 2005). The reality is that the overhauls have enabled the government to connect the dots more adeptly and to act in a more integrated fashion, but at the cost of some additional bloat.

In general, there is no reason to expect that reforms proposed by commissions necessarily make government policy "better" when they are adopted. On the one hand, the independence of panels can give them a

greater capacity than executive-branch agencies or congressional committees to advocate innovative approaches. On the other hand, commission recommendations, just like the proposals of any other body, can
sometimes be ill-advised. Indeed, my argument that political credibility,
rather than expertise, is the defining attribute of commissions implies
that panels should have a tendency to coalesce around proposals that
are politically feasible, which are not necessarily those that would do the
most to improve public policy.

Natural extensions of this book include evaluating the impact of
advisory panels other than national security commissions and assessing
whether reforms influenced by commissions tend to make the government more effective.

Lessons for Policy Makers

Finally, my findings yield a few lessons for policy makers seeking to establish a commission that prompts reform.

(1) *In the absence of a crisis, have low expectations.* Commissions
rarely catalyze change without the pressure for reform generated
by a crisis. Agenda commissions can still be useful, however, in
introducing new ideas, influencing public debate on an issue, or
laying down a marker that policy makers might return to if a crisis
emerges at a later date.

(2) *In a crisis, create the panel quickly and order it to report soon.* A
crisis creates a window of opportunity for reform that does not
last forever. Enabling the panel to report before that window closes
is critical to its ability to spur change. In this respect, executive-
branch commissions usually have an advantage over congressional
panels because the executive can set up panels more rapidly than
Congress. Representative Wolf's approach of earmarking commission funds to a research institute represents one creative way for a
legislator to avoid the delays typically associated with establishing
congressional panels.

(3) *Restrict the commission's scope.* Commissions are more likely to
prompt policy change if their scope is limited, because a narrow
mandate simplifies the reaching of consensus and the effective promotion of a panel's proposals, and makes it easier for a policy
maker to champion the recommendations successfully.

(4) *Prioritize political credibility over expertise in selecting commissioners.* Any commission needs a competent and knowledgeable staff.

But the most critical element of a panel's makeup is the reputation of its members. An ideologically diverse panel of people possessing national stature will usually impress the media and elected officials much more than a commission of outstanding nongovernmental experts. Commission chairs are especially important: Successful panels tend to be led by someone of nonpartisan reputation or by a pair of Republican and Democratic moderates. Because a commission's credibility depends heavily on its ability to issue a unanimous report, it can also be helpful to appoint some members with little experience on the issue at hand, who will be less likely to have entrenched stances on it. As former Senator Charles Robb (D-VA) observed, "People with other backgrounds don't come in with their favorite hobbyhorses in their pocket."[25]

(5) *Give the commission funding for advocacy and follow-up activities.* The work of most panels ends when they submit their reports. Yet commission proposals are more likely to be adopted if panel members promote the recommendations intensively and persistently. In some cases, dedicated commissioners and staff will engage in such advocacy on their own dime, but a panel can be a much more effective advocate if it has funds for promoting its proposals after it issues its report.

Of course, none of these steps will ensure that a panel's proposals lead to policy or organizational change. In the end, the impact of commissions is often unpredictable, in part because of their independence and in part because of the countless other factors that drive political developments. However, designing a commission thoughtfully is worthwhile considering the ability of some commissions to catalyze major reforms. During the last three decades, national security commissions have, among other effects, placed heavy pressure on President Reagan to withdraw U.S. troops from Lebanon; prompted an array of important diplomatic, aviation, and military security upgrades; spurred the largest government and intelligence reorganizations since 1947; and shaped Barack Obama's plan for ending the Iraq War. That is a remarkable track record for a set of advisory bodies that lacked formal power and cost American taxpayers an average of just $3 million.

[25] Interview of Charles Robb, July 23, 2007.

Appendix A

Construction of the Data Set

To construct my data set of national security commissions, I began with Amy Zegart's data set of commissions that reported between 1981 and 2001. Zegart's data set consists of commissions that addressed all issue areas and includes information on each panel's source of authority, dates of operation, and membership size, as well as Zegart's assessment of each commission's purpose. Her data set is drawn from the Encyclopedia of Government Advisory Organizations, and includes most national security commissions from 1981 to 2001.

I pulled out the national security commissions in Zegart's data set and supplemented that group in several ways. First, I searched the Encyclopedia of Government Advisory Organizations for national security commissions that reported between 2002 and 2006. Second, I conducted systematic searches of other valuable sources of information on commissions: a government database of annual reports mandated by the Federal Advisory Committee Act (available at http://www.fido.gov/facadatabase), and coverage of commissions in the *New York Times* and *Washington Post*. I searched these newspapers by using LexisNexis and identifying all articles between January 1, 1981 and December 31, 2006 that contained the words "panel" or "commission," and "security," "defense," or "military." These search terms turned up over 20,000 articles, each of which I scanned to determine whether it referred to a panel that fit my definition of a commission. This newspaper search and my search of the government database each turned up several commissions that were not listed in the Encyclopedia of Government Advisory Organizations. My use of these different sources gives me confidence that

I have identified all, or nearly all, of the national security commissions that operated between 1981 and 2006.

Third, I collected data for each commission on numerous variables not included in Zegart's data set, including the panel's budget, the size of its staff, the partisan balance of its membership, the proportion of sitting government officials among the membership, whether the report was unanimous, whether the House and Senate held hearings on the report, how much newspaper coverage the report received, and the two measures of commission impact described in Chapter 3. I used many of these variables in the statistical tests of my hypotheses.

Appendix B

National Security Commissions, 1981–2006

Name	Chair(s)	Date	Context	Authority source	Scope	Policy impact rating	Mean adoption score
President's Commission on Strategic Forces	Brent Scowcroft	1983	Agenda	Executive	Narrow	4.30	1.33
Commission on Security and Economic Assistance	Frank Carlucci	1983	Agenda	Executive	Broad	1.71	1.00
Commission on Beirut International Airport Terrorist Act of 23 October 1983	Robert Long	1983	Crisis	Executive	Narrow	3.42	2.00
National Bipartisan Commission on Central America	Henry Kissinger	1984	Agenda	Executive	Broad	3.05	1.67
Chairman of the Joint Chiefs of Staff Media-Military Relations Panel	Winant Sidle	1984	Crisis	Executive	Narrow	3.71	2.00
Chemical Warfare Review Commission	Walter Stoessel	1985	Agenda	Congress	Narrow	2.38	2.00
President's Blue Ribbon Task Group on Nuclear Weapons Program Management	William Clark	1985	Agenda	Congress	Narrow	3.13	1.33
Secretary of State's Advisory Panel on Overseas Security	Bobby Inman	1985	Crisis	Executive	Narrow	4.29	1.40
Commission to Review DoD Security Policies and Practices	Richard Stillwell	1985	Crisis	Executive	Broad	3.50	0.50

Commission	Chair	Year	Type	Branch	Scope		
President's Blue Ribbon Commission on Defense Management	David Packard	1986	Crisis	Executive	Broad	4.25	1.60
Secretary of State's Advisory Committee on South Africa	Frank Cary, William Coleman	1987	Agenda	Executive	Narrow	2.00	1.00
President's Special Review Board	John Tower	1987	Crisis	Executive	Narrow	3.63	2.00
Advisory Commission on Integrated Long-Term Strategy	Fred Ikle, Albert Wohlstetter	1988	Agenda	Executive	Broad	3.05	0.60
Commission on Merchant Marine and Defense	Jeremiah Denton	1989	Agenda	Congress	Broad	1.50	0.00
President's Commission on Aviation Security and Terrorism	Ann McLaughlin	1990	Crisis	Executive	Broad	4.03	1.80
Commission on the Assignment of Women in the Armed Forces	Robert Herres	1992	Agenda	Congress	Broad	1.33	0.33
United States Commission on Improving the Effectiveness of the United Nations	Jim Leach, Charles Lichenstein	1993	Agenda	Congress	Broad	2.00	0.00
Joint Security Commission	Jeffrey Smith	1994	Agenda	Executive	Broad	2.29	1.20
Commission on Roles and Missions of the Armed Forces	John White	1995	Agenda	Congress	Broad	2.78	0.83
Commission on the Roles and Capabilities of the United States Intelligence Community	Les Aspin, followed by Harold Brown	1996	Crisis	Congress	Broad	2.78	1.20
President's Advisory Board on Arms Proliferation Policy	Janne Nolan	1996	Agenda	Congress	Broad	1.50	0.00

Name	Chair(s)	Date	Context	Authority source	Scope	Policy impact rating	Mean adoption score
Small Satellite Review Panel	Robert Hermann	1996	Agenda	Congress	Narrow	2.75	0.00
White House Commission on Aviation Safety and Security	Al Gore	1997	Crisis	Executive	Broad	2.69	1.00
Commission on Protecting and Reducing Government Secrecy	Daniel Patrick Moynihan	1997	Agenda	Congress	Broad	2.31	0.00
President's Commission on Critical Infrastructure Protection	Robert Marsh	1997	Agenda	Executive	Broad	3.18	1.25
National Defense Panel	Philip Odeen	1997	Agenda	Congress	Broad	2.70	1.00
Federal Advisory Committee on Gender-Integrated Training and Related Issues	Nancy Kassebaum Baker	1997	Crisis	Executive	Broad	3.00	1.33
Long-Range Air Power Review Panel	Larry Welch	1998	Agenda	Congress	Narrow	4.00	2.00
Commission to Assess the Ballistic Missile Threat to the United States	Donald Rumsfeld	1998	Agenda	Congress	Narrow	3.00	N/A
Accountability Review Boards on the Embassy Bombings in Nairobi and Dar es Salaam on August 7, 1998	William Crowe	1999	Crisis	Executive	Narrow	4.13	2.00

Commission	Chair	Year	Type	Origin	Scope		
Commission to Assess the Organization of the Federal Government to Combat the Proliferation of Weapons of Mass Destruction	John Deutch	1999	Agenda	Congress	Broad	1.39	0.00
Congressional Commission on Military Training and Gender-Related Issues	Anita Blair	1999	Crisis	Congress	Broad	2.70	N/A
Joint Security Commission 2	Larry Welch	1999	Agenda	Executive	Broad	2.00	0.00
Special Panel on Military Operations in Vieques	Frank Rush	1999	Crisis	Executive	Narrow	3.60	1.40
Overseas Presence Advisory Panel	Lewis Kaden	1999	Crisis	Executive	Broad	3.29	0.83
Commission on the Advancement of Federal Law Enforcement	William Webster	2000	Crisis	Congress	Broad	1.75	0.00
National Commission on Terrorism	Paul Bremer	2000	Crisis	Congress	Broad	3.08	0.67
National Commission for the Review of the National Reconnaissance Office	Porter Goss, Bob Kerrey	2000	Agenda	Congress	Broad	2.21	1.00
USS Cole Commission	William Crouch, Harold Gehman	2001	Crisis	Executive	Broad	4.33	1.80

Name	Chair(s)	Date	Context	Authority source	Scope	Policy impact rating	Mean adoption score
Commission to Assess United States National Security Space Management and Organization	Donald Rumsfeld	2001	Agenda	Congress	Broad	3.33	1.00
U.S. Commission on National Security/21st Century	Gary Hart, Warren Rudman	2001	Agenda	Executive	Broad	3.19	0.67
Panel to Review the V-22 Program	John Dailey	2001	Crisis	Executive	Narrow	3.92	2.00
Commission for the Review of FBI Security Programs	William Webster	2002	Crisis	Executive	Narrow	3.50	1.33
Commission on the Future of the United States Aerospace Industry	Robert Walker	2002	Agenda	Congress	Broad	2.63	0.50
National Advisory Committee on Children and Terrorism	Angela Diaz	2003	Crisis	Congress	Narrow	1.97	0.75
National Commission on Terrorist Attacks upon the United States	Thomas Kean	2004	Crisis	Congress	Broad	4.61	1.00
Independent Panel to Review Department of Defense Detention Operations	James Schlesinger	2004	Crisis	Executive	Narrow	3.19	1.67
Commission on the Intelligence Capabilities of the United States regarding Weapons of Mass Destruction	Charles Robb, Laurence Silberman	2005	Crisis	Executive	Broad	3.90	1.67

Task Force on the United Nations	Newt Gingrich, George Mitchell	2005	Agenda	Congress	Broad	2.33	1.40
Commission on Review of Overseas Military Facility Structure of the United States	Al Cornella	2005	Agenda	Congress	Broad	2.13	0.60
Iraq Study Group	James Baker, Lee Hamilton	2006	Crisis	Congress	Broad	3.10	1.00

Note: "Date" refers to the year of the commission's final report. "Context" refers to whether the commission was a crisis commission or an agenda commission. "Authority source" refers to whether the commission was established by Congress or the executive branch. "Scope" refers to whether the commission's mandate was narrow or broad. "Policy impact rating" refers to the average rating of the commission's policy impact by commission participants and government officials with responsibility for the issue addressed by the commission, on a scale of one to five. "Mean adoption score" refers to the extent to which the commission's principal recommendations were adopted by the government within two years of the commission's report, on a scale of zero to two. See Chapter 3 for more information on these variables.

Appendix C

List of People Interviewed

David Abshire	Michael Clough	Bert Fowler
Marcy Agmon	William Coleman	Jim Freeman
Harold Agnew	Kenneth Colucci	Fred Frostic
Pete Aldridge	Lee Colwell	Caroline Gabel
Maynard Anderson	Al Cornella	Herald Gehman
Duane Andrews	William Crouch	Leslie Gelb
Michael Armacost	John Dailey	Ted Gold
Richard Armitage	Robert Dare	Jamie Gorelick
Norman Augustine	Lynn Davis	Arthur Grant
James Baker	Rhett Dawson	Gary Gray
Michael Bayer	Joan Dempsey	Brent Greene
Rand Beers	Jeremiah Denton	Richard Grunawalt
Patti Benner	David Deptula	Larry Halloran
Eric Biel	Mike Donley	Lee Hamilton
James Blackwell	John Douglass	John Hamre
James Bodner	Sidney Drell	Paul Hanley
Charles Boyd	Frank Duggan	Gary Hart
Paul Bremer	Lawrence Eagleburger	Donald Hays
Harold Brown	Mickey Edwards	Robert Hermann
Zbigniew Brzezinski	George Ellard	Diego Hernandez
James Busey	Marty Faga	Robert Herres
Daniel Byman	Richard Falkenrath	Andy Hoehn
Allen Cameron	Craig Fields	James Holloway
Frank Carlucci	Donald Finberg	Charles Horner
David Carpenter	Michèle Flournoy	Charles Huettner
Antonia Chayes	Cathal Flynn	Robert Hutchings
Ron Christmas	Steve Fogleman	Fred Iklé
Richard Clarke	John Foster	Bobby Inman

(*continued*)

William Itoh	Michael Munson	John Silber
Randy Jayne	Robert Murray	Anne-Marie Slaughter
Christopher Jehn	Douglas Necessary	Jeffrey Smith
Brian Jenkins	Hector Nevarez	Britt Snider
Loch Johnson	Robert Newberry	Lawrence Snowden
Lewis Kaden	Bryan O'Connor	Suzanne Spaulding
Gerald Kauvar	Philip Odeen	Ronald Spiers
Juliette Kayyem	Gordon Oehler	O.K. Steele
Thomas Kean	Bud Orr	Paul Stevens
Michael Kennedy	Joseph Palastra	Nina Stewart
Bob Kerrey	Leon Panetta	William Studeman
John Kester	Fred Pang	Peter Szanton
George Koleszar	Paul Piscopo	Dennis Thomas
Ann Korologos	Gene Porter	Mac Thornberry
Ken Krieg	Arnold Punaro	John Vessey
Jim Kurtz	Anthony Quainton	Charles Vest
Phil Lacombe	Thomas Reed	Robert Walker
Robert Lamb	Ben Rhodes	Sheryl Walter
Fred Lash	Robert RisCassi	George Ward
James Leach	Charles Robb	James Warlick
John Lehman	Timothy Roemer	Ted Warner
Donald Mahley	Jacques Rondeau	William Webster
Carolyn Maloney	Robert Rosenkranz	Larry Welch
Robert Marsh	Warren Rudman	John White
Gary Matthews	Frank Rush	Earl Whiteman
Rich McBride	Dan Ryan	Gregory Wierzynski
James McCarthy	Gary Samore	Philip Wilcox
Clark McFadden	James Schlesinger	Richard Williams
Robert McFarlane	William Schneider	Frank Wilson
Joe McGrail	Alan Schwartz	William Wise
Kenneth McKune	Brent Scowcroft	Lyn Withey
John McLaughlin	Daniel Serwer	Frank Wolf
Daniel Mica	Harry Shlaudeman	James Woolsey
Thomas Moorman	George Shultz	Philip Zelikow
Tony Motley	John Shumate	Barry Zorthian

Note: Other interviewees are not included on this list because they requested anonymity.

References

Accountability Review Boards. 1999. *Report of the Accountability Review Boards on the Embassy Bombings in Nairobi and Dar Es Salaam on August 7, 1998.* U.S. Department of State.

Allen, Mike. 2004. Bush Names Commission on Iraq Data. *Washington Post,* February 7.

Associated Press. 2003. 20 Years Later, Lebanon Bombing Haunts. *CNN.com,* October 21.

Atlas, Terry. 1985. Fortify U.S. Embassies, Advisers Urge. *Chicago Tribune,* June 26.

Baker, Peter, and Jon Cohen. 2006. Americans Say U.S. Is Losing War. *Washington Post,* December 13.

Balla, Steven J., and John R. Wright. 2001. Interest Groups, Advisory Committees, and Congressional Control of the Bureaucracy. *American Journal of Political Science* 45 (4): 799–812.

Bartels, Larry M. 1996. Politicians and the Press: Who Leads, Who Follows? Presented at American Political Science Association Annual Meeting. San Francisco.

Baumgartner, Frank R., and Bryan D. Jones. 1993. *Agendas and Instability in American Politics.* Chicago, IL: University of Chicago Press.

Beach, Derek. 2004. The Unseen Hand in Treaty Reform Negotiations: The Role and Influence of the Council Secretariat. *Journal of European Public Policy* 11 (3): 408–439.

Bearden, Milt, and Larry Johnson. 2000. Don't Exaggerate the Terrorist Threat. *Wall Street Journal,* June 15.

Beckman, Norman A. 1981. Policy Analysis for the Congress. In *New Strategic Perspectives on Social Policy,* edited by J. E. Tropman, M. J. Dluhy and R. M. Lind. New York: Pergamon Press.

Benjamin, Daniel, and Steven Simon. 2002. *The Age of Sacred Terror.* New York: Random House.

Bergen, Peter L. 2002. *Holy War, Inc.: Inside the Secret World of Osama Bin Laden.* New York: Simon & Schuster.

Best, Richard A., Jr. 2007. *Sharing Law Enforcement and Intelligence Information: The Congressional Role*. Congressional Research Service.

Bimber, Bruce. 1996. *The Politics of Expertise in Congress: The Rise and Fall of the Office of Technology Assessment*. Albany, NY: State University of New York Press.

Binder, Sarah A. 2003. *Stalemate: Causes and Consequences of Legislative Gridlock*. Washington, DC: Brookings Institution Press.

Birkland, Thomas A. 2006. *Lessons of Disaster: Policy Change after Catastrophic Events*. Washington, DC: Georgetown University Press.

Blanton, Dana. 2004. 08/05/04 Poll: Small Convention Bump for Kerry. *Foxnews.com*, August 5.

Bond, Jon R., and Richard Fleisher. 2000. *Polarized Politics: Congress and the President in a Partisan Era*. Washington, DC: CQ Press.

Bradley, Curtis A., and Judith G. Kelley. 2008. The Concept of International Delegation. *Law and Contemporary Problems* 71 (1): 1–36.

Brady, David W., and Craig Volden. 1998. *Revolving Gridlock: Politics and Policy from Carter to Clinton*. Boulder, CO: Westview Press.

Brinkley, Joel, and Philip Shenon. 2002. Ridge Meeting Opposition from Agencies. *New York Times*, February 7.

Broder, David S. 2001. Now Will We Pay Attention? *Washington Post*, September 21.

Broder, John M. 2006. Democrats Are Divided on a Solution for Iraq. *New York Times*, October 27.

Broder, John M., and Sheryl Gay Stolberg. 2006. Bush, In Meeting on Iraq, Rejects a Quick Pullout. *New York Times*, December 1.

Bumiller, Elisabeth, and Philip Shenon. 2004. Bush Now Backs Budget Powers in New Spy Post. *New York Times*, September 9.

Bumiller, Elisabeth. 2005. Overhauling U.S. Intelligence Gathering. *New York Times*, June 29.

Byman, Daniel L. 2006. Even the Wise Men Can't Save Us in Iraq. *Washington Post*, December 3.

Campbell, Colton C. 2002. *Discharging Congress: Government by Commission*. Westport, CT: Praeger.

Cannon, Lou. 1983. Political Pressure for Marine Pullout Likely to Increase. *Washington Post*, December 29.

Cannon, Lou, and David Hoffman. 1984. Troop Move Was Decided a Week Ago. *Washington Post*, February 9.

Causey, Mike. 1987. The Well-Ignored Report. *Washington Post*, September 10.

Chaiken, Shelly. 1980. Heuristic Versus Systematic Information Processing and the Use of Source Versus Message Cues in Persuasion. *Journal of Personality and Social Psychology* 39 (5): 752–766.

Checkel, Jeffrey T. 1997. *Ideas and International Political Change: Soviet/Russian Behavior and the End of the Cold War*. New Haven, CT: Yale University Press.

2001. Why Comply? Social Learning and European Identity Change. *International Organization* 55 (3): 553–588.

Chicago Tribune. 1999. Paying to Protect U.S. Missions. February 7.

Cialdini, Robert B. 2001. *Influence: Science and Practice*. Fourth ed. Boston, MA: Allyn and Bacon.

Clarke, Richard A. 2004. *Against All Enemies: Inside America's War on Terror*. New York: Free Press.

Cohen, Dara K., Mariano-Florentino Cuellar, and Barry R. Weingast. 2006. Crisis Bureaucracy: Homeland Security and the Political Design of Legal Mandates. *Stanford Law Review* 59 (3): 673–759.

Commission on Beirut International Airport Terrorist Act. 1983. *Report of the DoD Commission on Beirut International Airport Terrorist Act, October 23, 1983*.

Commission on the Advancement of Federal Law Enforcement. 2000. *Law Enforcement in a New Century and a Changing World*.

Commission on the Intelligence Capabilities of the United States Regarding Weapons of Mass Destruction. 2005. *Report to the President of the United States*. U.S. Government Printing Office.

Commission to Assess the Organization of the Federal Government to Combat the Proliferation of Weapons of Mass Destruction. 1999. *Combating Proliferation of Weapons of Mass Destruction*.

Crowe, William J., Jr. 1999. Two Embassies Down. *Washington Post*, May 4.

Davies, Frank. 2002. Intelligence Panels Start Hearings on 9/11 Lapses. *Star-Ledger*, June 4.

Dean, Alan L. 1969. Ad Hoc Commissions for Policy Formulation? In *The Presidential Advisory System*, edited by T. E. Cronin and S. D. Greenberg. New York: Harper & Row.

DeBose, Brian. 2006. Pelosi, Reid Push Security Agenda. *Washington Times*, March 30.

DeParle, Jason. 1983. Advise and Forget. *Washington Monthly*: May, 40–46.

DoD USS Cole Commission. 2001. *DoD USS Cole Commission Report*.

Draper, Robert. 2007. *Dead Certain: The Presidency of George W. Bush*. New York: Free Press.

Drew, Christopher. 1996. The Fate of Flight 800: Safety Stalled. *New York Times*, August 13.

Drew, Elizabeth. 2004. Pinning the Blame. *New York Review of Books* 51 (14).

Drew, Elizabeth B. 1968. On Giving Oneself a Hotfoot: Government by Commission. *Atlantic*: May, 45–49.

Druckman, James N. 2001a. The Implications of Framing Effects for Citizen Competence. *Political Behavior* 23 (3): 225–256.

2001b. Using Credible Advice to Overcome Framing Effects. *The Journal of Law, Economics, & Organization* 17 (1): 62–82.

Eggen, Dan, and Helen Dewar. 2004. Leaders Pick up Urgency of 9/11 Panel. *Washington Post*, July 24.

Epstein, David, and Sharyn O'Halloran. 1999. *A Transaction Cost Politics Approach to Policy Making under Separate Powers*. Cambridge: Cambridge University Press.

Epstein, Edward. 2005. National Security Gets Low Marks. *San Francisco Chronicle*, December 6.

Epstein, Susan B. 2001. *Embassy Security*. CRS Report for Congress.

Erlanger, Steven. 2001. 4 Guilty in Fatal 1986 Berlin Disco Bombing Linked to Libya. *New York Times*, November 14.

Falkenrath, Richard A. 2004/05. The 9/11 Commission Report. *International Security* 29 (3): 170–190.

Farrell, William E. 1984. Report Faults U.S. Embassy Security Plans. *New York Times*, September 22.

Federal Advisory Committee on Gender-Integrated Training and Related Issues. 1997. *Report of the Federal Advisory Committee on Gender-Integrated Training and Related Issues.*

Fenster, Mark. 2008. Designing Transparency: The 9/11 Commission and Institutional Form. *Washington and Lee Law Review* 65 (4): 1239–1321.

Fessenden, Helen. 2005. The Limits of Intelligence Reform. *Foreign Affairs*, November/December.

Filtner, David, Jr. 1986. *The Politics of Presidential Commissions.* Dobbs Ferry, New York: Transaction Publishers, Inc.

  2004. Why the Cynics Are Wrong about Presidential Commissions. *History News Network*, February 9.

Fingar, Thomas, and Mary Margaret Graham. 2010. Getting Smarter on Intelligence. *Washington Post*, April 30.

Fritz, Sara. 2001. Studies Often Warned of U.S. Vulnerability. *St. Petersburg Times*, September 17.

Garrett, Geoffrey, and Barry R. Weingast. 1993. Ideas, Interests, and Institutions: Constructing the European Community's Internal Market. In *Ideas and Foreign Policy: Beliefs, Institutions, and Political Change*, edited by J. Goldstein and R. O. Keohane. Ithaca, NY: Cornell University Press.

Gilligan, Thomas W., and Keith Krehbiel. 1990. Organization of Informative Committees by a Rational Legislature. *American Journal of Political Science* 34 (2): 531–564.

Goldberg, Jeffrey. 2002. In the Party of God. *New Yorker*, October 14.

Goldstein, Judith. 1989. The Impact of Ideas on Trade Policy: The Origins of U.S. Agricultural and Manufacturing Policies. *International Organization* 43 (1): 31–71.

Goshko, John M., and Fred Hiatt. 1984. Criticism of Security at Embassy Rises. *Washington Post*, September 22.

Graham, Hugh Davis. 1985. The Ambiguous Legacy of American Presidential Commissions. *The Public Historian* 7 (2): 5–25.

Gray, Jerry. 1996. Republicans Weaken House Bill on Combating Terrorism. *New York Times*, August 3.

Haas, Peter M. 1992. Introduction: Epistemic Communities and International Policy Coordination. In *Knowledge, Power and International Policy Coordination*, edited by P. M. Haas. Columbia, SC: University of South Carolina Press.

Hall, Peter A. 1989. Conclusion: The Politics of Keynesian Ideas. In *The Political Power of Economic Ideas: Keynesianism across Nations*, edited by P. A. Hall. Princeton, NJ: Princeton University Press.

Halperin, Morton H. 1961. The Gaither Committee and the Policy Process. *World Politics* 13 (3): 360–384.

Halperin, Morton H., and Priscilla A. Clapp. 2006. *Bureaucratic Politics and Foreign Policy*. Second ed. Washington, DC: Brookings Institution Press.

Hawkins, Darren G., David A. Lake, Daniel L. Nielson, and Michael J. Tierney, eds. 2006a. *Delegation and Agency in International Organizations*. Cambridge: Cambridge University Press.

Hawkins, Darren G., David A. Lake, Daniel L. Nielson, and Michael J. Tierney. 2006b. Introduction. In *Delegation and Agency in International Organizations*, edited by D. G. Hawkins, D. A. Lake, D. L. Nielson and M. J. Tierney. Cambridge: Cambridge University Press.

Hilsman, Roger. 1993. *The Politics of Policy Making in Defense and Foreign Affairs: Conceptual Models and Bureaucratic Politics*. Englewood Cliffs, NJ: Prentice Hall.

Howell, William G., and Jon C. Pevehouse. 2007. *While Dangers Gather: Congressional Checks on Presidential War Powers*. Princeton, NJ: Princeton University Press.

Ignatius, David. 1984. CIA Is Expanding Anti-Terrorism Effort but Lacks Data from Inside the Groups. *Wall Street Journal*, January 31.

Ikenberry, G. John. 1993. Creating Yesterday's New World Order: Keysenian 'New Thinking' and the Anglo-American Postwar Settlement. In *Ideas and Foreign Policy: Beliefs, Institutions, and Political Change*, edited by J. Goldstein and R. O. Keohane. Ithaca: Cornell University Press.

Investigations Subcommittee of the House Committee on Armed Services. 1983. *Adequacy of U.S. Marine Corps Security in Beirut*. U.S. Government Printing Office.

Iraq Study Group. 2006. *The Iraq Study Group Report*. New York: Vintage Books.

Jacobson, Sid, and Ernie Colon. 2006. *The 9/11 Report: A Graphic Adaptation*. New York: Hill and Wang.

Johnson, Loch K. 2004. The Aspin-Brown Intelligence Inquiry: Behind the Closed Doors of a Blue Ribbon Commission. *Studies in Intelligence* 48 (3): 1–20.

Joint Inquiry. 2002. *Report of the U.S. Senate Select Committee on Intelligence and U.S. House Permanent Select Committee on Intelligence*. U.S. Government Printing Office.

Kahneman, Daniel, Jack L. Knetsch, and Richard H. Thaler. 2000. Anomalies: The Endowment Effect, Loss Aversion, and Status Quo Bias. In *Choices, Values, and Frames*, edited by D. Kahneman and A. Tversky. Cambridge: Cambridge University Press.

Kamen, Al. 2001. Back from the Brink of Obscurity. *Washington Post*, September 14.

Kaplan, David E., and Kevin Whitelaw. 2004. Intelligence Reform – At Last. *U.S. News & World Report*, December 20.

Kean, Thomas H., and Lee H. Hamilton, with Benjamin Rhodes. 2006. *Without Precedent: The Inside Story of the 9/11 Commission*. New York: Knopf.

Keeler, John T. S. 1993. Opening the Window for Reform: Mandates, Crises, and Extraordinary Policy-Making. *Comparative Political Studies* 25 (4): 433–486.

Kempster, Norman. 2001. Vast Restructuring Urged to Shield U.S. from Terror Attack. *Chicago Tribune*, February 1.

Kennicott, Philip. 2009. Breaking the Diplomatic Ties That Bind Design. *Washington Post*, July 19.

Kiewiet, D. Roderick, and Matthew D. McCubbins. 1991. *The Logic of Delegation: Congressional Parties and the Appropriations Process*. Chicago, IL: University of Chicago Press.

Kingdon, John W. 1995. *Agendas, Alternatives, and Public Policies*. 2nd ed. New York: Longman.

Kirchhoff, Christopher. 2009. Fixing the National Security State: Commissions and the Politics of Disaster and Reform. Ph.D. dissertation, Cambridge University.

Kitts, Kenneth. 2006. *Presidential Commissions and National Security: The Politics of Damage Control*. Boulder, CO: Lynne Rienner Publishers.

Koffler, Keith. 2001. Bush Makes Plea to Graham on Homeland Security Position. *National Journal*, October 25.

Koremenos, Barbara, Charles Lipson, and Duncan Snidal. 2001. The Rational Design of International Institutions. *International Organization* 55 (4): 761–99.

Krehbiel, Keith. 1991. *Information and Legislative Organization*. Ann Arbor, MI: University of Michigan Press.

    1998. *Pivotal Politics: A Theory of U.S. Lawmaking*. Chicago, IL: University of Chicago Press.

Lamb, Robert E. 2000. Have We Inmanized Yet? *Foreign Service Journal*: June, 36–41.

Lardner, George, Jr. 1990. Anti-Terrorism Procedures Already Exist, Experts Say. *Washington Post*, May 16.

Larsen, Otto N. 1975. The Commission on Obscenity and Pornography: Form, Function, and Failure. In *Sociology and Public Policy: The Case of Presidential Commissions*, edited by M. Komarovsky. New York: Elsevier.

Legro, Jeffrey W. 2005. *Rethinking the World: Great Power Strategies and International Order*. Ithaca, NY: Cornell University Press.

Lehman, John F., Jr. 1988. *Command of the Seas*. Annapolis, MD: Naval Institute Press.

Lewis, David E. 2003. *Presidents and the Politics of Agency Design: Political Insulation in the United States Government Bureaucracy, 1946–1997*. Stanford, CA: Stanford University Press.

    2007. Testing Pendleton's Premise: Do Political Appointees Make Worse Bureaucrats? *The Journal of Politics* 69 (4): 1073–1088.

Lindsay, James M. 1994. *Congress and the Politics of U.S. Foreign Policy*. Baltimore, MD: Johns Hopkins University Press.

Lippman, Thomas W. 1999. Clinton Increases Embassy Security Fund. *Washington Post*, June 5.

Loeb, Vernon. 2000a. Panel Advocates Easing CIA Rules on Informants. *Washington Post*, June 6.

    2000b. Senator Presses for Bill to Combat Terrorism. *Washington Post*, October 3.

    2001. Cheney to Lead Anti-Terrorism Plan Team. *Washington Post*, May 9.

Lundberg, Kristen. 2005. *Piloting a Bipartisan Ship: Strategies and Tactics of the 9/11 Commission*. John F. Kennedy School of Government.

Mann, Thomas E., and Norman J. Ornstein. 2006. *The Broken Branch: How Congress Is Failing America and How to Get It Back on Track.* Oxford: Oxford University Press.

Marcy, Carl. 1945. *Presidential Commissions.* New York: King's Crown Press.

May, Ernest R. 2005. When Government Writes History. *New Republic*, May 23.

Mazzetti, Mark. 2009. Intelligence Turf Battles Test Spy Chiefs. *New York Times*, June 8.

McCain, John. 2002. Probe Deep, and Fairly. *Washington Post*, May 22.

McFadden, Robert D. 1989. Bomb Victim Relatives Urge Tighter Security. *New York Times*, March 18.

McFarlane, Robert C., with Zofia Smardz. 1994. *Special Trust.* New York: Cadell & Davies.

McNeil Jr., Donald G. 2001. The Lockerbie Verdict: The Overview; Libyan Convicted by Scottish Court in '88 Pan Am Blast. *New York Times*, February 1.

McPhee, Mike. 2001. Hart: Media Ignored Terror Study. *Denver Post*, September 19.

Milbank, Dana. 2004. Keeping the Power. *Washington Post*, July 27.

Milbank, Dana, and Dana Priest. 2004. Bush to Back Probe of Iraq Data, Officials Say. *Washington Post*, February 1.

Mintz, John. 1999. Panel Cites U.S. Failures on Security for Embassies. *Washington Post*, January 8.

Mitchell, Alison. 2002a. Democrats Say Bush Must Give Full Disclosure. *New York Times*, May 17.

———. 2002b. Letter to Ridge Is Latest Jab in Fight over Balance of Powers. *New York Times*, March 5.

Moe, Terry M. 1989. The Politics of Bureaucratic Structure. In *Can the Government Govern?* edited by J. E. Chubb and P. E. Peterson. Washington, DC: Brookings Institution.

Moe, Terry M., and Scott A. Wilson. 1994. Presidents and the Politics of Structure. *Law and Contemporary Problems* 57 (2): 1–44.

Moose, Richard. 1999. Security for Diplomats. *Washington Post*, December 23.

Mufson, Stephen. 2001. Overhaul of National Security Apparatus Urged. *Washington Post*, February 1.

Nagourney, Adam. 2004. Kerry Sees Hope of Gaining Edge on Terror Issue. *New York Times*, July 25.

Nakamura, Ken. 2004. Legislative Update: The FY 05 Omnibus and State and Commerce Funding. American Foreign Service Association.

National Commission on Terrorism. 2000. *Countering the Changing Threat of International Terrorism.*

National Commission on Terrorist Attacks upon the United States. 2004. *The 9/11 Commission Report.* New York: W.W. Norton & Company.

New York Times. 1984a. A Statement by Mondale on Lebanon. January 1.

New York Times. 1984b. Text of Democrats' Draft Resolution. February 2.

New York Times. 2005. A Profile in Timidity. April 1.

Newmann, William W. 2003. *Managing National Security Policy: The President and the Process.* Pittsburgh, PA: University of Pittsburgh Press.

Olson, Mancur. 1965. *The Logic of Collective Action: Public Goods and the Theory of Groups.* Cambridge, MA: Harvard University Press.

Omang, Joanne. 1986. $1.1 Billion Voted to Improve Embassy Security. *Washington Post*, June 26.

Overseas Presence Advisory Panel. 1999. *America's Overseas Presence in the 21st Century*. U.S. Department of State.

Page, Susan. 2006. USA More Pessimistic on Iraq War. *USA Today*, December 12.

Paltrow, Scot J. 2005. Many Antiterror Recommendations Wither. *Wall Street Journal*, April 26.

Parker, Laura. 1989. Airlines Got Early Bomb Alert; FAA Described Device Month before Crash of Pan Am Plane. *Washington Post*, March 17.

Parker, Laura, and David B. Ottaway. 1989. Aftermath of Flight 103: Probe, Relatives Stymied. *Washington Post*, July 9.

Patashnik, Eric M. 2008. *Reforms at Risk: What Happens After Major Policy Changes Are Enacted*. Princeton, NJ: Princeton University Press.

Peterson, Cass, and Martin Schram. 1984. Marines Called "Vulnerable"; Mondale Urges Lebanon Withdrawal. *Washington Post*, January 1.

Pew Research Center for the People & the Press. 2004. 9/11 Commission Has Bipartisan Support.

Pfiffner, James P. 2009a. Partisan Polarization, Politics, and the Presidency: Structural Sources of Conflict. In *Rivals for Power: Presidential-Congressional Relations*, edited by J. A. Thurber. Lanham, MD: Rowman and Littlefield.

2009b. Presidential Commissions: Keys to Success. Center for the Study of the Presidency.

Phillips, Don. 1990. Transportation Chief to Take Control of Security. *Washington Post*, May 28.

Pincus, Walter. 2009. Primacy of CIA Station Chiefs Confirmed, Ending Interagency Row. *Washington Post*, November 13.

Pincus, Walter, and Peter Baker. 2005. Data on Iraqi Arms Flawed, Panel Says. *Washington Post*, April 1.

Popper, Frank. 1970. *The President's Commissions*. New York: Twentieth Century Fund.

Posner, Richard A. 2005. *Preventing Surprise Attacks: Intelligence Reform in the Wake of 9/11*. Lanham, MD: Rowman & Littlefield.

Preble, Christopher. 2005. *The Uses of Threat Assessment in Historical Perspective: Perception, Misperception and Political Will*. Princeton Project on National Security.

President's Blue Ribbon Commission on Defense Management. 1986a. *An Interim Report to the President*.

1986b. *A Quest for Excellence: Final Report to the President*.

President's Commission on Aviation Security and Terrorism. 1990. *Report of the President's Commission on Aviation Security and Terrorism*.

President's Commission on Strategic Forces. 1983. *Report of the President's Commission on Strategic Forces*. U.S. Government Printing Office.

Priest, Dana. 1997. Civilian Committee on Military Favors Separate Female Training. *Washington Post*, December 16.

Priest, Dana, and Susan Schmidt. 2002. 9/11 Panel Criticizes Secrecy on Saudi Links. *Washington Post*, December 12.

Purdum, Todd S. 2004. The Next Hard Step. *New York Times*, July 23.

Relyea, Harold C. 2003. Organizing for Homeland Security. *Presidential Studies Quarterly* 33 (3): 602–24.

Reynolds, Maura. 2006. Poll Finds Majority in U.S. Backs Timetable for Pullout. *Chicago Tribune*, December 13.

Rich, Andrew. 2004. *Think Tanks, Public Policy, and the Politics of Expertise.* Cambridge: Cambridge University Press.

Riker, William H. 1986. *The Art of Political Manipulation.* New Haven, CT: Yale University Press.

Risen, James. 1999a. Embassy Security Budget Is Far Less Than Panel Urged. *New York Times*, February 5.

   1999b. U.S. to Seek $264 Million for Building of Embassies. *New York Times*, June 5.

   2002. Dissent on Assigning Blame As 9/11 Panel Adopts Report. *New York Times*, December 11.

Roberts, Steven V. 1983. Legislators Say Reagan Must Reassess U.S. Role. *New York Times*, October 24.

Rogers, David, and Robert S. Greenberger. 1983. Report on Bombing of Marines Will Erode Backing in Congress for Mideast Policy. *Wall Street Journal*, December 29.

Romano, Lois. 2006. The Woman Who Would Be Speaker. *Washington Post*, October 21.

Rosenbaum, David E. 2005. Commissions Are Fine, but Rarely What Changes the Light Bulb. *New York Times*, October 30.

Rosenfeld, Stephen S. 1981. Feeling Insecure about Security? *Washington Post*, August 14.

Rosenthal, A. M. 1990. The League of Terror. *New York Times*, May 27.

Salant, Jonathan D. 1989. Flight 103 Mourners: Terrorists Grow Bolder. *Post-Standard*, August 3.

Schelling, Thomas C. 1960. *The Strategy of Conflict.* Cambridge, MA: Harvard University Press.

Schlesinger, Robert, and Susan Milligan. 2004. Probe Sought on Intelligence System. *Boston Globe*, January 29.

Schram, Martin. 1979. Young Resigns as U.N. Ambassador. *Washington Post*, August 16.

Seale, Patrick. 1992. *Abu Nidal: A Gun for Hire.* New York: Random House.

Secretary of State's Advisory Committee on South Africa. 1987. *A U.S. Policy toward South Africa.* U.S. Department of State.

Secretary of State's Advisory Panel on Overseas Security. 1985. *Report of the Secretary of State's Advisory Panel on Overseas Security.* United States Department of State.

Seib, Gerald F. 2008. In Crisis, Opportunity for Obama. *Wall Street Journal*, November 21.

Shapiro, Margaret, and Fred Hiatt. 1983. President Defends Policy in Lebanon, Backs Gen. Kelley; Joint Chiefs Opposed Marines' Beirut Role. *Washington Post*, December 21.

Shear, Michael D. 2008. McCain Embraces Regulation after Many Years of Opposition. *Washington Post*, September 17.

Sheehan, Michael A. 2008. *Crush the Cell: How to Defeat Terrorism without Terrorizing Ourselves*. New York: Crown Publishers.

Shenon, Philip. 1999a. Report on Security Suggests Closing Some U.S. Embassies. *New York Times*, January 9.

———. 1999b. Spending to Avert Embassy Attacks Assailed As Timid. *New York Times*, February 19.

———. 2008. *The Commission: The Uncensored History of the 9/11 Investigation*. New York: Twelve.

Short, James F., Jr. 1975. The National Commission on the Causes and Prevention of Violence: Reflections on the Contributions of Sociology and Sociologists. In *Sociology and Public Policy: The Case of Presidential Commissions*, edited by M. Komarovsky. New York: Elsevier.

Simon, Herbert A. 1955. A Behavioral Model of Rational Choice. *The Quarterly Journal of Economics* 69 (1): 99–118.

———. 1982. *Models of Bounded Rationality*. Cambridge, MA: MIT Press.

Stanley, Alessandra. 2006. Where the Tube Beats YouTube. *New York Times*, December 24.

Stevenson, Richard W. 2002. Signing Homeland Security Bill, Bush Appoints Ridge As Secretary. *New York Times*, November 26.

Tallberg, Jonas. 2006a. *Leadership and Negotiation in the European Union*. Cambridge: Cambridge University Press.

———. 2006b. The Power of the Chair: Formal Leadership in International Cooperation. Presented at European University Institute Workshop on the Council of Ministers. Florence.

Tama, Jordan. 2011. The Power and Limitations of Commissions: The Iraq Study Group, Bush, Obama, and Congress. *Presidential Studies Quarterly* 41 (1).

Taubman, Philip. 1983a. O'Neill Considers Backing a Change in Marine Mission. *New York Times*, December 30.

———. 1983b. Pentagon Delays Publishing Report on Beirut Attacks. *New York Times*, December 24.

Templeton, Jean M. 2005. Pursuing Policy Change: The Illinois Death Penalty. Ph.D. dissertation, University of Illinois at Chicago.

Tolchin, Martin. 1983. Social Security: Compromise at Long Last. *New York Times*, January 20.

Tsebelis, George. 1995. Decision Making in Political Systems: Veto Players in Presidentialism, Parliamentarism, Multicameralism and Multipartyism. *British Journal of Political Science* 25 (3): 289–325.

Tutchings, Terrence R. 1979. *Rhetoric and Reality: Presidential Commissions and the Making of Public Policy*. Boulder, CO: Westview Press.

U.S. Commission on National Security. 1999. *New World Coming: American Security in the 21st Century*.

U.S. Commission on National Security. 2000. *Seeking a National Strategy: A Concert for Preserving Security and Promoting Freedom*.

U.S. Commission on National Security. 2001. *Roadmap for National Security: Imperative for Change*.

United States Senate Select Committee on Intelligence. 2004. *Report on the U.S. Intelligence Community's Prewar Intelligence Assessments on Iraq*.

Updike, John. 2004. The Great I Am. *New Yorker*, November 1.

VandeHei, Jim. 2004. 9/11 Commission Roiling Campaign Platforms. *Washington Post*, August 9.

Verba, Sidney. 1961. *Small Groups and Political Behavior: A Study of Leadership.* Princeton, NJ: Princeton University Press.

Von Drehle, David, and Mike Allen. 2002. Bush Plan's Underground Architects. *Washington Post*, June 9.

Wall Street Journal. 1984. The Lebanon Debate. January 26.

Warner, Michael, and J. Kenneth McDonald. 2005. *US Intelligence Community Reform Studies since 1947.* Center for the Study of Intelligence.

Washington Post. 2000. Proposal on Sanctions Rejected, June 5.

Weaver, R. Kent. 2000. *Ending Welfare As We Know It.* Washington, DC: Brookings Institution Press.

Weinberger, Caspar. 1990. *Fighting for Peace: Seven Critical Years in the Pentagon.* New York: Warner Books.

Weisman, Steven R. 1984. Reagan Orders Marines Moved to Ships Off Beirut But Widens Air and Sea Role. *New York Times*, February 8.

Wildavsky, Aaron. 1966. The Two Presidencies. *Trans-action*: December, 7–14.

Wolanin, Thomas R. 1975. *Presidential Advisory Commissions: Truman to Nixon.* Madison, WI: University of Wisconsin Press.

Woodward, Bob. 2006. *State of Denial: Bush at War, Part III.* New York: Simon & Schuster.

Wrenn, Harry L. 1984. Strategic Force Modernization: The Scowcroft Commission Recommendations and Alternatives. Congressional Research Service.

Wright, Lawrence. 2006. *The Looming Tower: Al-Qaeda and the Road to 9/11.* New York: Vintage Books.

Wright, Robin. 2001. *Sacred Rage: The Wrath of Militant Islam.* Second ed. New York: Simon & Schuster.

 2008. Since 2001, a Dramatic Increase in Suicide Bombings. *Washington Post*, April 18.

Wu, Chenghuan, and David R. Shaffer. 1987. Susceptibility to Persuasive Appeals As a Function of Source Credibility and Prior Experience with the Attitude Object. *Journal of Personality and Social Psychology* 52 (4): 677–688.

Zaller, John R. 1992. *The Nature and Origins of Mass Opinion.* Cambridge: Cambridge University Press.

Zegart, Amy B. 2004. Blue Ribbons, Black Boxes: Toward a Better Understanding of Presidential Commissions. *Presidential Studies Quarterly* 34 (2): 366–393.

 2005. September 11 and the Adaptation Failure of U.S. Intelligence Agencies. *International Security* 29 (4): 78–111.

 2006. An Empirical Analysis of Failed Intelligence Reforms before September 11. *Political Science Quarterly* 121 (1): 33–60.

 2007. *Spying Blind: The CIA, the FBI, and the Origins of 9/11.* Princeton, NJ: Princeton University Press.

Zeleny, Jeff. 2007. 2 G.O.P. Senators Press to Change U.S. Role in Iraq. *New York Times*, July 14.

Index

9/11 attacks, 10, 113, 182: aviation security and, 105; Bremer Commission and, 129, 131–132, 137; Crowe Panel and, 118; DNI and, 165; families of victims of, 157, 159, 174, 175; Hart-Rudman Commission and, 139–140, 148–153, 154, 156; Joint Inquiry and, 157–160; scale of, 157, 171–176; window of opportunity for reform and, 139–140, 176

9/11 Commission, 10, 21, 110, 137, 156–176, 182: advocacy and, 39, 157, 159, 174–175, 176; Bush, George W. and, 156, 159–160, 163, 165, 166–169, 170; congressional hearings and, 164–169; consensus of, 157, 160–162, 172; DNI and, 5, 21–22, 139, 164–169; embassy bombings and, 113; impact assessment of, 5, 171–176; Intelligence Reform Act and, 167–170, 172–174; Joint Inquiry and, 156–160, 164; media and, 161, 164–165, 171–172, 175; political credibility and, 164, 172–173, 174–175, 176; public interest in, 6; recommendations of, 163–171; report card of, 170, 175; report of, 163–171; turf protection and, 165, 183; window of opportunity for reform and, 156–157, 175, 176

9/11 Commission Implementation Act (2007), 170–171

9/11 Public Discourse Project, 169, 174, 175

Abu Nidal Organization, 97

Accountability Review Boards on the Embassy Bombings in Nairobi and Dar es Salaam (1998) (the Crowe Panel). *See* Crowe Panel

advocacy, 40–41, 43, 52: 9/11 Commission and, 39, 157, 159, 174–175, 176; Bremer Commission and, 130; Crowe Panel and, 110, 114, 116–120, 121, 137; domestic policy commissions and, 192; in executive *vs.* congressional commissions, 24–25; Hart-Rudman Commission and, 154; impact and, 8, 65, 67, 68, 70, 71, 195; Inman Panel and, 91–94, 96–97; Lockerbie Commission and, 103, 106, 108; mandates and, 26–27; political credibility and, 39–40; unanimity and, 59–61; *USS Cole* Commission and, 137

Afghanistan, 112

agency (control variable), 52, 65, 68. *See also* congressional commissions; executive commissions

agenda commissions, 8, 14–16, 17, 194: Chemical Warfare Review Commission and, 50; Commission to Assess United States National Security Space Management and Organization and, 59; Deutch-Specter Commission and, 62–63; domestic policy and, 191; impact of, 54–55, 59, 65, 66, 68, 181; President's Advisory Board on Arms Proliferation Policy and, 50; Scowcroft Commission, 28–30, 38–39; Secretary of State's Advisory Committee on South Africa